MW01482326

Mothers,
in East German Women's Films

NEW DIRECTIONS IN NATIONAL CINEMAS

Jacqueline Reich, editor

Mothers, Comrades, and Outcasts in East German Women's Films

Jennifer L. Creech

INDIANA UNIVERSITY PRESS   *Bloomington & Indianapolis*

This book is a publication of

INDIANA UNIVERSITY PRESS
Office of Scholarly Publishing
Herman B Wells Library 350
1320 East 10th Street
Bloomington, Indiana 47405 USA

iupress.indiana.edu

♾ The paper used in this publication
meets the minimum requirements of
the American National Standard for
Information Sciences—Permanence of
Paper for Printed Library Materials,
ANSI Z39.48–1992.

Manufactured in the
United States of America

Library of Congress Cataloging-in-
Publication Data

Names: Creech, Jennifer L., [date]- author.
Title: Mothers, comrades, and outcasts in
     East German women's films / Jennifer L.
     Creech.
Description: Bloomington : Indiana
     University Press, [2016] | Series:
     New directions in national cinemas |
     Includes bibliographical references and
     index.
Identifiers: LCCN 2016017124| ISBN
     9780253023018 (pbk. : alk. paper) |
     ISBN 9780253022691 (cloth : alk.
     paper) | ISBN 9780253023179 (ebook)
Subjects: LCSH: Motion pictures for
     women—Germany (East). | Motion
     pictures—Germany (East)—History. |
     Women in motion pictures.
Classification: LCC PN1995.9.W6 C74
     2016 | DDC 791.43/6522—dc23 LC
     record available at https://lccn.loc
     .gov/2016017124

1 2 3 4 5   21 20 19 18 17 16

For Violet Mae, Charlotte Yvonne, and Violet Gail

The direct, natural, and necessary relation of person to person is the *relation of man to woman.* . . . From this relationship one can therefore judge man's whole level of development.

—Karl Marx, *Economic and Philosophic Manuscripts of 1844*

Contents

Preface

In the opening sequence of Egon Günther's 1972 film, *Der Dritte* [*Her Third*], the viewer watches the female protagonist, Margit, at work as a mathematician in a computer engineering lab. Overlaid with a blue filter, the camera captures the lab and the engineers—equal numbers of men and women—in medium shots, in discussion while working with the computers that fill the room. In voice-over, we hear the film's director, Günther, asking the lab's director about specifics regarding job skill differences, wages, and gender parity. The camera then cuts to medium shots of Margit and her colleagues leaving the lab, taking the streetcar, and walking home.

Arriving at home, Margit enters her dark apartment, turning on lights that reveal its emptiness, occasionally turning toward the camera in medium close-up, baring a face that looks tired, beat. She is alone. She turns on the television and returns to the kitchen to make a solitary meal, but the dialogue from the television piques both her and the viewer's interest. We see her peer around the kitchen doorway to get a closer look at the man and woman on screen. The camera cuts to the screen-within-the-screen: we—the diegetic and extra-diegetic viewers—see a Russian captain standing on the forest floor, looking up at his younger female compatriot, an army nurse, teasing her, suggesting she is afraid to walk along the narrow trunk of the fallen tree on which she stands.[1] A high-angle close-up emphasizes his desiring gaze as he exclaims, taunting, "you *are* afraid!" The camera cuts to to a low-angle medium close-up of the nurse shaking her head. As she asserts, "I don't need your pity, thanks!" the camera cuts to a medium shot of Margit watching, somewhat disinterestedly, focusing more on her dinner plate than on the drama unfolding before her. As the camera cuts back to the film-within-the-film, we see and hear the nurse assert that she can—and *will*—jump over a large crevice in the earth on her own. Yet there stands the captain, legs broadly spread, straddling the crevice, tauntingly second guessing her: "On your own?! On your own?!" Grabbing her around the waist, he pulls her to him, her limp body hanging over the abyss, her legs motionless between his. The camera tracks lower into the earth, presenting this dynamic scene of his desire. He sizes her up with his eyes, then bends her to the side, kissing her passionately. The camera hovers below until he sets her down, safely, on the other side and, as both diegetic and extra-diegetic spectators watch, she moves unsteadily away from him along the edge of the abyss.

The camera cuts back to Margit and we register minute changes in her formerly disinterested spectatorship: she now leans slightly forward, and her movements, as she eats, are more agitated. She pushes her plate away and picks up a newspaper, but her eyes constantly move from the page back toward the television as the captain demandingly whispers, "Mascha, come here!" We see the nurse in close-up, her eyes racing from side to side, as she contemplates his command aloud, asking "Why should I?" Yet the answer is obvious to both the diegetic and extra-diegetic spectators. The camera cuts back to Margit and we see her visibly restless: she readjusts her position and quickly flips through the newspaper, all the while watching the TV from above and around the pages. Finally, she sets the paper aside and stands, removing her plates from the table as we hear the captain half-commanding, half-pleading "Go away. Go away, Mascha. Do you hear, Mascha? Leave. I'm asking you to leave." Margit reenters the frame, and we see that she has brought her glasses with her. She sits down, cleans her glasses on her breast pocket, and proceeds to get a better look at the captain's aggressive pursuit of his desired object. The camera cuts to a medium shot of Margit's hand turning off the light. She turns toward the camera, in the dark, and walks slowly over to the wall of windows. Crossing her arms over her chest, hugging her shoulders close, and shivering, she looks out over Berlin *Plattenbau* at night, and the camera follows her gaze: a broad cityscape of windows, some lit, most dark. Margit sighs.

In these first eight minutes, the average viewer likely feels challenged to make sense of a narrative that does not begin with a typical exposition, inexplicably mixes generic conventions, and focuses on the banality of a single woman's after-work routine. Why, for example, does the film begin with a documentary realist scene—formally stylized, yet framed by the humorously interrogative voice of the film's director—followed by the cinematic play of the film-within-the-film? Why, some may wonder, is a cinematic classic playing on primetime television? What, we ask, is the relationship between the shots of Margit at work and those of Margit at home? Between Margit, as a protagonist, and the female protagonist on the screen-within-the-screen? How is Margit's lonely stance in front of the secondary screen of high-rise apartments related to what we have seen of her thus far—Margit as a laboring and a spectating subject?

In these first minutes of his film, Günther self-consciously emphasizes many of the issues this book attempts to confront. First, he calls attention to film as a medium of pleasure. The seemingly objective documentary form in the opening shots are complicated by the director's own playful banter with those who assist in constructing the narrative. Similary, spectatorial enjoyment is emphasized, as we watch Margit resist and ultimately succumb to the pleasures of viewing. Further, by intercutting the celebrated work of Russia's most acclaimed director, Andrei Tarkovsky, with his own, Günther's work embodies the socialist ideal of art "for the masses," art as "pleasurable . . . cheerful and militant learning," proving (as Brecht had many years prior) that art and entertainment must not be mutually exclusive.[2]

Second, Günther's film emphasizes the role of narrative film as a sociopolitical medium. While Tarkovsky's narrative reproduces a traditional understanding of the feminine as primary object of the desiring male gaze, Günther's documentary realist introductory scene coupled with an emphasis on Margit's resistant viewership opens up a space for the film's larger critique of generic conventions and socialist femininity. The play between Günther's own film and Tarkovsky's invites the viewer to think more concretely about narrative conventions that govern spectatorship as a site of subject formation. Genres, narrative conventions, teach viewers through identificatory structures *how* to be and *what* to want, and spectators register affective responses in their reception of— and resistances to—the texts they encounter in the social field. Prior to presenting us with Margit as a pleasure-seeking spectator, Günther constructs her socioeconomically, as one who labors. The contradictions between those aspects of socialist identity—labor and desire—will be borne out by Margit over the course of the film. As Günther's film shows, and as this book will attempt to articulate, femininity is a particularly nuanced site of contradictions between the two.

A single mother raising two teenage girls from two previous relationships, Margit spends the rest of the film pursuing "her third." Finding her colleague Hrdlitschka handsome and apparently successful, she decides to determine his suitability from afar—observing him at work, following him on the train, researching how he spends his free time. When she eventually decides that he is worth the pursuit, she realizes that in order to achieve her goal and satisfy her desire, she must uncomfortably navigate conflicting ideas about socialist femininity, namely the active role she must play as a productive, emancipated member of socialist society and the passive role that is expected of her in the game of love. In the penultimate sequence, she outlines this contradiction in a monologue directed at both her daughters and Hrdlitschka after her daughters have caught her performing this passive femininity by pretending not to be the brilliant mathematician she is:

> I have been working for two years as an engineer. I use a computer, sometimes we call him Emil. I'm a mathematician. I work, think, and feel in accord with the principles and politics of the socialist technological revolution. But if I like a man, if I need him in my life, if I want him, I will still make a fool of myself if I tell him so. No, to attain my goal I must conceal my love and bury my desire because it might repel him. Right? He's the only one allowed to be proactive. I have to wait and be a good girl, just like Granny was, and hope that fate is kind … that I will be noticed, that he will find me desirable. I can only make myself noticeable to him if I'm quiet and reserved in matters of the heart. If he touches me, I'm supposed to resist him, avert my eyes, say "no." Otherwise he will be disgusted; he's had experience with *that* sort of thing. Mom and Dad taught him what to think of girls like that. Can't you see I don't want that? I can't do that? … I *want* you to notice me! To *know* me!

Hrdlitschka looks on, simultanesouly amused, flattered, and impressed by her passion, the boldness of her confession, and the truth of her critique. As the film's climax, Margit's monologue gives voice to the contradictions of a femininity defined by new socialist ideologies of egalitarianism and emancipation, and by residual gender ideologies (re)produced through social structures (the nuclear family) and narrative conventions (romance, fairy tales, etc.).

Margit's self-critique leads the viewer to the film's final sequence, which is introduced by the intertitles, "Love" and "and Marriage." Here, we see the happy couple at their wedding reception, eating, drinking, and being merry. Yet the film's final scene threatens to disrupt the happy ending. The camera cuts to a medium shot of Margit posed like a saint with her hands pressed to her mouth, as if in prayer.[3] Her best friend, Lucie, enters the room with two bowls of cherries and joins her on the bed. Margit makes a joke that her daughters are thrilled; after all, it's their first father! Margit and Lucie laugh, and we suddenly hear a snore; the camera pans down to reveal Hrdlitschka passed out on the bed between them. Margit strokes his head and encourages him to go back to sleep. Margit sits back up and says with a sigh, "Well, I guess we'll have to wait and see. Right, Lucie?" Her face registers hesitant optimism; a cloud of doubt covers her eyes. Margit and Lucie return their attentions to the cherries as the film's theme plays.

Her Third thus holds out the hope for a happy ending, only to qualify and suspend it. The wedding now over, Margit settles into the reality of marriage, which is, like the end of the film, open and uncertain. Margit's final speech act—an overt questioning of the possibility of a happy ending—refuses to resolve the contradictions of socialist femininity through anticipated narrative conventions. As a result, the confluence of emancipation and self-fulfillment, which has proven over the course of the film to be overdetermined by both labor *and* desire, is not contained and resolved. Instead, it remains, like Margit's words, a tentative potential that hovers between characters and spectators alike.

Heiner Carow's *Bis daß der Tod uns scheidet* [*Until Death Do Us Part*] (1978) similarly uses an open ending when addressing the problem of emancipation and self-fulfillment within the context of the failed marriage of its protagonists, Sonja and Jens. Six years after the release of the German Democratic Republic (GDR)'s greatest cult romance, *The Legend of Paul and Paula* (dir. Heiner Carow, 1972), Carow's second romantic drama begins and ends with a wedding. The film focuses on the conflicting desires of Sonja and Jens as they navigate both individual and collective expectations of socialist marriage, beginning with Sonja's desire to return to work after one year at home with their infant. Sonja's desire meets with resistance from Jens, whose longing for a traditional bourgeois marriage is based on his own bad experiences as a latchkey kid. Realizing this, Sonja resolves to appease him, playing the role of the seductive housewife and attentive mother. Yet she secretly enters a qualification program in order to return to work in a higher position, thinking that Jens will be happy about a career advance and a larger income. His response to her secrecy, however, is physical abuse. Her further attempts to placate him with homemade dinners and racy lingerie are thwarted by his consistent visits to bars and his subsequent alcoholism. Sonja decides to return to work secretly, and when Jens finds out, he beats her. After an evening of violence, Jens forces himself on her, and her fear of bearing a child disabled by his alcoholism eventually leads her to secretly abort the pregnancy. Frustrated with her situation and unable to leave him, Sonja watches silently as her drunken husband mistakenly drinks acid that she put into a seltzer bottle. The film ends with Sonja confessing to her act at her best friend's wedding reception.

Both the opening and closing sequences of Carow's film depict wedding ceremonies, framing the film with an overt emphasis on the institutional and communal meanings of marriage. The opening sequence begins with an off-camera voice-over monologue, during which the viewer hears a female judge reading the preface to the vows:

> Dear bride and groom, in every person's life there are many highlights; a very special highlight of your lives is this day. You, dear pair, have considered honestly whether or not your character traits, ways of thinking, and attitudes toward marriage and family life are in accord. With the development of our society new forms of family life have emerged. The equality of men and women, and your educational and professional possibilities create the necessary and supportive conditions for you to build a happy and lasting marriage. You hope for a happy and harmonious marriage based on mutual love, respect, loyalty, and understanding. Because these are the pillars of a good marriage. These, your wishes, are also those of our society, at whose center stands the individual.

In this ceremony, the personal and the public are merged in the individual wish and communal concern for "mutual love, respect, loyalty, and understanding." In the context of the monologue, marriage is defined as having acquired social meanings in East Germany that differentiate it from those in the West. The wedding official's assertion that Sonja and Jens have already determined that their personalities, beliefs, and positions on marriage and family are harmonious is a foreshadowing of the film's central conflict: the gap lying between Jens' and Sonja's romantic expectations.

However, when read in the context of the film as a whole, and in concert with Sonja's final confession, the social preconditions for this gap in desire become the basis of the film's critique, and the contradictions between a socialist subjectivity based in labor and one based in desire seem unresolvable. For, over the course of the film, it becomes increasingly obvious that the social and political ideology of marriage in the East cannot fully contain—and thus, successfully domesticate—personal desire. Throughout the film, Sonja and Jens seek answers to their problems in the community, to no avail. A better job for Jens, better qualifications for Sonja, and a new apartment are each presented as a likely solution, representing the official assumption that progress follows from material change, symbolized in work and the products of labor. Just as the woman's right to education and job training will supposedly lead to emancipation, a better job and a new apartment should guarantee familial bliss. Yet Carow's film reveals that this emphasis on work as a cure for all social ills fails to deal with emotional and romantic expectations in the domestic space. Real problems of desire and abuse cannot be assuaged by a new job or apartment, and the narrative unresolvability of love—the film's refusal of a happy ending—is directly linked to the State and the community's failure to confront this irreconcilability.

Similar to Margit's monologue in *Her Third*, Sonja's confession at the wedding reception of her best friend, Tilly, uses mise-en-scène and framing to resist the generic convention of a happy ending. The scene begins with Tilly receiving a marital advice book that Sonja had received at her own reception but that failed—like the advice of friends and family—to provide her with answers to her domestic problems. When she asserts that the book was no help at all, Jens' foreman pushes back, saying, "Why are you complaining? . . . You have a nice flat, money, a healthy child! Everyone's nice to you. Who's to blame then?" Sonja responds by overtly questioning this materialist solution: "Why look for guilty parties? Why didn't it end happily? I want to know why it happened this way! We both wanted it to work. We all did. I went by the book. I relied on that book. It still went wrong! I still poisoned him! Why did I poison him if you all wanted the best? I knew what was in the bottle and I let him drink it!" The response of the community is collective disavowal: one woman looks sternly in Sonja's direction, then turns her back and begins cleaning up dishes; another woman stands up from making out with her lover and leaves the room in frustration, followed by another; Finally, in an attempt to redirect attention, Jens' foreman turns to the crowd and shouts, "A polonaise!" leading the party out the door and into the street, singing. As we watch Sonja and Jens left alone in the apartment, the voice-over from the opening sequence returns, saying, "Dear bride and groom, in every person's life there are many highlights, a very special highlight of your lives. . . . " The camera then pans from Jens and Sonja to another screen-within-the-screen: the framed window becomes a second screen through which the diegetic and extra-diegetic viewers witness the relocated wedding party.

Like *Her Third*, Carow's *Until Death Do Us Part* refuses to provide the viewer with narrative resolution. The collective's choice to turn away and ignore the film's problem is, in fact, what the spectators are forced to confront in the end. The spectator is left to choose: either to work through the film's engagement with the contradictions of socialist subjectivity—bourgeois family values, infidelity, alcoholism, and domestic abuse—or to accept the pat alternative, Tilly's own "happily-ever-after" ending—evasively stylized, framed by the window, and located, literally, outside of the film's problem. Like the exchange between Margit and Lucie, the problem of self-fulfillment is located at the intersection of the individual and the collective, where labor and desire compete for primacy as the foundation for socialist subjectivity.

Acknowledgments

During my gap year as a Fulbright Teaching Assistant in Göttingen from 1996–1997, I was invited to participate in a weeklong seminar on East German women, offered by the Fulbright Program. The seminar, populated by other young female Fulbright assistants, focused on the history of women's experiences, women's literature, and films about women in the context of East German socialism. It was there that I first recognized the stark differences between gendered socialization and narrative approaches to everyday life in the East and West, which sparked my interest in this fascinating body of films.

While studying at the University of Minnesota, I had the opportunity to work with a variety of scholars whose intellectual interests greatly influenced my own. My advisers, Richard McCormick and Arlene Teraoka, provided me with helpful guidance as I began formulating my focus, and their critical feedback was essential to my progress while writing. Rembert Hueser and Keya Ganguly proved to be excellent readers; their comments and suggestions for analyzing these films in the context of a transnational cinematic landscape and period-specific film theory helped me to see the continuities and discontinuities between my objects of study and the larger cinematic history in which they are embedded.

I am grateful to the Department of German, Scandinavian & Dutch at the University of Minnesota for awarding me a yearlong grant in 2001–2002, and to the Deutscher Akademischer Austauschdienst (DAAD) for awarding me a second yearlong grant, in 2002–2003, to study and pursue research at the following institutions: the Humboldt Universität zu Berlin, the Bundesarchiv-Filmarchiv, the Stiftung Archiv der Parteien und Massenorganisationen der DDR (SAPMO), and the Hochschule für Film und Fernsehen—Konrad Wolf (currently the Filmuniversität Babelsberg—Konrad Wolf). In addition to funding two years of indispensable archival research, these grants enabled me to participate in a graduate student colloquium run by Gabrielle Jähnert, Director of the Zentrum für transdisziplinäre Geschlechterstudien at the Humboldt Universität, and to study with Birgit Dahlke, whose expertise in gender relations and East German literature proved essential for my own intellectual growth.

While in Berlin, I had the rare opportunity to pursue archival research under the guidance of Helmut Morsbach, founder and director of the DEFA-Stiftung in Berlin. Helmut helped me to navigate the Bundesarchiv-Filmarchiv, enabling and expediting my access to films, production stills, and marketing materials. Suggesting contacts at SAPMO and introducing me to directors, he was a vital and tireless supporter of my archival work, as well as a thoughtful and caring mentor. He fervently affirmed my research at a time in which East German cinema was still largely marginalized in the academy, and he pushed me to think critically about using Western theoretical approaches to interrogate Eastern texts. I am forever grateful for his generosity, his wealth of knowledge, and his unbounded enthusiasm for my work.

During these two years in Berlin, I also had the extraordinary chance to establish contact with various artists and intellectuals who were willing to share their thoughts and expertise with me. I extend my sincerest "tausend Dank" to Frank Beyer, Egon Günther, Eva Kaufmann, Ralf Schenk, Elke Schieber, Ursula Schröter, Tamara Trampe, and Dieter Wolf. I am so very grateful to each of them for taking time to meet with me, for speaking candidly about their experiences at the DEFA studios, and for encouraging me in my research on this important topic. Indeed, I have stood on the shoulders of giants.

On this side of the Atlantic, I wish to give special thanks to the DEFA Film Library at the University of Massachusetts-Amherst for providing me and other North American scholars with access to films and film journals from the former East Germany. I am especially grateful to Barton Byg, Sky Arndt-Briggs, and Hiltrud Schulz for their assistance in acquiring research copies of films, accessing stills for reproduction, and for their organization and facilitation of the biannual DEFA Summer Film Institute. I have benefitted greatly from their expertise and professional support.

In the final stages of revision, this book was shaped by the insights of various colleagues at the University of Rochester, including Joel Burges, Susan Gustafson, Kathleen Parthé, Ryan Prendergast, and Sharon Willis. Thank you all for taking precious time away from your own work to support me in mine.

To Jason Peck, thank you for being an intellectual mentor, a domestic support during our many years together, and an excellent father to our three children. Above all, thank you for always showing such enthusiastic interest in my object of study and for exploring East German culture with me. As Manfred Krug once said, "I'd even go see a DEFA film with you."

To my parents, Kenneth and Charlotte Creech, I wish to express the utmost appreciation. Without your personal sacrifice and careful guidance, I would never have been able to achieve what I have today. My love of reading, writing, and learning is a direct result of your hard work as parents. I love you. Thank you.

To my children Syler Joel, Violet Gail, and Harlan Wayne, thank you for your patience and for understanding when Mommy needed to work instead of play. Thank you for being proud of me and for saying so. I love you all to pieces.

And to Sebastian, my comrade in arms: I thank the cosmos every day for throwing us into orbit together. Thanks for believing in and striving for utopia with me.

Note on Translation

When translations of secondary sources (historical, critical, and theoretical works) were available in English, quotes were taken from the English versions. Translations of secondary sources not available in English (journalistic and newspaper sources, archival documents, film histories, and critical essays) are mine. For films, subtitles were quoted when appropriate. However, in cases where subtitles were inadequate, missing, or misleading—particularly when regional dialect played a role in my analysis—the translations are mine.

Mothers, Comrades, and Outcasts
in East German Women's Films

Introduction: Rescuing History from the Ruins

> Films can preserve memory and function as vehicles of History. They can also serve as a means of forgetting, a medium to stylize, distort or erase the past.
> —Rentschler, *Ministry of Illusion*

> "History" has failed us. . . . We would do well to bring the ruins up close and work our way through the rubble in order to rescue the utopian hopes . . . because we cannot afford to let them disappear.
> —Buck-Morss, *Dreamworld and Catastrophe*

Decades after the fall of the Berlin Wall, socialist cinema is a specter that continues to haunt Europe. While the East German studio system, the *Deutsche Filmaktiengesellschaft* (German Film Corporation—DEFA), is widely studied by colleagues in the fields of German and Cinema Studies, for the majority of the contemporary movie-viewing population, the history of Eastern bloc cinema is a vast gray area littered with a few familiar, often censored works of well-known auteurs, who, in spite of the repressive tactics of a totalitarian regime, were able to assert their artistic vision. For most contemporary viewers, both in the United States and abroad, the Academy Award–winning film *The Lives of Others* (dir. Florian Henckel von Donnersmarck, 2006) reveals the cold, hard truth of art under a communist dictatorship: plug away in the privacy of your domestic enclave, smuggle your work out to the Western democratic presses, and don't let any dangerous women with Stasi lovers stand between you and your great (resistant) work of art.

This book is an intervention borne out of my own enjoyment of so-called women's films in their numerous manifestations, and of theoretical and lay reactions to these films and to women's films in general. But it also has to do with an absence of scholarly interest in these films, which caused me to wonder why they are so often overlooked. My archival research at the *Bundesarchiv-Filmarchiv* in Berlin included viewing over thirty films from 1965–1989 that might fall under the term "women's film"—the protagonist was a woman, the director was a woman, and/or the film involved romance and, therefore, was supposedly intended for an audience of women. While my opinion has since changed, at an earlier stage of my research, my findings suggested one possible answer to the lack of interest in these texts—some of them might not be considered artistically and narratively engaging; in short, they were simply "bad" films and could have easily been categorized under DEFA's B-list, if ever it had had one.

But many of them were not B-list films, and it was difficult not to include an examination of many more films in this project. In fact, popular—if not theoretical—interest in these films continues to assert itself in the form of daily reruns on several television channels broadcast from the former East German states.[1] And while recent studies have suggested the theoretical value of considering DEFA women's films, they have only partially considered the films' critical engagement with real, existing socialism, with little attention paid to international cinematic trends and theories, and with only marginal consideration of their potential as agents of social change.[2] This book therefore is part of an emerging reconsideration of Eastern bloc culture, in particular the debate about "other" women's films as representative of the "typical" and "everyday" texts that have been neglected or ignored. In doing so, this book attempts to broaden our understanding of DEFA's women's films by engaging with certain problems that arise in critical and theoretical literature about them, about feminism and film, and therefore, about women as a part of critical filmmaking practices in the former East.

This book attempts a rescue. In response to the mounting tide of historical memory loss, this book contributes to a growing body of work that reconsiders the former East German cinema from a post-unification perspective. It sets out from various assertions: that DEFA was willfully ignored by the West, in particular by West Germany, throughout the forty years of its existence; that in the post-unification period DEFA is only now emerging from its marginalization within the canon of German film history despite its enduring popularity; that this marginalization of Eastern bloc and East German culture is related to the general hegemony of Western intellectual trends in the post–Cold War era and the specific naturalization of Western German history and culture in post-unification Germany; that the recovery and reconsideration of Eastern bloc culture is necessary for engaging the ideological, intellectual, and political standstill of "post-historical" positionalities; and finally, that gender is crucial for understanding the critical dimensions of these cultures, for positing a radical politics of representation, and for considering the possibilities of utopian hope in the current moment.[3]

Each of these critical interventions are important for the project at hand. Barton Byg and Leonie Naughton have both criticized the marginal reception of DEFA as particularly fraught after unification. Byg has argued that, while DEFA films are typically absent from recent definitions of a unified German *Kulturerbe* (cultural tradition), those films that do get incorporated are the banned films, along with several antifascist films, and a handful of neorealist-inspired films. These texts continue to serve as the exceptions to East German cinematic culture, leaving the typical and everyday films to fill the dustbin of history, except in instances when the "unabashed use of the legacy of the GDR on film" becomes a fruitful opportunity to "promote 'German' culture as the culture of democracy and freedom."[4]

As Naughton has argued, this negation of the experiences of lived socialism resulted in mass feelings of loss as East German cultural identity was eroded and utopianism was voided from the post-*Wende* ideological and political landscape.[5] Upon unification, East Germans were expected to assimilate to a Western-defined German identity, one that devalued material life in the former GDR and invalidated positive memories linked to personal histories. Amid feelings of loss and bewilderment at the sweeping denunciation of most things East German, acts of mourning and nostalgia for a life that once was are dismissed as misguided by a post-unification discourse that asserts the victor's perspective of history.[6]

This "normative (West) German postwar history that runs from catastrophe to civility" is indicative of a larger discursive framework, in which socialism is equated with fascism through the concept of "totalitarianism."[7] This post-socialist, post-historical sleight of hand affirms the moral superiority of Western ideological and political discourse, and effects what Žižek has termed the *Denkverbot* [prohibition of thought] that sustains today's liberal-democratic hegemony:

> [T]he moment we show a minimal sign of engaging in political projects which aim seriously to challenge the existing order, the answer is immediately: 'Benevolent as it is, this will inevitably end in another Gulag!' The ideological function of constant references to the Holocaust, the Gulag, and more recent Third World catastrophes is thus to serve as the support of this *Denkverbot* by constantly reminding us how things could have been much worse. . . . What we encounter here is the ultimate example of what Anna Dinerstein and Mike Neary have called the project of *disutopia*: not just the temporary absence of Utopia, but the political celebration of the end of social dreams.[8]

That is, in rejecting any critical re-evaluation of the supposed victory of liberal democracy over totalitarianism, the current ideological and political hegemony asserts its totalizing (totalitarian) view of history, making any critique, and therefore any significant change, impossible.

Further, it conceals the ideological problems at the heart of the discursive binary of totalitarianism versus liberal democracy. As Susan Buck-Morss has argued, both Eastern and Western bloc cultures were deeply rooted in a Western modernizing tradition of progress, and both establish their legitimacy through a monopoly on violence.[9] In deconstructing sovereignty through an interrogation of violence and the rule of law—rather than the actual rule of the people—Buck-Morss attempts to recover the utopian dreams from the ruins of history without resuscitating violent sovereignty:

> There is real tragedy in the shattering of the dreams of modernity—of social utopia, historical progress, and material plenty for all. But to submit to melancholy at this point would be to confer on the past a wholeness that never did exist, confusing the loss of the dream with the loss of the dream's realization. . . . We cannot afford to let [the utopian hopes of modernity] disappear . . . without the narration of continuous progress, the images of the past resemble night dreams. . . . Such images, as dream images, are complex webs of memory and desire wherein past experience is rescued and, perhaps, redeemed.[10]

Rescuing that dream is especially important in the twenty-first century, at a time in which the compartmentalization and splintering of the masses into discrete, seemingly incompatible groups (through the marketing of commodities and lifestyles, through social networks and media outlets) cynically furthers personal utopianism as the supposed inverse of a collective utopia for all.[11] It is in this theoretical context, through the dialectical reconsideration of the personal and the public, and of the tensions between utopian desire and social critique, that I return to DEFA's women's films. For these films in particular underscore both the tensions and possibilities of critique within a leftist, feminist framework of "the personal is political." In particular, I am interested in how they might inform our contemporary discourse of Western liberal democracy that is seemingly unfettered by rigid ideologies. For example, how do DEFA women's films raise issues that we have supposedly dealt with in this post-feminist, post-historical visual landscape? More specifically, how might a reconsideration of DEFA's *Frauenfilme* as a lost moment of critical reflection on the failures and possibilities of socialism and socialist utopianism help us to reconsider a structure of feeling that is now lost in post-socialist liberal democracy?[12]

WOMEN'S FILMS AND FEMINIST FILM THEORY

Since the 1980s, scholarship on DEFA has grown exponentially. The University of Massachusetts-Amherst's DEFA Film Library currently cites over three hundred scholarly works that address DEFA in some manner, and recent film histories have begun to establish parity between the West and East German film canons.[13] The proliferation of work on DEFA speaks to the artistic breadth of the East German cinema. Yet given the explosion of interest in DEFA, only a handful of the works listed focus specifically on women in East German film and media.[14] And while DEFA women's films importantly foreground a kind of Eastern bloc feminist consciousness in regards to marriage, career, partnership, and friendship, they were and continue to be read primarily in terms of their sociohistorical context.[15] The most insightful readings of West German women's films, by contrast, push beyond the sociohistorical to engage feminist and film theories, focusing on the ways in which gender is mobilized by the cinematic apparatus. These important feminist approaches to works by Helke Sander, Helma Sanders-Brahms, Jutta Brückner, Rainer Werner Fassbinder, and others interrogate formal structures that determine gender's meaning: gaze, voice, alienation, language, narration, fetishism, surrealism, and melodrama.[16]

Situating DEFA's women's films within both a national and a transnational context, we can discover political and aesthetic continuities and divergences within the East, as well as between East and West. This makes several things possible. First, it enables us to demystify the cultural homogeneity of the Eastern bloc: we begin to see the national and regional specificities of Eastern bloc filmmaking, discerning local historical and political ideologies as manifested through the concept "woman."[17] Second, we begin to problematize the notion of Central and Eastern Europe as the "other" Europe, the "impoverished cousin to the 'real' thing," using "woman," the Other of the cinema, as our point of departure.[18] This serves to deconstruct "Europeanness" as "legitimately and 'purely' Western" and also enables us to see the development of the East European cinemas in their larger context: as texts situated in a transnational political and cinematic history. Further, an emphasis on "women of the second world" also destabilizes our understanding of feminism as a phenomenon or concept that is inherently Western. Given feminism's tainted reception in the second world, in particular by female directors whose work is often labeled "feminist," it is especially important to reconsider what "feminist" or "feminine" filmmaking might mean or look like in the former Eastern bloc.[19] Finally, and perhaps most importantly, this broader contextualization offers us the opportunity to "rediscover and put into new perspectives theories that may have been cast aside as no longer useful or popular in mainstream film theory in order to address intra- and intercultural negotiations over representations that are more specific to the East European cultural terrain."[20] By returning to fundamental concepts in feminist and film theory—including Mulvey's definition of the male gaze, Silverman's interrogation of the female voice, de Lauretis' analysis of narration, Kristeva's conception of "women's time," Rich's assertion of a "lesbian continuum," as well as numerous theoretical models of "feminist documentary filmmaking"—this book also attempts a reconsideration of those foundational concepts through the lens of socialist women's films.

Considering DEFA's women's films through the lens of feminist theory developing during the period of their production, we can accomplish several things. First, we can discover how and to what extent these films were already engaging with that emergent feminist theory, whether consciously or not. This enables us to historically and theoretically contextualize both the films and the dominant discourse of feminist film theory in the 1970s and 80s. The original and diverse contribution of socialist women's films to women's studies and cinema studies can be more fully understood only within the larger context of the emergent theories of their time. Conversely, engaging with evolving theoretical models of the period from the lens of socialist women's films enables us to evaluate their residual potential (and limitations) for understanding second-world women in/and cinema. Interestingly and in contrast to the "counter-cinema" films of the New German Cinema, DEFA women's films are both not explicitly feminist and are also meant to meet the entertainment needs of a broad, feature-film audience.[21] In particular, the notion of the *Frauenfilm* in the GDR and the Federal Republic of Germany (FRG) are extremely divergent as a result of ideologically disparate notions of feminism and of film as a medium of politics and entertainment. Feminist consciousness in the West grew organically out of the West German feminist and student movements, not as a result of state policies.[22] The notion that the "personal is political," therefore, developed organically from a desire to raise feminist consciousness and to assert the "politics of the personal" (access to abortion, political lesbianism, resistance to discrimination against women and mothers in the workforce, etc.). In applying this theory of politics to their aesthetic praxis, West German feminist filmmakers asserted the private sphere as a social, political, and economic space that encompassed more than romantic desire and domestic bliss. In contrast, the women's films of DEFA did not have to assert the primacy of sociopolitical changes for women's emancipation since those changes had seemingly already occurred and had, in fact, not alleviated women's social alienation. Instead, for DEFA filmmakers the need was to assert the primacy of self-determination, especially if that meant constructing a successful, albeit covert, critique of the dominant socialist ideology of collectivisim through the female protagonist.[23] It is this very emphasis on the feminine as a site of critique that already aligns

DEFA's women's films with other "alternatives to dominant cinema which may be regarded as relevant to a feminist cultural politics" even if those alternatives are not "informed by a consciously feminist intent."[24] A contextualization of women's films from the second world of East Germany thus makes a contribution to both the history of women's film and the history of feminist film theory from a transnational perspective.

Given the social and economic differences in the former East, these Western theoretical approaches will undergo somewhat of a transformation in a different cinematic and sociohistorical context. Narrative choices in terms of voice, audience address, and narrative trajectory, as well as formal choices such as camera work, lighting, and sound, will likely vary, as different audiences are targeted and different notions of "political cinema" pertain to the East and West. The questions raised by emerging Western feminist theory at the time that now seem rote and passé will likely lead to rather different analyses in the context of second-world cinema. For instance, how do various cinematic structures—gaze and voice, viewer identification and pleasure, tensions between auto-biography and documentary truth—function in these Eastern films differently from how they have been debated in Western feminist film theory? Can the gaze be aligned with woman's desire? Can popular film encourage male identification with female protagonists? Does the "talking heads" technique have any emancipatory potential for women on screen, given documentary debates about transparency and truth? The difference in gender construction in East Germany necessitates a more thorough look at how cinema in particular constructs those gendered positions, as well as a reconsideration of how femininity and woman are aligned with agency, authority, and pleasure in these texts. By reconsidering this difference in theoretical function, we can discover how these films respond to potential blind spots and fill historical gaps in feminist film theory, while also illustrating the variety of critical potential present in the women's films of the former East Germany.

In addition, we may consider the critical potential of mass-marketed feature films. By engaging primarily Western feminist theories of film, I emphasize the importance of reading DEFA within an international cinematic context, particularly in relation to the Hollywood tradition and to the traditions of the Eastern bloc. I have chosen to do so, given DEFA's attempt to set itself apart from Hollywood, while at the same time attempting to create socialist blockbusters that could rival the Western imports that were immensely popular in the GDR.

A return to these films will also enable us to reconsider the role of DEFA in post-unification German culture, and most importantly, in post-socialist culture as a whole. If, in contrast to Buck-Morss, we mainain the clear ideological distinctions between democracy and dictatorship, then we relegate the utopian potential of the socialist project to the dustbin of history. An interdisciplinary, intertextual, theoretically rigorous engagement with DEFA women's films provides an avenue for rethinking the seemingly obvious ideological distinctions between West/East, individual/collective, private/public and liberal democracy / totalitarianism. The resistance to an either/or is something these films offer in abundance. In their dialectical engagement with gendered subjectivity, East German women's films offer a model for a critically engaged yet entertaining cinema. Like their cousins in Hungary, Poland, and the former Czechoslovakia, as well as West Germany, they embody to varying degrees the attempt to marry theory with praxis, work with pleasure, politics with entertainment.[25] In resisting the ceaseless march of progress demanded by socialist ideology (and perpetuated in a different form in the current liberal-democratic model of globalization), their protagonists demand a reconsideration of terms: who is the (socialist) individual? What are her desires? How can she achieve self-fulfillment? Are individual and collective desires commensurate? These films remind us that feminism and socialism are complex, potentially productive bedfellows, and that attempting to outsmart the Central Committee often provides for more engaging art than does meeting the bottom line.

Finally, DEFA's women's films deserve thoughtful consideration in the context of post-unification German cinema, particularly vis-à-vis the works of the Berlin School and their recurrent deployment of female protagonists in articulating alienation and stasis under global, neoliberal capitalism. The Berlin School's observational emphasis on the quotidian nature of everyday life and on "unattached, undistinguished and wayward" protagonists shares both aesthetic and narrative affinities with East German women's films under consideration here. The reinvigorated interest and investment in critical realism in the work of Maria Speth, in particular, underscores the importance of female protagonists as sites for working through the contradictions of lived experience.

ANSWERING THE "WOMAN QUESTION": EMANCIPATION MADE IN GDR

In order to understand the complexity of DEFA women's films as sites of political critique, we must first understand the complexity of gender under socialism, in particular the definition and image of "woman" as it was used in official discourse to posit East German socialism as the singular site of women's emancipation after fascism. Beginning in the immediate postwar period, "woman" came to symbolize the *Überlebensgesellschaft* [society of survival] in postwar Germany. The *Trümmerfrauen* [rubble women] densely populate the images of postwar destruction and reconstruction: rebuilding German cities stone by stone, they represent survival and the possibility of a new beginning. For both East and West, women came to embody the hope and promise of life after the horrors of the previous decade, a caesura in the lives of the German *Volk*. As such, "woman" became the first image of the future.[26] Depictions of the rubble women regularly show them standing in lines for food, precariously carrying buckets of water over mountains of rubble, squirreling food away, bartering on the black market, and doing "men's work" in men's clothing, asserting woman's crucial role in rebuilding and redirecting German society in the immediate postwar period.[27] Always depicted in groups rather than as individuals, the rubble woman became a postwar symbol of cooperation and solidarity.

Yet, as Ina Merkel argues, this did not immediately correlate to women becoming the archetype of the "New Man" during the period of the *Wiederaufbau /Aufbau* [reconstruction]. While women were depicted as the subjects of survival in the immediate postwar period, they were not necessarily the symbols of the new society to come:

> The legends of the rubble women's superhuman achievements and the legendary reconstruction pathos of the younger generation are meaningfully connected to each other, but they differ greatly in their imagistic presentation. The rubble woman is recognizable by her bent back, her well-worn shoes, her tattered skirt that is too short, her shapeless body in a thick coat. Rubble women are matronly,

old women. The reconstruction helper, by contrast, is a young man burning
for action, who stands with his feet spread and firmly planted, calling others to
volunteer in reconstruction work on a Sunday [*Sonntagseinsatz*], with the instru-
ments of reconstruction—hammer, trowel, plane—already in his hand.[28]

Thus, there is a clear division between images of the maternal and
matronly femininity of the transition period and the robust, active
masculinity of the *Aufbau* period. During the *Aufbau*, men became representative of the *Sondereinsatz* [special actions], whereas women were
representative of the *Alltagsarbeit* [everyday work], and both were val-
ued differently. The "New Man" could be seen actively structuring the
new social order, giving it a "new content, a goal, a future."[29] Men were
conceived as the productive constructors of society, whereas women
ultimately remained tied to reproductive work and the reestablishment
of life per se.

This image of matronly femininity is also present to a certain extent
in the *Trümmerfilme* [rubble films] of the immediate postwar period. Set
amid the urban ruins of a recently defeated Nazi Germany, these films
thematized political defeat, material devastation, and psychic loss. Taking the perspective of a "depoliticized humanism," the rubble films primarily focused on coming to terms with the fascist past at an individual,
rather than social, level and involved "the bracketing of the political and
the containment of history [which] culminated in the exculpation of
ordinary Germans as victims of anonymous forces. The real victims and
perpetrators . . . remained unnamed."[30]

Similar to the images that Merkel describes, it is the figure of the
postwar mother in the rubble films who simultaneously bridges and displaces the horrific past and the future-oriented present. As Pinkert and
Hell argue, the postwar (Stalinist) mother is a recurring narrative device
that serves to repair the psychic rupture caused by fascism and enables
the construction of a cohesive postwar history as family narrative. By
becoming the embodiment of loss, silence, and victimization associated with fascism and the "home front," the postwar mother affirms the
paternal Stalinist figure, who takes the place of the absent "bad" (fascist)
fathers and enables postwar sons to imagine themselves within a legiti-
mate familial and political telos of revolutionary antifascism.[31] Yet, as a
marker of generational and gender difference, matronly femininity was

not associated with political agency or productivity in the films of the late 1940s and 50s. Cast within the domestic and familial sphere, these women were "exposed to but not actively participating in the realm of history or social change."[32]

In contrast to their mothers, however, postwar daughters represent a shift from the past to the future and are generally "harnessed to the political and economic agenda of the *Aufbau*."[33] This new generation of young women "embod[ies] the emotional and intellectual sensibilities that enable a fantasy socialism in which affirmative affects such as peace, truth, understanding, courage, and calm, are nurtured and in which . . . everyone reaches happiness."[34] By the late 1950s and 60s, most films about female protagonists were situated in the period of the *Aufbau* and constructed a cinematic imaginary of social stability, wherein future progress was due, in large part, to women's successful integration into public realm as active citizens and productive workers. This idealistic depiction of youthful femininity was constructed within the context of socialist realism, which demanded that cinema represent reality not as it is, but rather, as it ought to be, through "typical stories and characters; effective mechanisms of identification; ample opportunities for idolization and heroization," etc.[35] Building on the Soviet cinema of the 1930s, East German films of the Stalinist era construct these new women as hard-working comrades, who embody the ideal of emancipated socialist femininity and whose happiness is to be found not in the romantic twosome but in the "warm embrace of the collective."[36]

The generational discrepancy between a matronly femininity associated with loss and a youthful femininity associated with productivity and antifascism reveals an attempt to break with the past and begin afresh with a new generation committed to socialist ideals. Using female protagonists as the benchmark for achieving those ideals certainly aligned with Marxist philosophy, which asserted that the "direct, natural, and necessary relation of person to person is the *relation of man to woman* . . . from this relationship one can therefore judge man's whole level of development."[37] These films thus conformed to and reinforced the emphasis on women's social, political, and economic equality set forth as one of the primary goals of the new East German government.[38] Drawing on the long history of women's involvement in the workers' movements of the late nineteenth and early twentieth centuries, the *Sozialistische Einheitspartei Deutschlands* [Socialist Unity Party], or SED, established women's formal equality in the first East German constitution in 1949: women were constitutionally granted equal access to education, work, and equal pay. In fact, women were privileged in the constitution as requiring "special protections" in regards to labor so as to guarantee that each woman would be able "to combine her task as a citizen and worker with her duties as a wife and mother."[39] The SED focused its policies primarily on the political and economic equality of men and women in all aspects of life, privileging women's economic independence in particular, which was to be achieved through women's equal participation in the processes of production and in all aspects of social and political life. This, the SED believed, could be achieved through the development of a comprehensive social network that would make it easier for a woman to combine her "natural" role as mother with her "social" role as a laboring socialist subject. The *Gesetz über die Mutter- und Kinderschutz und die Rechte der Frau* [*Law for the Protection of Mothers and Children, and Women's Rights*] in particular privileged women's special needs as citizens who are assumed to be or to become mothers, including: the decriminalization, availability, and affordability of abortion within the first three months of pregnancy (1972); free access to the pill beginning at the age of fourteen; the "baby year" (11th Party Congress of the SED, 1976), wherein women were granted up to three years of paid maternity leave with the guarantee of returning to their positions at work thereafter; one-time maternity payments for the first and each additional child, ranging from 500 to 1000 East German marks, and additional monthly subsidies ranging from ten to fifty East German marks; numerous child services for children aged six months through school age, such as full-time daycare services, children's health clinics, orphanages, and kindergartens (*Law for the Protection of Mothers and Children, and Women's Rights*, 1950); as well as the outsourcing of domestic labor to social services.[40] Each of these provisions should enable women to juggle their natural and social roles. Already by the 1950s this translated into women's enrollment in various fields of study at the universities, including traditionally masculine fields in the hard sciences, and large numbers of women had begun to enter the workforce. By the 1960s, 68 percent of women were working outside the home, and by the fall of the Wall in 1989, that number had risen to 91 percent.

As early as the 1970s, the SED had begun to assert that women and men's equality had been achieved. The typical media image of femininity in the 1970s was the superwoman, and the primary strategy of such images was to show women's seemingly effortless ability to combine their careers with their roles as wives and mothers. The SED's focus on the unity of economic and social policies had cemented the notion of women's emancipation as being primarily based on their ability to combine participation in the workforce with motherhood. This meant that emancipation and gender equality were strictly conceived in terms of making *working motherhood* manageable; men were never conceived of as *working fathers*—they were simply *workers*. Men's emancipation from patriarchy was not considered a problem that needed solving.

Consequently, a very obvious gender inequality persisted under socialism, and both official and unofficial East German discourses fostered this continuity. Although women were not discriminated against in terms of university and vocational training, and they significantly overtook both previous generations' and West German women's access to formal training and qualifications, they continued to be disadvantaged with regard to occupational fields and seniority, and earned on average one third of what men earned.[41] While women were constitutionally guaranteed "equal pay for equal work," they typically made less money than men because they were disproportionately represented in lower-wage jobs, primarily as a result of gendered differences in job-related qualification structures. Despite women's official equal access to all professional fields, most women ended up in traditionally feminine fields that were paid less than the traditionally masculine fields: women were often "pink-collar" workers—salespeople and skilled laborers in the textile fields and in electronics. Many women worked below their qualification levels in order to manage their second shifts at home, and fewer women chose to pursue advanced qualifications because of the time investment, resulting in lower wages and fewer opportunities to advance professionally. Finally, while the gendered division of domestic labor was supposedly eradicated through woman's official emancipation, provisions such as the *Haushaltstag* [housework day] and up to four weeks paid leave from work to care for a sick child were enacted with only mothers in mind, formally instituting women's (and not men's) "double burden."[42]

Further, because the GDR was a *Mangelgesellschaft* [society of shortage/lack], women often ended up working a "second shift" at home that involved much more than routine housework. This was primarily due to the fact that many of the social services (cleaning services, tailors, domestic and car repairs) and consumer goods (fresh fruits and vegetables, baked goods, fast food) taken for granted in the West often had to be performed, prepared, grown, or made by individuals at home, and women performed a disproportionate amount of this work, sometimes averaging as many as 38–47 hours of housework per week. Three quarters of that work was performed by mothers working full-time (40–44 hours per week) outside the home.

Yet women did experience some emancipation despite these discrepancies in gender equality, in particular with regards to marital and sexual norms in the East. While early marriage was encouraged by the state, there was a high rate and social acceptance of divorce, and a tendency toward "patchwork families" by the late 1960s. And although marriage remained the main form of sexual partnership, extramarital affairs were common, there was more gender symmetry in terms of infidelity, and many couples experimented with swinging. This somewhat liberal sexual climate was primarily a result of the fact that, by the mid-1960s, sexologists in the GDR had successfully pushed for the establishment of so-called "Marriage, Family and Sexual Counseling Centers" all over East Germany.[43] And while the East Germans did not experience a sexual revolution, a "sexual evolution" had begun by 1969 with the publication of Siegfried Schnabl's *Mann und Frau intim. Gesundes Geschlechtsleben, gestörtes Geschlechtsleben* [Man and Woman, Intimately: Issues of Healthy and Unhealthy Sex Life]. In this groundbreaking text, Schnabl, a prominent East German psychotherapist and sexologist, argued for the decoupling of sex from reproduction and the recognition of sex as the most intensive form of interpersonal closeness and relaxation. As a result, an entire public discourse surrounding sex, love, and partnership exploded in newspapers and magazines, including advice columns answered by prominent sexologists. The question of women's sexual satisfaction held a dominant position at the center of this discourse that, regardless of its somewhat traditional emphasis on love, nevertheless emphasized that "women were independent and could make decisions about their bodies, which resulted in an incomparable sexual openness."[44]

It is unsurprising then that East German women's contradictory experiences of gender and sexual (in)equality led to a popular, non-institutionalized, and sociohistorically determined feminist consciousness. As a result of their official emancipation, East German women came into consciousness as gendered subjects with expectations of equality that often conflicted with their material experiences and with the concept of the *allseitig entwickelte sozialistische Persönlichkeit* [the "all-round developed socialist personality"].

By the late 1960s and early 1970s, the question of women's possibilities for *Selbstverwirklichung* [self-actualization or -realization] under socialism had become a primary concern, in particular for women writers. Irmtraud Morgner, Brigitte Reimann, Helga Schubert, Helga Schütz, and Christa Wolf engaged the "woman question" as a thematic focus, an aesthetic paradigm, and as an affective disposition. Maxi Wander's opening words to her collection of interviews with East German women, *Guten Morgen, du Schöne* [Good Morning, Beautiful] encapsulate these women writers' personal and political investments in answering the "woman question":

> We first become conscious of conflicts once we can afford to overcome them. We have come to see our position as women in a more differentiated way since the moment we were faced with the opportunity to change it. . . . It is not against men that we want to emancipate ourselves, but rather in the struggle with them. What matters to us is our disentanglement from old gender roles, what matters to us is human emancipation generally speaking.[45]

Wander's collection was part of a larger wave of documentary literature that has been largely understood as a response to the lack of a public sphere in the GDR. Similar collections by Christine Lambrecht, Christine Müller, Gabriele Eckart, Irina Liebmann, Meta Borst, and Erika Rüdenauer revealed a broad-based need for women (and occasionally, men) to express fulfilled and unmet desires and hopes in regards to family, work, and sexuality, and to reflect on old and new forms of living together and living alone.[46]

Similar to the women captured in the documentary literature, the female protagonists created by East German women authors struggle with "emancipation from above" and its effect on gender roles and romantic love, on women's "double burden," and on motherhood as a natural or enforced role. They grapple with existential questions such as these: What does it mean to be a woman under socialism? What new conflicts and hurdles result from the change in women's demands in work, in society and in partnership? Can women, under the given circumstances, really achieve self-actualization?[47]

Yet, as an aesthetic paradigm, the "woman question" took on varied forms, and was certainly not limited to attempts to realistically document women's experience under real existing socialism. Fairy tales, myths, legends, science fiction, and surreal narrative styles emerged, wherein the depiction of East German reality often remained starkly germane. In the works of Christa Wolf and Irmtraud Morgner, in particular, modernist and postmodernist aesthetic tendencies come to the fore. These aesthetic choices find their bases in a fundamental refusal of the institutionalization of instrumental reason, the socialist insistence on a rigorously realistic worldview, and the "mimesis of the hardened and alienated."[48] For both Wolf and Morgner, this resistance is directed against a "coalition of horror, male domination, violence, war and pure technical rationality" and is embodied both by the narrative form and the female protagonist.[49] Their call to arms: "power to fantasy!" One of Morgner's protagonists, the siren Arke in *Amanda: Ein Hexenroman*, articulates the revolutionary kernel of fantasy as follows:

> What made life difficult was not simply the development of abstract thought, but rather its claim to exclusivity, that not only hindered the further development of figurative thinking, but actually destroyed it. It depressed me that the history of thought continues to progress in the same vein as the rest of history: warlike. . . . The remainder that was destroyed is the figurative appropriation of the world.[50]

For Morgner, the use of fantastic realism functions as an aesthetic subversion of (socialist) realist forms. As a method of feminist writing practice, she uses fantasy to critique instrumental reason, always historically bound to patriarchy, by defamiliarizing the everyday. With the mixing of generic modes—history, montage, novellas, songs, poems, myth, legends, dreams, newspaper and research reports, interviews, and passages from educational books, including nutritional and behavioral research—the politics of Morgner's aesthetic practice become apparent, revealing the "emergence of a free association of individuals characterized by creative fantasy."[51] Further, her "concern with the possibility and usefulness of a definition of woman and the consequences of such a definition for political practice" infuses what Von der Emde has characterized as her postmodernist feminism.[52] Morgner's female protagonists travel through time as female troubadours, witches, sirens, and goddesses to ironically comment on the seemingly transhistorical nature of gender and sexual difference.[53] Morgner's feminist demand that women "enter into history," Von der Emde argues, is enacted through self-reflexivity, the attempt to move beyond a binary logic of "either/or" to "both/and," and the use of parody, situating her within a postmodernist aesthetic politics.[54]

As the GDR's most prolific and influential feminist writer, Christa Wolf similarly embodies the confluence of aesthetic experimentation and gender critique. While her two early novels, *Moskauer Novelle* [*Moscow Novella*] (1961) and *Der geteilte Himmel* [*Divided Heaven*] (1963), represent a critical yet progressive identification with socialism in a more realist style, beginning in the 1970s her writing engaged other forms (most notably, science fiction and myth) and revealed a feminist perspective increasingly defined by her growing interest in feminist theory and in the Frankfurt School's critique of Western civilization as a process of reification.[55] As a marker of those qualities excluded by instrumental reason in Western civilization, qualities that come to be identified as belonging to nature, the feminine functions for Wolf as both the "Other" of Enlightenment and, as a result, that which resists the Enlightenment's "universal subject of history" becoming an "I" steeped in immediate historical experience.[56]

As the representation *par excellence* of Wolf's feminine aesthetic, *Cassandra* synthesizes myth, lyrical prose, and feminist politics to resist the barbarity of rationality under Western civilization. Wolf takes up her resistance at the level of form, exploring "the possibility of 'feminine' writing in opposition to the Western culture of war and its dominant art form, the heroic epic."[57] Plot, Wolf argues, becomes the narrative support of patriarchy: "The advent of property, hierarchy, and patriarchy extracts a blood-red thread from the fabric of human life.... The blood-red thread is the narrative of the struggle and victory of heroes, or their doom. The plot is born. The epic, born of the struggles for patriarchy, becomes *by its structure* an instrument by which to elaborate and fortify the patriarchy."[58] Wolf thus sees in the epic form a systemic support for masculine thought as "abstract rationality's will to dominate nature and its tendencies toward ever greater homogenization."[59] As a mode of resistance, Wolf opposes to the linear narrative of the epic a new aesthetic of women's writing, based in material experience, that does not "create large-scale, vital, ideal figures [and] no longer wants to tell coherent stories held together by war and murder and homicide," one that is no longer interested in "history as the story of heroes."[60] Instead, it is an attempt to "turn women from objects into subjects of narration," to "transform the woman-made-myth, and thereby object, into an autonomous subject with a voice."[61]

By the 1970s, "woman" had been transformed from a vessel of socialist realist ideology into a mouthpiece for critical resistance to the status quo. While a fantastical and postmodernist approach was generally lacking in the East German cinema, it is certain that the female protagonist advanced as DEFA's most scathing critic of real existing socialism.

AFTER THE FREEZE: 1965 AND BEYOND

In October 2005, the Museum of Modern Art (MoMA) in New York City offered the first comprehensive US retrospective on East German cinema. Entitled "Rebels with a Cause," the series brought together scholars of the period (1946–1992), as well as directors and actors who had worked at DEFA, to present the films and reflect on the political complexities of artistic production in the state-owned studios. Having produced over 750 films, many of them at the famous Studio Babelsberg, DEFA is noted in recent international critics' surveys to have produced more than a dozen films voted among the 100 best German films ever. The title of the retrospective, "Rebels with a Cause," conjures a vision of a cinema that is raw, defiant, and engaged, which DEFA, in some respects, certainly was. But what is most interesting about the retrospective was the film chosen to open the series. One might have expected to witness one of DEFA's most overtly rebellious films about youth struggling between the lure of decadent West Berlin and idealist, antifascist East Berlin, or one of the numerous banned films narrating the trials and tribulations of the East German subject resistant to the state. Instead one meets Margit who, after two failed relationships, rediscovers herself through flashbacks recounting eighteen years of her life.

MoMA's decision to open its DEFA retrospective with Egon Günther's *Her Third*, a film about East German women's emancipation, implies that this woman, Margit, be read as "a rebel with a cause." That is, it assumes a particular perspective from which to reconsider the notion of rebellion or resistance in East German film: it proposes that a woman's discovery of herself, through the blossoming and failure of intimate relationships, is in itself a form of rebellion. In doing so it proposes, as feminist theory and feminist film theory have been arguing for decades, that films emphasizing the personal are also political. This perspective on rebellion engages traditional Western notions of Eastern resistance that recognize only overt attacks on the regime as political. This residual Cold War approach, while contradicted by MoMA's retrospective, is still common among some DEFA scholarship.[62] Although the variety of approaches to DEFA includes issues as disparate as coming to terms with the fascist past, the socialist appropriation of German literary and cultural history, and the problem of youth culture in a socialist state, one particular trope repeatedly returns in these analyses: that of cinema as an instrument or a hostage of the state. Regardless of the film under consideration, the state often looms in the background, either as the puppet master or symbolic father threatening the artists' creativity or political vision. This is understandable, given the oft quoted "Lenin sentence" that film is "the most important art."[63] In fact, DEFA's history encourages such a reading, given the studio's strong connection to the state: in 1945 the studios were created and consolidated under the Soviet Military Administration (SMAD) and were transferred in 1946 to the *Zentralkomitee* [Central Committee] (ZK) of the SED. Eventually, in 1954, DEFA came under the direction of the SED's *Ministerium für*

Kultur [Ministry of Culture] (MfK).[64] Within the context of the new Marxist-Leninist state, film was seen as a pedagogical tool to reeducate a public that had been manipulated by the fascist cinema of the recent past. DEFA also saw itself in conscious opposition to the Hollywood cinematic tradition, which, according to the SED's *Kulturpolitik* [cultural policy], was not simply corrupt due to its inherent commerciality but was also aligned with the Nazi's *Universum Film-Aktien Gesellschaft* (UFA) tradition of entertainment as a "fascist opiate of the masses." This "most important art" was to become a voice of antifascist, anti-Western resistance that would aid in the building of socialism by shaping the new socialist individual:

> Those films that not only mirror contemporary political processes, but rather intervene in these processes on behalf of the Party, are ... essential; cinema [is] an instrument of propaganda, ... a "collective agitator and organizer" in Leninist terms. ... Film, according to Lenin, should, from this point forward, strictly adhere to Party doctrine and demands: there is no room for *petit bourgeois* entertainment in the battle for the "New Man."[65]

Given the SED's perspective on film's political function as educator and agitator, it is understandable that critics continue to return to an analysis of DEFA within the larger context of East German cultural policy and state censorship. The most discussed period of East German cinema is the period surrounding the 11th Plenary of the SED's Central Committee in December of 1965, often referred to as the *Kahlschlag* [clear-cutting].[66] This term has been used to reflect the SED's aggressive campaign for control over artistic production in the mid-1960s, a period during which official denunciations and professional dismissals of artists, as well as the immediate removal of films from circulation and the prohibition of others from initial distribution ravaged DEFA studios. Those films that were banned or shelved have become markers of a critical East German cinema that was lost to the maneuverings of a totalitarian state. These "*Kaninchenfilme*" [rabbit films], a term derived from the title of one of the banned films, *Das Kaninchen bin ich* [*The Rabbit Is Me*] (dir. Kurt Maetzig, 1965), are viewed by some as East Germany's lost new wave, a burgeoning avant-garde that was quickly replaced with politically and aesthetically meager fare. These two opposing ideas—film as a tool of the state and a medium of resistance against the state—recur throughout various analyses of DEFA, and the period of the *Kahlschlag* has come to serve as a convenient marker for some critics in asserting the end of DEFA's potential as a medium of critical resistance.[67]

However, for others—such as the curators at MoMA—the so-called rabbit films have not become symbols of the final days of East Germany's "critical" cinema. Where some critics view films that deal with the so-called private sphere as a retreat from truly political engagement, others see these films as an articulation of "an alternative East German self-understanding, which functioned as a means of resistance to, and of accommodation with, the conformist pressures of the socialist system."[68] Like other recent works, *Mothers, Comrades & Outcasts* reconsiders the notion of politics in DEFA films by moving beyond an analysis that recognizes only overtly political attacks on the socialist system.[69] In questioning this residual Western understanding of *political* as having to do with society at large, a designation often interchangeable with banned films or films critical of the regime, this book argues for a recognition of the private as political, for the critical potential of films that deal with personal or individual problems of everyday life.[70] Rather than suggesting that DEFA was the instrument of a totalitarian state or that artistic freedom was undermined by the SED dictatorship, I, along with other contemporary critics, argue that state power in the GDR was not limitless, and that artists and intellectuals, and East German citizens in general, actively participated in the formation of the social fabric.[71]

To do so, I will first address the complexity of DEFA as a state institution. While acknowledging the structural limitations placed on artists, including external and internal censorship, I will consider artists' relative autonomy within the institution. Second, I will reflect on the importance of viewer expectations in establishing artists' relative autonomy, given that DEFA, like any studio system, needed to produce profitable films for a viewing public. In particular, I will show how female protagonists played a key role as critics of the socialist system in this popular cinema, particularly in the years following the *Kahlschlag* of 1965. Finally, moving beyond my discussion of female protagonists and popular film as social critique I will consider how these films might contribute to past and present debates about socialist culture and feminist film theory.

DEFA—THE INSTITUTION

Part of my interest in DEFA has to do with its vertical monopoly of production, promotion, and distribution. The centralized nature of filmmaking in the GDR forces one to reconsider the possibilities for social critique from within a state-run institution. Those critics who argue that filmmakers were controlled by the state often juxtapose filmmakers with other artists working individually in different media: writers, visual artists, and musicians, for example. These assertions regarding artistic individuality are only partially valid. For example, while writers were limited by the state in terms of publishing options and possible *Berufsverbot* [professional blacklisting] should they choose to publish abroad, feature and documentary filmmakers were dependent on the studio system for all aspects of their trade. In short, because filmmaking is a collaborative process that necessitates expensive production materials, trained specialists in a variety of technical fields, as well as a collective space for its reception by a viewing public, DEFA was a highly structured, overmanaged institution that often placed undue burdens on its artists. However, while it is seemingly one of the least likely places to uncover social critique, given the various possible levels of censorship, it is in this overtly bureaucratic atmosphere that social critique takes on a more ambiguous, and therefore more viable, character.

The sheer size of DEFA makes an imposing impression, with the second largest film studio in Europe—*Mosfilm* in Moscow was the largest—including twelve feature film studios, two animation studios, three synchronization studios, two mixing studios, and enormous storage capacity housing over 850,000 props, costumes, and furniture.[72] While an average of only 16–18 films were produced each year (in comparison to over 100 per year in the FRG), a total of over 650 films were made, including coproductions with studios from both Eastern- and Western-bloc countries.[73] DEFA employed over 2400 film specialists (out of 3500 total employees) annually, and the studio premises, approximately 108 acres, included an emergency room, two daycare centers, two kindergartens, a sauna, hair salon, laundromat, deli, KONSUM shop, bank, shoemaker, and a restaurant.[74] DEFA's bureaucracy was as imposing as its premises. At various stages of the filmmaking process, there were official decision-making procedures, be it over the development of subject matter, the acceptance of the screenplay, the budgeting for film (measured in meters) and for actors' salaries, as well as the number of days filming on location, and the often precarious *Studioabnahme* [studio acceptance procedure].[75, 76]

And yet, even in this highly monitored, official environment, the question of state control becomes blurry, and the party line itself becomes a question of interpretive departure, particularly within the *Künstlerische Arbeitsgruppen* [artistic working groups] (KAGs). In the KAGs, differing, often contradictory opinions were shared that, taken as a whole, could be productive for the writer and director: "While one dramatic advisor fears hidden messages behind every turn, relentlessly seeks them out and tries to hinder them, the other exerts equal amounts of energy seeking opportunities to say that which, officially, may not be said."[77] As a result, the possibility of critique was not altogether lost in this obsessively controlled environment, and the exceptional artistic director who seeks to "speak the unspeakable" simply finds others ways of doing so.[78] Further, even though the general director had the final say in a film's production and release, the KAG often had leverage against sweeping censorship. This was usually the result of certain writers' and director's social status: writers and directors whose works were well received by the public had "a power that the studio could not easily defy."[79]

In fact, critics who were former members of DEFA studio, like Jungnickel, Ralf Schenk, Schönemann, Trampe, and Wischnewski often discuss the power struggle between filmmakers and the state in questions of censorship and artistic creation, suggesting that neither had total control of the films produced. Some of the relative power of the filmmakers vis-à-vis the censorship apparatus came about as part of the decentralization process in 1962–1963 through the development of the KAGs that were intended to mirror the decentralization of the studios in Poland and Czechoslovakia.[80] However, the tension between artistic and state power was based in the East German foundational myth of antifascism and film's role as the "most important art." Directors' power lay partly in their choice between the two systems, only one of which could serve as the material foundation for moving Germany toward a utopian future. A director's choice not to emigrate, but rather to participate aesthetically in the antifascist struggle by supporting the socialist state was recognized as a political choice of the highest order, and for many artists it was the only viable choice given the recent German past. And yet the *Kahlschlag* of 1965/1966 remains the cloud over possible artistic independence, even for the "socialist" filmmaker:

> Our motivations, born out of everything that can be shortened into the phrase "Germany 1945," had become unintelligible. . . . this Party, this movement, this utopia had become ossified in a ritualized system and was decaying into the chimera of omnipresent, police-state violence. But we saw no alternative. That is, namely, what was most terrible: the utopia had not been fully achieved, hope still seemed possible: at some point reason would have to prevail. Marx is certainly reason and thinking! Also, there were no alternatives because West Germany at the time, for us—and at that point for many—was no alternative. For later generations the GDR ceased being an alternative space for thinking and living, and became a type of prison, a strictly police-secured, enforced place of residence. For us, there had been possibilities for decision making and *engagement*. With the 11th Plenary a serious, longstanding identity crisis began.[81]

In fact, as "the most important art," film functioned as a double-edged sword. As a product of a state-run studio, it was mandated to enforce official ideology. Yet the material circumstances of cinematic reception meant that film also had the potential to incite resistance to official ideology: "where art is received by several hundred people simultaneously, insurrection lies in wait just beyond the door."[82]

Schönemann sees this second, revolutionary potential thwarted by a paranoid, dictatorial state. Her admission that certain directors could assert their projects in opposition to state power is countered by her skepticism regarding DEFA's overall ability to incite discussion and debate in the society at large. This, she argues, is because DEFA was a state-owned institution and artists, as a result, could not assert their individual artistic vision, but instead had to bend to institutional will.[83] Naughton similarly highlights the practical restrictions placed on filmmakers as a result of the nationalization of the film industry, their financial and technical dependence on the state, and their resulting self-censorship and compromise.[84]

Yet, while Schönemann and Naughton do an excellent job of pointing out the constraints of artistic resistance, we must also problematize the notion of "artistic freedom" that seems to underlie these arguments. One issue that presents itself is that of Party politics and privilege. Schönemann asserts that only those artists who were longstanding members of the SED and DEFA could produce work that incorporated a perspective critical of East German reality.[85] However, in the case of both Egon Günther and Helke Misselwitz, whose work I will discuss in detail, this is clearly not the case. At the time of his first film's production, *Lots Weib* [*Lot's Wife*] (1965), Günther was not a longstanding nor ranking member of the SED. Misselwitz, who was close to one of DEFA's most experimental and censored documentary filmmakers, Jürgen Böttcher, was a rising, though hardly well-established filmmaker at the time of *Winter adé*'s [*Goodbye to Winter*'s] filming in 1988. Further, directors like Böttcher, a longtime member of the SED who had put in many years at DEFA, regularly experienced difficulty from the Ministry of Culture while producing his films. Party membership and tenure at DEFA were neither prerequisites nor a guarantee for state acceptance of an artist's critical vision.

Another issue is that of the institutional nature of artistic practices. While artists in other fields had easier access to the necessary materials for creating their art, they were still forced through official channels if their art was to be consumed. Simply put: in order for art to be received by a public, it had to be published, exhibited, or recorded. To achieve this, artists could go through a *Volkseigener Betrieb* [state-owned company—VEB], send their work abroad, show it in "apartment exhibitions," or in the most extreme circumstances, emigrate to continue working.[86] Outside of artistic institutions (publishing houses, museums and galleries, recording studios and labels, underground networks, etc.) art did—and does—not exist. While authors might have had difficulty finding a publisher for overtly critical texts, there remained the possibility of publishing abroad. Yet this too would limit the distribution to Western audiences and the Eastern-bloc black market, still practically curtailing their artistic expression in the GDR and likely leading to professional blacklisting. Therefore all artists, working alone or otherwise, had to deal with the state in the last instance.

Filmmakers, on the other hand, were dependent on the state-owned studios to achieve their artistic goals.[87] Not only does feature filmmaking almost always require the technical and financial backing of a studio, it also requires the expertise of many individuals, who enjoy financial and professional security within the studio system.[88] Thus, filmmaking makes obvious what other artistic media often obscure: the collective nature of both producing and consuming art. While the East German author and visual artist often seem to be "individuals" working against a centralized, "totalitarian" system, the collective nature of filmmaking forces one to recognize that all artistic processes are social, that all artists and their texts are in some way institutionally contained. All texts must therefore be read within an institutional framework, which includes economies of production, distribution, and, finally, reception.

BETWEEN THE PARTY AND THE PEOPLE

Reception, or the question of audience, is one of the most important aspects of uncovering DEFA's critical potential. The prospective audience for cinematic texts as opposed to literary texts or other visual arts was much larger in the GDR, given the material conditions of film reception.[89] That the average East German citizen consumed more films than other artistic media asserts the cinema's role within an official public sphere that "enjoyed at best a very limited and fragile hegemony."[90] Rather than read DEFA solely as an institution constrained by the state to which it was subservient, one must also consider it a site of negotiation between the desires of the Party to educate and politicize the public, the desires of filmmakers to engage critically with society and international cinematic trends, and the desires of viewers to be entertained.

In fact, the acknowledged importance of film spectatorship, its cultural and political implications, was the focus of Lothar Bisky and Dieter Wiedemann's seminal sociological study, *Der Spielfilm: Rezeption und Wirkung* [*Narrative Film: Reception and Effects*], published in East Germany in 1985. In an attempt to fill a void in East European film research, Bisky and Wiedemann's study attempted to answer the following questions:

> To what can we ascribe the widespread consumption of film? What is film's role in cultural life? What are the cultural implications of this pervasive use of film? And what does it mean that millions of people today find themselves caught up

in discussions about lifestyles and ideological problems or aesthetic criteria in
an attempt to understand the diverse questions of socialist values and ways of
living, as a result of meaningful cinematic experiences?[91]

Relying on statistics and interviews collected through various state agencies, Bisky and Wiedemann's study of spectatorship painted a portrait
of the sociocultural characteristics of East German film viewers that is
both broad and deep. Considering factors as diverse as age, gender, class,
education, and frequency of viewing, as well as access and preference for
other forms of leisure, Bisky and Wiedemann point to film as the primary
source of leisure for East Germans across all age groups, with viewers
aged fourteen to thirty-five making up 86 percent of the population that
regularly visited the theaters.[92] Given that "by age 25, the film viewer in
the 1980s has . . . seen at least two thousand films," the spectator's role in
the success of DEFA films was crucial.[93]

The issue of viewer expectations was, in fact, part of the impetus for
opening up the centralized process of film production in the early 1960s,
prior to the *Kahlschlag*. During the late 1940s and the 50s, DEFA was
strongly urged to adhere to the socialist realist form sanctioned by the
Central Committee. In its attempt to define itself in clear opposition to
the UFA and Hollywood film traditions as markers of fascist and commercial entertainment industries, DEFA had asserted itself as a vanguard
of socialist cinema. During the 1950s, DEFA came under scrutiny during
the "formalism debates" for cinematic trends that tended away from socialist realism. According to the socialist realist rubric, the artist should:
"portray life—not academically, not as dead or 'objective' reality, but
rather as the *objective reality in its revolutionary development. The* truthful,
historically concrete artistic depiction must be combined with the task
of ideologically transforming and educating the working people in the
spirit of socialism."[94] The hero(ine) should be positive and exemplary, the
emphasis not on East German reality per se, but rather on representing
the ideals of socialism and building a future based on those ideals.

As Barton Byg has argued, the ideal of socialist realist art manifested
as a desire on the part of the Party rather than as an actual formal practice, and by the early 1960s, it had become obvious to the leaders at DEFA
that the viewing public was paying no attention to this "most important art."[95] Television was giving DEFA serious competition, especially

Western television programs and film imports.[96] In fact, the problem of meeting viewer expectations and competing with international films persisted from the 1960s through the 1980s.[97] In the early 1960s, the result of increased competition and decreased film viewership was an attempt to win back the viewers, not simply on the part of filmmakers, but also on an institutional level: "As a result a broad front arose, not just within the studio, but one that ... reached into the depths of the Ministry, and everyone agreed: we had to find film material, especially in the stories of contemporary life, that was open, serious, full of conflict, honest and aware of problems, and we had to craft those stories in a way that would reach the spectators again."[98] The failure of DEFA was located not simply in Party ideology and didacticism, but also in the poverty of stories and characters with which the viewers could identify and the absence of complicated and artistic cinematography. The loss of viewers "demanded a new cinematography that takes the problems of daily life seriously, that accepts the viewer as a partner."[99] Michail Romm's thesis, "Man is complicated," became the mantra for winning back the viewers' attention.

While some critics have attempted to draw a strong line between the pre- and post-*Kahlschlag* films of the early- to mid-1960s, often asserting an artistic retreat from political engagement to the safety of everyday, primarily domestic issues, these early theorizations about viewers' expectations reveal a continuity in pre- and post-1965 cinema that often goes undiscussed. In the 1980s, Bisky and Wiedemann's research made much the same argument regarding viewership as was made in the early 1960s, suggesting that viewers' basic expectations of the cinema were entertainment, good artistic realization, and realistic portrayal of reality:

> Analysis shows that most [East German] viewers expect entertainment, suspense, humor *and* a good artistic implementation. To put it more simply, "entertainment" and "art" are the basic expectations of film viewers ... both expectations "coexist" alongside each other, are interfused, do not rule each other out. ... Comparisons with earlier research findings reveal an increase in expectations in regards to artistic and aesthetic pleasure. ... Exceptional stories told in films exhibit sufficient points of reference to viewers' social experiences, to their opinions, wishes, and hopes. These reference points enable identification and encourage viewers' attentive participation in the narrative. As a result, the narratives take on personal meanings for viewers both during and beyond the moment of reception.[100]

In particular, the "realistic portrayal of reality" became the focus of two cinematic trends in DEFA filmmaking in the 1960s: the *Gegenwartsfilm* [film of contemporary life] and the *Alltagsfilm* [film of everyday life]. As has been argued elsewhere, these two genres reveal a fundamentally different approach to the Marxist-Leninist notion of the cinema, and most important, to critiques of the socialist system. The term *Gegenwartsfilm* "implies a strong sense of historical progression: the present as a mediating stage between the past and the future. *Alltag*, while it does not exclude the passage of time, emphasizes ahistorical existence.... The Party's ideology, the country's economic organization, and indeed the entire ordering of society through the state were based on a progressive vision of history."[101] That is, the *Gegenwartsfilm*, while dealing with the difficult issues of contemporary socialist life, also fulfilled certain ideological expectations by asserting a progressive vision of East German socialism moving toward a utopian communist future. The *Alltagsfilm*, on the other hand, dispensed with the notion of historical progress, alluding instead to the halted, banal, and stagnant nature of life under real existing socialism. While the *Gegenwartsfilm* offered viewers a critical perspective, it continued to embody the utopian striving at the heart of the socialist project. The *Alltagsfilm*, on the other hand, ultimately refused to engage the utopian aspects of the socialist project, often revealing a more skeptical or even cynical relationship to socialism as an emancipatory system.

Feinstein's reading of *Born in '45 [Jahrgang '45]* (dir. Jürgen Böttcher, 1965) suggests that this shift toward *Alltag* already begins in the films of the mid-1960s. He argues that it is particularly in the "everyday" of these films that the viewer could find a "truer" East Germany, one that spoke to the viewers' lived experiences in a stagnating socialist society: "*Alltagsfilme* . . . abandon[ed] the task of depicting a society rapidly moving toward the future . . . [and] dispense[d] with an essential moral realm informed by official ideology . . . to allow the immediacy of ordinary existence almost complete autonomy."[102] *Born in '45* centers around the ennui and "vague longing" of one couple and lacks "a clearly articulated political theme. In contrast to pictures like *Berlin—Ecke Schönhauser* [*Berlin-Schönhauser Corner*] (dir. Gerhard Klein, 1957) or *Divided Heaven* (dir. Konrad Wolf, 1963), everydayness did not supplement or compete with a narrative driven by ideological logic."[103]

Feinstein sees the genuine and lasting popular resonance of such films as evidence of the way in which *Alltagsfilme* articulated "an alternative East German self-understanding" that was both a form of critical resistance and acceptance. In foregoing the didacticism of the 1950s, the new *Alltagsfilme* created a sense of authenticity and "truth" by dealing with unofficial discourses of real, existing socialism, a "truth situated in the texture of daily experience":[104]

> I imagine a feature film like this: two people get to know each other and after a while they have their first big argument. Well, then they're both too proud, and they won't go to each other and explain that everything . . . you know, to, like, apologize and make up. They don't trust themselves. And then there has to be something about work, what she does and what he does. Well, and then one night she meets this other guy, a young guy, and then she notices after a while that she doesn't really like him as much as the first guy, the guy she was with earlier. Now she has to, like, go back to him and explain how things are, you know? And then they end up getting back together. And then they can't yet end the film. Then they have to show, like, how they live, how the family grows, what kinds of problems they have. And . . . yeah, I don't know what else.[105]

Thus, the shifting of the political register from overt, pedagogical morals, to an engagement with the intimate, problem-rich experiences of everyday life under socialism also illustrates the subversive potential of the *Alltagsfilm* in contrast to the *Gegenwartsfilm*. These changes in approach to political filmmaking were accompanied by a further shift to a new socialist subject: woman.

THE *ALLTAGSFILM* AND THE PUBLIC/PRIVATE DIVIDE

The most popular *Alltagsfilme* in the 1980s, argue Bisky and Wiedemann, had two things in common: a linear narrative structure and sufficient points of reference in regards to viewers' social experiences, opinions, wishes, and expectations.[106] A new socialist hero had entered the scene in the mid-1960s, who was sometimes ambiguous and passive, and at other times brash and cheeky. This new hero dispensed with the ideological tropes of the socialist realist heroes of the 1950s and offered the spectator a "feeling for life and the world" that could be experienced as *wirklichkeitsnah* [close to reality]:

> Upon critical reflection, one sees that the artistic idea at the heart of these films is primarily the hero(ine), who is searching for something, breaks loose, categorically champions certain ideals and repudiates other patterns of behavior. In the films' structures of conflict, s/he appears mostly as a catalyst, through whom those ideals and patterns of behavior are judged and made clear. As a result of this [narrative] function, not only does the basic conflict in the story come to a head, but rather the character succeeds in bringing in many elements of real life into the narrative, elements that communicate a "feeling for life" and a "sense of the world." More powerful than the arranged conflict in the narrative are the various "small" dramatic situations and conflicts . . . that are taken directly from life and that excite the viewer precisely because they excite him/her in real life. The ethic of these films . . . not to depict life as idyllic and not to descend into didacticism . . . has found its thankful viewing public.[107]

While film continued to be seen as the "most important art" by the SED, its use value had changed. No longer the medium through which the GDR would imagine its infinite progress toward a utopian future, *Alltagsfilme* created a space within which the spectator could see his or her individual struggles in a society that seemed to be standing still.

As a result, the relationship between the cinematic apparatus and the viewing public was altered. Rather than educating the individual through the collective narrative, the collective was now constructed through the problems of the individual, and everyday life often became the point of departure for discussing the contradictions in socialist society. Bisky and Wiedemann focus on the films' abilities, as collectively received cultural objects, to enable viewers' reflective comparison of the films' content with the content of their own lives. The public, collective nature of reception would then lead to "often intensive discussions" that typically moved beyond what was happening in the actual film: public discussion of personal problems, as well as the incongruities of real, existing socialism. For Bisky and Wiedemann, "these films . . . influence the collective understanding of moral expectations, of educational questions, and of what it means to say that 'the individual is at the center of it all.'"[108]

The shift from larger questions of socialist society to smaller issues of the everyday cannot, therefore, be read as a retreat from political engagement given that it engages specifically with the supposed private problems and desires of the larger public. The masses' discontent with lived socialism is thematized in the everyday struggle of the individual. While some critics insist that the distinction between the *Gegenwartsfilm* and the *Alltagsfilm* is one between political engagement and political retreat, one can alternatively see this shift to the private as a political intervention that challenges the failure of socialism to reimagine the ideological distinction between public and private. In fact, this dichotomy has been the focus of feminist critique for many decades, and has often revolved around the problematic division of the social into separate spheres, namely the public versus the private sphere, which are then conflated with the political and the personal and consequently gendered masculine and feminine. Western feminist interrogations of these ideological dichotomies have focused on whether or not they are spatial, symbolic, or rhetorical constructs; and whether they are universal features of human society or, rather, connected to particular forms of social organization associated with the rise of the family, private property, and the state.[109]

However, the public/private distinction was also directly targeted by nineteenth-century communist theorists and twentieth-century socialist and communist parties as an essential point for transforming bourgeois, capitalist society into a collectively-oriented social space. Extending state control into spaces and activities previously deemed private "was understood as a means of ending or reducing social inequality and especially the oppression of women. Changing the conceptual or discursive linkage of women's work to private and men's to public was one of the goals of communist planners and ideologues."[110] And yet, as Susan Gal and others have shown, the ideological distinction between public and private was perpetuated in the former Eastern bloc, albeit with different discursive meanings, and regardless of the state's attempt to transform society into a collectively-oriented social space.[111] Further, Gal argues that these discursive meanings were constantly in flux:

> "Public" and "private" are not particular places, domains, spheres of activity, or even types of interaction. Even less are they distinctive institutions or practices. [They are] . . . indexical signs that are always relative: dependent for part of their referential meaning on the interactional context in which they are used. . . . the public/private dichotomy is . . . a fractal distinction. . . . Whatever the local,

historically specific content of the dichotomy, the distinction between public
and private can be reproduced repeatedly by projecting it onto narrower contexts and broader ones.[112]

Gal has suggested that, in the former Eastern bloc, another layer of this
ideological distinction was its alignment along axes of power, in the discursive opposition between a newly powerful "them" who ruled the state
and the victimized "us," who were subject to state power:

> Private activities, spaces, and times were understood by people throughout the
> region as "ours" and not the state's. Different moral principles and modes of
> motivation and reward were considered appropriate to work spaces and social
> relationships considered "ours" as opposed to those considered the purview
> of the state. People loafed in official jobs, but on their private plots practiced
> extremes of overwork ("self-exploitation"). The imperative to be honest and ethi-
> cally responsible among those who counted as "us" contrasted with the distrust
> and duplicity in dealings with "them" and with the official world generally.[113]

I argue that an emphasis on seemingly private spaces in DEFA films
from the mid-1960s onward reveals filmmakers' attempts to deal with the
politics of the personal and should not be interpreted as a retreat from
political themes. In fact, depicting the "politics of the personal" was
partly to blame for *Born in '45*'s being banned. The problem with portraying the everyday was the lack of an overt political message, which opened
up space for ambiguity and critique that could be revealed in every marital, familial, fraternal, or professional narrative. In the case of *Born in '45*,
"the [HV Film] office blasted the artists for approaching the material
with such 'a profoundly indifferent, skeptical-subjective attitude'. . . .
Equally troubling from the agency's perspective was the depiction of a
'social milieu' that was 'far removed from the characteristic traits of our
socialist reality.' The settings were 'sad, unfriendly, dirty and ill kept.'"[114]
Thus constructed, critique now lurked within characters' vague desires
and amid the gray tones of their small, dilapidated apartments.

WOMEN'S FILMS AND THE POLITICS OF THE PERSONAL

Much like literature in the 1960s and 1970s, which saw significant artistic
and political changes, films of the period were dominated by growing
numbers of female protagonists. As film narratives shifted from public to

private spaces, heroes increasingly became heroines. This was, as I have already argued, mainly due to the fact that socialist society had never completely divorced itself from the dichotomies public/private, political/personal and male/female. In emphasizing the private or domestic sphere as a political space, these films made a valid attempt to uncover the contradictions in socialist society that were most often linked to women's, rather than men's, everyday experiences.

As such, the films are are often framed in terms of emancipation, the "woman problem," and the resulting contradictions of lived socialism. Interestingly, these narrative struggles often led to engagement with seemingly different problems. Wolfgang Engler has theorized gender relations and women's emancipation, as manifested in romantic relationships, as representative of a more general crisis of East German identity. This identity, according to Engler, was disrupted in the shift from a capitalist to a socialist society, in which money and consumer goods could no longer be used as a basis of social differentiation and identity formation. Engler suggests that social equality, economic independence, and existential security were the bases of a social network that made interpersonal relationships different in the GDR.[115] He argues that, as a result, East Germans could no longer rely on things (titles, income, consumer goods) to define themselves, but were forced to face the *Echtheit* [authenticity] of others around them.[116] This radical social equality, he argues, altered gendered relationships by turning former romantic and sexual traditions on their heads, resulting in a tension between inherited notions of romance and expectations developed under a new social order. As a result, feminine and masculine were no longer clearly defined categories whose naturalness was located in social behaviors.

The shift from man to woman as the subject of desire and agency was expressed most frequently in the recurrent association of woman with emotionality and passion. The focus on emotionality, however, was perceived by critics not only as a woman's issue, but rather as a question at the heart of socialist humanism, a question that filmmakers could most successfully pose through the figure of a female protagonist:

> These are ... general questions regarding life in our times and in our society that are ... handled through the female characters. Changes in social life are more intensely mirrored in the lives of women ... heroines represent the absolute

developmental possibilities of the individual under socialism, without losing
their characteristics as women, which have developed, gender-specifically, over
centuries of material occurrences.[117]

Like their literary comrades of the period, DEFA female protagonists
represented the shift from explicit to ambiguous social critique, a subtle
highlighting of the system's failure to produce the so-called all-round
developed socialist personality.[118]

The term *Frauenfilm* or "women's film" had begun to be used in the
1970s and 80s by a variety of filmmakers and film critics to describe a
new genre of *Alltagsfilm* that specifically engaged the "woman question"
in order to move beyond it:

> In coming-of-age stories, in stories about family life and partnership problems,
> the everyday dominates; the everyday, whose honest portrayal demands com-
> munication in the public sphere, but which is not afforded such by journalistic
> media. . . . DEFA women's films wanted to be seismographs of social conditions.
> Insofar as women in these films act out against inherited ways of thinking,
> against complacency and withdrawal into the private sphere, they support a
> process in which more and more citizens became aware of living under a stagnat-
> ing system, a system that was precisely dependent on inherited, residual forms
> of being and thinking in order to survive. . . . The female characters . . . stand
> on the lower rungs of society, transgress moral codes, neglect their children,
> steal, drink, and deny the hard and fast rules of a society that extols work as the
> primary purpose in life.[119]

Schieber gives the term *Frauenfilm* a particular meaning here. While the
term certainly alludes to the primacy of the female protagonist (even
in stories that involve a male protagonist), it does not assume a female
audience, nor does it privilege so-called women's issues, which, given
residual gender stereotypes, generally included questions of romance,
child rearing, and domesticity. While such domestic concerns might be
the focus of the majority of women's films, they often serve a mediating
role in introducing larger social issues. The women's films thus function as a kind of *Ersatzöffentlichkeit* [alternative or compensatory public
sphere]—though even this term is insufficient, given research that asserts the numerous public spaces in the GDR—within which official
silences are spoken and social critique was practiced.[120] Margit Voss uses
the term *Frauenfilm* in much the same way as Schieber. She sees this trend
in DEFA toward a female protagonist paralleled in films from the West

that are more politically engaged and socially critical.[121] For her, female protagonists are represented as those who actively seek self-awareness, while their male counterparts "flee into a world of memory, resignation and renunciation."[122] Woman, therefore, functions as a marker of social conflict and contradiction, opening up a space for critical thought that her male counterpart often rejects.

The film critic Maya Turovskaya gives a rather different definition for the *Frauenfilm*. She considers a variety of constellations that appear in so-called women's films: "the ordinary pain" women experience in marital and familial relationships; the tensions between traditional, bourgeois, and modern, socialist notions of femininity; women as "the stronger sex;" and the difficult, "unfeminine" happiness of the emancipated woman. However, for Turovskaya one key to understanding the women's film is the role women play in the filmmaking process. She argues that the gap between the emancipation represented on film and women's actual access to the art of filmmaking reveals the ultimate impossibility for feminist filmmaking.[123] The relative lack of female directors represents for Turovskaya the real failure of cinema as a medium of social change in the Eastern bloc. Turovskaya sees a clear distinction between films made by women and those made by men, and goes on to argue that the proportionately small number of women making films results in the impossibility of a feminist cinema.[124] While taking this position within a socialist economy in the late 1980s reveals an important resistance to the male-dominated cinema culture in the Eastern bloc at the time, it does not reflect the very concrete impact that women had on East German cinema as both screenwriters and dramatic advisers.[125] And as I will show, particularly in the first chapter, both male directors and male cameramen were equally able to create films that privileged the female voice and look, often asserting a feminist challenge to official gender ideologies at the time.

Whether one accepts Schieber's interpretation of the women's film as an emancipatory, socially engaged genre, or agrees with Turovskaya that women behind the camera is what matters, the result of this shift toward woman as the new socialist heroine reconfigures the relationship between viewer and spectator in ways that affect both DEFA and film theory. In discussing this shift, Hans-Rainer Mihan, along with other film critics, alludes to the female protagonist's ability to encourage spectator identification. Woman's emotionality, as a result of her social position, they suggest, is more believable than that of her male counterparts. In constructing woman as the socialist individual, these films encourage both same-sex and opposite-sex identification with the female protagonist. As I will discuss at length in the first chapter, by placing "woman," rather than "man" at the center of the narrative, "she" rather than "he" becomes the locus for spectator identification.

This identificatory relationship between viewer and hero(ine), between the narrative on screen and the viewer's personal narrative, held a privileged place in East German film criticism. Often hearkening back to Lenin's notion of the "most important art," East German film criticism repeatedly emphasized the importance of viewer identification for pleasurable viewing, and the ability of narrative cinema to shape and form the individual, once the need for pleasurable identification had been met.[126]

By returning to a select group of DEFA's women's films with these considerations in mind, this book attempts to excavate a moment in cinematic history in an effort to "preserve memory" and rescue the utopian hopes—as well as the critical dissidence—of a past moment. It is my hope that *The New York Times* will be proven wrong in its assertion that "with few exceptions . . . most [DEFA films] are now long forgotten," and that the popularity and success of contemporary films about the former GDR, like *The Lives of Others* and *Barbara* (dir. Christian Petzold, 2010), will encourage us to revisit these East German texts.[127] This book will help readers to focus in particular on femininity's crucial role in East German social critique, in the cinematic politics of representation, and in the feminizing of narrative agency, authority, and (viewing) pleasure.

In the first chapter, "Happily Ever After," I focus on female desire as an emergent concern of the East German New Wave. Contextualizing Egon Günther's *Lot's Wife* (1965) within the French and West German New Waves and focusing on the New Waves' privileging of female protagonists and their critical engagement with the Hollywood model, my analysis also serves as the basis for a reconsideration of two of the most important cinematic constructions for feminist film theory: gaze and voice. In my analysis of Günther's film, I show how the female protagonist is used as a narrative tool to critique the ideology of the public/private distinction under socialism. In this chapter, I assert that the female protagonist does not function as the object, but rather as the subject of the gaze and of voice. More specifically, I show how gaze and voice function to align the spectator with Katrin, mapping personal desire onto the viewing public, thus visually and narratively undercutting the ideological dichotomy of public/private.

In the second chapter, "The Lonely Woman?" I consider the problem of motherhood in Evelyn Schmidt's *Das Fahrrad* [*The Bicycle*] (1982) and Hermann Zschoche's *Bürgschaft für ein Jahr* [*On Probation*] (1981). These texts, I argue, represent the failure of socialism to deal with the material specificity of motherhood, that is, with the problem of *reproduction* as an inherent, though marginalized, aspect of production. Following Julia Kristeva's assertion that "the specific character of women could only appear as nonessential or even nonexistent to the totalizing and even totalitarian spirit" of socialist ideology, I argue that these films problematize production as the foundational moment of socialist subjectivity by focusing instead on reproduction.[128] In *The Bicycle*, Evelyn Schmidt articulates motherhood as an alternative discourse of subjectivity that compensates for the protagonist's, Susanne's, lack of fulfillment in her romantic and professional endeavors. For Susanne, motherhood provides a respite from an otherwise alienated existence marred by social and economic marginalization and hopelessness. Mothering offers Susanne affective pleasures that serve an *ersatz* function in a discourse of socialist subjectivity centered around labor. Hermann Zschoche's *On Probation*, however, provides a much bleaker narrative of single motherhood. The film's protagonist, Nina, is able to enjoy motherhood only insofar as she can perform acts of maternal love outside of socialist norms and expectations, and unnoticed by members of her community. As a woman whose maternal abilities are questioned throughout the film, Nina ultimately experiences motherhood as yet another alienating experience to be lived out under the watchful eye of the paternalist state. *On Probation* suggests that woman is bound to her biology through a social discourse that simultaneously assumes her natural inclination to reproduce while also punishing her failure to successfully perform her biological responsibilities in socially acceptable ways. In contrast to the resistant role that motherhood offers Susanne in *The Bicycle*, motherhood for Nina in *On Probation* serves as a form of disciplinary constraint that is inherently linked to her perceived biological essence.

In chapter three, "Women Working, Seeing, Loving," I give considerable attention to Iris Gusner's *Alle meine Mädchen* [*All My Girls*] (1979) as a rare iteration in the East German cinema of what Adrienne Rich has termed the lesbian continuum. Produced by one of the few all-female artistic groups at DEFA, the *Gruppe Berlin*, Gusner's *All My Girls* attempts to address several cinematic concerns: representing the masses as a form of entertainment, representing women as those masses, and representing female desire. In my analysis, I consider how the female brigade is constructed as the new "mass subject" and argue that woman becomes the marker for *Mensch* [man/human] in this film about a female collective in a light bulb factory. I argue that the film constructs an alternative position of viewing pleasure that does not rely on voyeurism or masochism, but rather encourages both the enjoyment of and identification with the female collective on screen, regardless of the viewer's gender, and in doing so, reimagines the all-round developed socialist personality as one that results from interpersonal (often homosocial) relationships rather than labor. Considered within the context of the well-known documentary protocol by Maxie Wander, *Guten Morgen, du Schöne*, and other DEFA films that emphasize relationships between women, including Egon Günther's *Her Third* (1972) and Heiner Carow's *Bis daß der Tod uns scheidet* [*Until Death Do Us Part*] (1978), my reading of *All My Girls* uncovers the often disavowed primacy of same-sex relationships for East German women.

In the fourth and final chapter, "Real Women," I focus on one of DEFA's most important documentary films, *Goodbye to Winter* (1988). I consider how the film engages with the history of documentary filmmaking at DEFA, while also applying cinematic techniques that are both international and feminist. Misselwitz' film moves away from the idealist aesthetics of socialist realism to create an aesthetics of "critical truth." I argue that the film uses a collage of interviews to investigate women's lives as sites of social contradiction and rupture, thus constructing an alternative, oral history of women in the GDR that can be experienced by the viewer as "authentic" vis-à-vis official discourses of gender.

1

Happily Ever After? The Emancipatory Politics of Female Desire in *Lot's Wife*

Is it now clear to all comrades . . . that this isn't about literature nor is it about
lofty philosophy, rather, that this is about a political struggle between two
systems? . . . It's about securing East German freedoms. . . . But we have freedoms that move beyond those of the West; we just don't have freedoms for the
insane. . . . We have no freedoms for counterrevolutionaries, absolutely not.
  —Walter Ulbricht, 11th Plenary of the Central Committee

[The SED leaders] had the wish and illusion: Why can't these boys make us a
film that would finally help us to govern! And that makes it clear that we live in
the best of all possible worlds?—They didn't understand that no one was going
to do that, that it just wouldn't work, that art *has* to be subversive.
  —Egon Günther, "Die verzauberte Welt"

THE NEW WAVES

The emergence of DEFA's women's films represents one particular piece
of a larger shift in European cinematic history of the postwar period.
While I will situate DEFA primarily within the East European and West
German contexts in the chapters that follow, it is imperative to consider how DEFA's aesthetic and political engagements of the mid-1960s,
the period from the thaw into the freeze, are also related to cinematic
trends extending into Western Europe as well. From the mid-1950s until
well into the 60s, DEFA films exhibited clear influences from both Italy
and France, as well as from West Germany. Beginning with the first
"Berlin film," *Berlin—Ecke Schönhauser* [*Berlin—Schönhauser Corner*]

(dir. Gerhard Klein, 1957), and followed by numerous others, the East German cinema experienced a less than decade-long New Wave that revealed influences as diverse as Italian Neo-Realism, *cinema verité*, documentary realism and the magical realism typical of the Czechoslovakian cinema.[1,2] The film that I discuss in this chapter, Egon Günther's *Lot's Wife* (1965), exhibits affinities with and differences from the trends in the French and West German cinemas at that time, particularly with regards to female desire as a structure for the film's narrative logic and political engagement.

The cinematic similarities that transgress the boundaries between East and West during the 1960s are both aesthetic and content based, born out of a break with the past and a celebration of the "new" and the "modern," a desire to construct new modes of representation for a postwar generation coming of age.[3] Like their East German counterparts, the French and West German filmmakers of the early 1960s were themselves participating in a form of patricide and parthenogenesis: in resisting *Papas Kino* (the Oberhausen Manifesto and the New German Cinema) and the *cinéma de papa* (the "young Turks" at the *Cahiers du cinéma*), West European filmmakers were, with varying and often divergent political goals, remaking the cinema in their own image. Theirs was a cinema of youth, a modern cinema that both resisted and manipulated traditional generic forms, and was simultaneously preoccupied with issues of gender and sexuality (at the level of film content), and aesthetic innovation (at the level of film form).

For the core cohort of the French New Wave—Truffaut and Godard, in particular—breaking with the *cinéma de papa* involved at first constructing a less overtly political cinema, one that was characterized by a rejection of history and an affirmation of the present whose dominant cultural traits were mannerism, stylization, formalism, and reflexivity.[4] Like many of their colleagues in East and West Germany, the directors of the French New Wave rediscovered the Hollywood films of their childhood and their youth, engaging with particular genres in innovative new ways.[5] Interestingly, by fetishizing individual Hollywood filmmakers— most notably Alfred Hitchcock and Howard Hawks—as the epitome of artistic individualism, the cinéastes at *Cahiers* came to privilege what they described as cinematic *auteurism*, which, ironically, had its roots in the Hollywood dream factory. Distinct from the East European emphasis on a collectively-oriented socialist cinema that would serve as an alternative to the Hollywood model, and from the West German emphasis on auteurism as a rejection of Hollywood spectacle and as a path toward constructing a representative, democratic public sphere, the auteurism of the French New Wave is primarily characterized by distinct directorial styles that emphasize form, generic play, and abstraction rather than overt political engagement.[6] However, it was in this very style, the formal results of their "individual talents"—the use of the jump cut, playful use of eye-line matches, disruption of continuity in editing, the use of text on screen, confusion of diegetic and extra-diegetic sound, and (often abstract) close-ups of beautiful female faces in long takes—that one observes a clear influence on other national new waves. In addition, the French New Wave's focus on particular characteristics of everyday life has its affinities in other East and West European cinemas of the period, including plots set in the immediate present; antiheroes as protagonists; a (primarily apolitical) refusal of institutions; nihilism and the absence of altruism; the increased presence of young, emancipated female protagonists; and an emphasis on the private sphere and individual problems, which focused on the banality of the everyday, the failure or rejection of the nuclear family, and issues of sexual emancipation.[7]

The rebirth of the French and West German cinemas in the 1950s and 60s was clearly also a response to a diverse range of definite sociocultural changes, including the various postwar "economic miracles" based in an American-style consumerism; the advent and social coup of youth culture; fomenting political resistance in the form of various social movements; as well as major changes in film production and distribution, including the introduction of lightweight cameras and onsite sound technology, and state and regional subsidies for the reestablishment of a national film culture that could compete with American imports.

In both France and West Germany, political and social movements provoked resistance to anti-authoritarianism, to the war in Vietnam, to colonialism, and to the residues of fascism in the newly democratized West. Feminist demands emerged from and grew alongside these movements, influencing the role women would play in the cinematic landscapes of both countries. While their counterparts in East Germany had already been benefitting from and learning to critique a paternalistic vision of women's equality handed down from the Party, women in Western Europe were decidedly constructing, as a grassroots movement, the second wave of feminism. Campaigns for equal rights and fair pay; access to contraception, abortion, and child care services; as well as equal representation in politics, access to typically masculine professions, and resistance to the exploitation of women in the workplace were only some of the demands being made by the West European feminist movements in the 1960s. Women's sexual emancipation and their various approaches to resisting patriarchy—avoiding marriage, embracing contraception, living in all-female communes, choosing lesbianism—reverberated in the films of the New Waves, which were produced almost exclusively by male directors.

Interestingly, while women in both France and West Germany were reporting similar experiences of inequality and sexism, their respective national cinemas produced visually similar yet politically different discursive meanings of woman and femininity. This can be partly explained by the different national experiences of the war and postwar period, the role of cinema as a national (exportable) art form, and the role of cinema as a site of public discourse. For the core cohort of the French New Wave—Truffaut, Godard, Chabrol, Rohmer, and Rivette—breaking with the past did not carry the same political gravity as it did for West and East German filmmakers, whose sense of historical responsibility weighed heavily in their cinematic politics. And although many of the radical thinkers of the 1960s and 70s who ushered in new political debates about academic knowledge, cultural elitism, and patriarchal power, were French—Bourdieu, Derrida, Foucault, Irigaray, Kristeva—their theorization of gendered, sexual, economic, political, and aesthetic discourses were not necessarily mirrored in the aesthetic politics of the French New Wave.[8]

Instead, the French New Wave maintained a rather superficial relationship to gender politics. While amorous and sexual relations were often the focus of their films, the role of female desire and narrative agency was often contained by the point of view of a male protagonist. For James Monaco, "Truffaut's men are ... continually involved in an existential struggle to reaffirm their egos ... the women appear as art works, mysterious and confusing, variable and a little frightening . . . women and art become indistinguishable."[9] For Geneviève Sellier, the female protagonists represent "the male hero's fears and desires made concrete, and the viewer only has access to them through his gaze."[10] When women are the main protagonists, "the director's gaze functions . . . like that of a sociologist, who describes, with more or less pity or distance, the social and sexual alienation of the female character (and eventually her "emancipation" through love), in the lineage of *Madame Bovary.*"[11]

However, the French auteurs' interest in female problems, most notably women's sexual emancipation, served as an important influence for both East and West European cinemas beginning as early as the late 1950s. Roger Vadim's *Et Dieu . . . créa la femme* [*And God Created Woman*] (1956) is particularly interesting in this respect. Brigitte Bardot's raw expression of sexuality is presented by Vadim quite voyeuristically, most notably in the opening scene of her sunbathing nude and during the scene in which she dances the mambo. In the latter scene the camera, representing the points-of-view of her husband and her lover as the diegetic surrogates for the male viewer, holds a close-up of her bare legs as they uncontrollably gyrate to the driving beat, a scene that clearly manifests Mulvey's theorization of the cinematic male gaze. Yet Bardot simultaneously registers the sociological importance of a new model of sexually uninhibited femininity, which "provided liberating effects that were discussed in many popular magazines for young women" at the time mostly because she fell outside of hitherto acceptable categories of French femininity.[12] Louis Malle's *Les Amants* [*The Lovers*] (1958) was also groundbreaking in its representation of female desire: while receiving cunnilingus from her lover, Jeanne Moreau is presented in a facial close-up, providing the viewer with overt evidence of her sexual pleasure. More important for the films that came after, and for this chapter in particular, however, was Malle's use of the female voice-over. Spoken by Moreau about the character she is playing, the female voice-over privileges the heroine's perspective while also providing a distancing effect that presents her choice to escape the confines of her bourgeois marriage without moral judgement. This use of voice-over, along with the final shot of Moreau's character driving off into an uncertain future, is mirrored in Günther's cinematic choices in *Lot's Wife*, though with rather different political meanings.[13]

Of all the French influences one might detect in the East German New Wave, Godard's is most obvious. Both formal and narrative elements of *Vivre sa vie* [*My Life to Live*] (1962) and *Une femme mariée* [*A Married Woman*] (1964) can be rediscovered in Günther's film in particular. The protagonist of the first film is played by Anna Karina, the other by Macha Méril, both of whom Günther's protagonist, played by Marita Böhme, physically and stylistically resembles. The staging of femininity and masculinity, and of the three women's alienation in their intimate relationships, is highly stylized in each of the three films, through the use of black and white film, close-ups of the women's faces, and extreme close-ups of their bodies broken into various parts, as seen in Figures 1.1 through 1.6.

Yet while the visual and narrative elements are similar, the relationship between politics and gender is quite different. Godard does provide his female protagonists with a voice, using a male voice-over in the first film and a female voice-over in the second, and films them in such a way as to emphasize the alienation and commodification of romance and

Figure 1.1. *My Life to Live*. Dir. Jean-Luc Godard, France, 1962.

Figure 1.2. *A Married Woman*. Dir. Jean-Luc Godard, France, 1964.

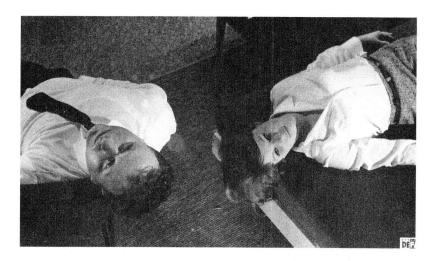

Figure 1.3. *Lot's Wife*. Dir. Egon Günther, DEFA, 1965. ©DEFA-Stiftung/Horst Blümel.

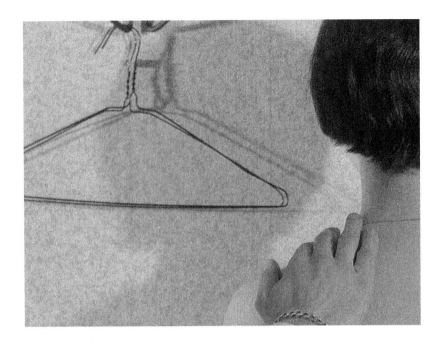

Figure 1.4. Nana, with a client's hand on her shoulder. *My Life to Live.*

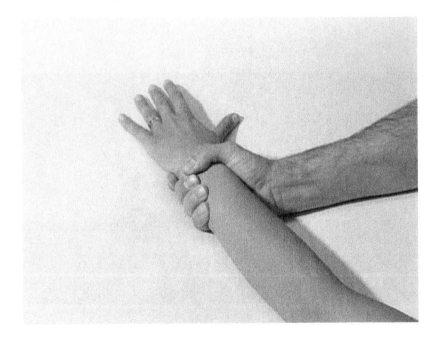

Figure 1.5. Charlotte's hand, held by her lover. *A Married Woman.*

Figure 1.6. Richard's hands just before he forces himself on Katrin. *Lot's Wife*. ©DEFA-Stiftung/Horst Blümel.

sex, more so than his other New Wave colleagues.[14] In *My Life to Live*, this is particularly so, as sex is removed from marriage (Anna Karina's character, Nana, is divorced) and placed decidedly within the realm of commodification: Nana has become a prostitute in order to support herself. Yet, as Sellier argues, the use of the male voice-over and of intertitles introducing each of the twelve tableaux maintains a sociological distance that makes Nana less "understandable" since she remains an object of (male) observation.[15]

In *A Married Woman*, Charlotte's voice serves as the extra-diegetic commentary for many of the images. Yet the abstract nature of her words—a stream of consciousness that does not make overt connections between sound and image—constructs her obtusely, maintaining a narrative distance between her and the viewer. In addition, the camera clearly fetishizes Charlotte's childlike beauty: the markers of her femininity—knees, legs, belly button, face, eyes, mouth, hands, arms—are presented in long takes and in close-up. Although we are encouraged to witness her body as being somewhat contained—her lover's hand grasping her wrist or his hands pressing against her abdomen—she is primarily presented as an object of his, and by extension, our desire.

Further, Charlotte's own desire to escape her marriage floats between the film's politics, rather than being connected to the larger issues Godard seems to want to address in the film. Discussions of the Holocaust and the Auschwitz trials in Frankfurt are interspersed with scenes of Charlotte having sex with her lover and her husband; comparing, with geometrical precision, the size of her breasts with the "perfect bust" measurements in a woman's magazine; shopping for bras; and listening to two young women at the local coffee shop discuss their first experiences of sex. The relationship between female desire and politics is only made obvious through the camera's gaze and through the alignment of feminine desire with an ahistorical, anti-intellectual relationship to the world, in particular to the past. This is made clear in two scenes introduced with the intertitles: *I. Memory* and *II. The Present*. The first is introduced by Charlotte, who argues that "The past isn't amusing, the present is more important," which is followed by Charlotte's husband's soliloquy on memory. Smoking a cigar and describing his experience of the Auschwitz trials, he remarks on the unbelievable inability of perpetrators to remember anything of their crimes and of false memory. He ends by saying he remembers everything: his first flight, a childhood vacation, the day they met, the dress she wore. This is followed by the second scene, *II. The Present*, in which Charlotte asserts that memory is not for her, she prefers the present because it is more exciting, because things die, and because of love: love has to be lived, and one lives in the present. One has to be aware, it's difficult to live in the present, she argues, but she loves to live in the present because it gives her no time to think, and because it's impossible to understand. Charlotte's face, presented in medium close-up, glows; she is youthful and unencumbered in her soliloquy. The alignment of masculinity with memory and understanding, and its juxtaposition with femininity as contingent and as object (rather than subject) of history and the gaze, reveals the underlying political meaning of femininity for Godard: women are fascinating because they are ungraspable, they provide aesthetic pleasure but are unknowable, and, most important, they are "incapable of knowing or taking responsibility for their desire."[16] Godard reveals here that the feminine exists outside of (masculine) politics, because she exists outside of a history: she is a contingent, commodified object to be fetishized by the camera, but not understood, since she cannot even understand herself.[17] Günther's film, on the other hand, takes a different route by privileging feminine desire as a means of potential resistance to a socialist ideology of labor—an ideology built upon a memory of the past that must not be repeated in a future utopia—and by using the female voice-over to overdetermine the narrative logic of the film. As such, Katrin Lot resembles several West German protagonists of the time, whose femininity is more directly aligned with an overt politics of coming to terms with the past in the present.

This national difference in the New Waves' use of the feminine is clearly related to differences in France and Germany's national relationships to history. The specificity of Germany's responsibility for the war and mass genocide, its superficial engagement with that responsibility and disavowal of collective guilt in the immediate postwar period, and the West German experience of American occupation made coming to terms with the past the highest priority for the generation of West German filmmakers coming of age in the 1960s. Developing an aesthetic politics that proclaimed the cinema an alternative public sphere was the pressing agenda. In asserting the need for "freedom from the conventions of the established industry, freedom from the outside influence of commercial partners [and] freedom from the control of special interest groups," the signatories of the Oberhausen Manifesto (1962) refused Hollywood and UFA aesthetics and asserted that "the old film is dead." Referencing the rebirth of film in France, Italy, Poland and Czechoslovakia, Alexander Kluge asserts the need to "free film from its intellectual isolation ... militate against the dictates of a strictly commercial orientation operative in the film industry ... [and] allow for conditions which make film aware of its public responsibility. . . . Film should embrace social documentation, political questions, educational concerns, and filmic innovations."[18]

For West German filmmakers, Alexander Kluge and Helke Sander in particular, the public responsibility that the New German Cinema should assert often involved the use of a female protagonist as the means for coming to terms with present social contradictions whose foundations often lie in the past. Kluge's first three feature films, *Abschied von Gestern* [*Yesterday Girl*] (1966), *Artisten unter der Zirkuskuppel: ratlos*

[*Artists Under the Big Top: Perplexed*] (1968), and *Gelegenheitsarbeit einer Sklavin* [*Part-time Work of a Domestic Slave*] (1973) all privilege female experience as the site for working through the problems of emancipation within the public sphere, or, more specifically, emancipation as a problem of the public/private dichotomy. For Kluge, emancipation is not located necessarily in the specifically female experience of the private sphere; rather, like his East German contemporaries, the female protagonist becomes a mode through which to consider "the productive power of fantasy and its ability to advance the utopian promise of a society committed to the fulfillment of human desires."[19]

Utilizing women "as the representatives of a tradition of human productivity presumably less damaged by the existing power structures," Kluge constructs the protagonist of *Yesterday Girl*, Anita G., as having little access to the supposedly public sphere.[20] In each of her interactions with social institutions—the university, the space of labor, the police—Anita is "Other": lacking access, she cannot forge a truly emancipatory relationship between theory and praxis. Unable to successfully apply knowledge to her lived experience, unable to make ends meet and secure a stable home, and finally forced to seek refuge within the confines of the prison, Anita represents the failure of the present democratic West Germany to come to terms with its authoritarian past.

Similar to his French contemporaries, Kluge also makes regular use of the close-up, focusing on Anita's beautiful, childlike face.[21] Yet he rarely uses the close-up as a method of fetishization. Instead, Anita, played by Kluge's sister, Alexandra, is constructed with Brechtian distance both via performance and cinematography. Constantly presented as performance—rehearsing lines in the opening scene, responding with "correct" answers to her judge and jury, repeating the appropriately moral answers of her Catholic sponsor in the halfway house (see figure 1.7), and learning about opera from her lover, a local minister of culture—Anita's face in close-up simultaneously reveals the beauty and the performativity of the feminine in the cinema and in the public sphere. Further, Kluge's decision to completely obscure from vision Anita's sole romantic encounter in the film—she and her lover presumably have sex under a blanket—reveals his resistance to the fetishization of the female body as a part of his cinematic politics.

Figure 1.7. Anita discussing morality with her Catholic sponsor. *Yesterday Girl*. Dir. Alexander Kluge, West Germany, 1966.

In *Artists Under the Big Top: Perplexed*, the protagonist Leni Peickert similarly struggles to combine theory and practice. Seeking to protect the work of fantasy against economic necessity by constructing a "reform circus" that escapes the commodification of art, Leni imagines the circus as an alternative space to spectacle and attempts to enact a utopian public space. Kluge's aesthetic choices simultaneously do the same by overtly connecting Leni with the fantasy-provoking function of film form. This is most clearly articulated by Marc Silberman:

> Kluge's laconic logic undermines the illusionism of the commercial cinema
> . . . the linking of associations creates a web of memory meant to provoke the
> spectator into a more active participation in constructing the film. . . . Although
> thematizing exhibitionism and visibility through the focus on the circus, Kluge
> undermines the visual opulence characteristic of the commercial cinema with a
> restrained camera, ascetic images, intentionally mismatched shots, or disjunc-
> ture of image and sound. . . . The female protagonist . . . provokes disruption
> because she refuses to discredit any experience. . . . Kluge's belief that aesthetic

perfection and synthetic totality exclude the role of the spectator motivates his practice of filmmaking as much as it does Leni Peickert's efforts to reform the circus.[22]

Thus, the female protagonist enacts, in her allegorical public space, the same attempt to provoke fantasy that Kluge's film aesthetics attempts to provoke in the cinematic spectator.

This resistance to spectacle is obvious in his filming of the female protagonist, particularly during two auditions: one as a showgirl, the other as a clown. In the first, Leni is dressed in a sequined leotard, flowing frontless skirt, heels, and a large feather headdress and must perform actions following the director's cues. Opening with a close-up of Leni applying heavy eyeliner, the camera remains in close-up as we hear the director telling her to "make it beautiful with the feathers." Leni provides the director and viewer with a forced smile in profile and as the camera zooms out, we see that her performance of femininity requires great effort. Shot with jump cuts, Kluge presents the repetitive nature of her struggle as she continuously readjusts the cumbersome headdress and nearly falls off the ladder she is asked to traverse multiple times. Throughout the scene, we hear the director asking her to move her hands differently, to be more graceful, to take off the skirt, and repeatedly telling Leni her performance is "no good." Finally, the director takes over, showing Leni how femininity is to be performed correctly.

In another scene, she responds to a newspaper ad for "troop entertainment" abroad. She should have "an open mind" and be willing to "try new things." She performs, in close-up, a brief slapstick act with wordplay. The director's response is to ask, while gesturing across his chest, if she doesn't have "something special" to offer? Perhaps she has a blouse that is open in front, and she could wear star pasties with a string of pearls? In both of these scenes, Kluge points to the problem of femininity as spectacle, thus underscoring that it is only from the perspective of the "Other" that radical change in the public sphere can be enacted.

Here we see a clear distinction between the function of the female protagonist in the French and the West German cinema of the time. While the first is overtly apolitical yet reveals its gender politics via the cinematic gaze and voice projected onto the female protagonist, the second uses the feminine as a (naturalized) "Other" to provoke in the spectator a political

Figure 1.8. Leni performs during her second audition. *Artists Under the Big Top: Perplexed.* Dir. Alexander Kluge, West Germany, 1968.

response.[23] Günther's film, like its East German contemporaries, draws on both of these traditions. His film reveals an overt rejection of classical Hollywood's narrative and cinematic structures, as well as an emphasis on the feminine as a mode of accessing the "new" and "modern." Günther's alignment of the camera with the female protagonist and his use of female voice-over resists the fetishization of the feminine, enabling her desire to structure the narrative logic and the film's political critique.

WOMEN IN EAST GERMANY'S NEW WAVE

In his address to the 11th Plenary of the Central Committee, Walter Ulbricht initiated the *Kahlschlag*, one of the most discussed periods of censorship in the history of East German cultural politics. The plenary began on December 15, 1965. Originally conceived and convened to discuss economic issues, namely the resolution of the second stage of the *Neues Ökonomische System der Planung und Leitung* [New Economic

System of Planning and Management—NÖSPL], the three-day plenary became the site of a culture war waged by the Party against artists in the name of "socialist morality." The confluence of the economic and the cultural was inherent to turning the plenary into a cultural *Kahlschlag*. Through the rationalization and modernization of its economy and administration via the NÖSPL, the SED had relinquished total control of both and had "successfully" handed over a significant amount of control to workers, including filmmakers and artists, through the KAGs. And after the building of the Wall four years prior, the SED had loosened its grip on cultural critique, enabling—encouraging, even—a new wave of modernist artworks that interrogated East German reality with formal and narrative inventiveness.[24] The 11th Plenary functioned as a public forum for the political denunciation of artists, whose works revealed a "skepticism" and "nihilism" that could be directly mapped onto the upward trend in antisocialist sentiment and criminality among East German youth. This "East German modernity" was radical and uncompromising in its critique of gray-haired functionaries and unconscionable careerism, of the penal code and incarceration, of opportunism and cynicism in the educational system, of duty and class privilege. The modernization and rationalization of the economy and administration that had begun a few years before had, by December 1965, led to the financial and cultural support of a whole year's worth of provocative films. These films unflinchingly validated their protagonists' wishes and hopes, in particular the conditionality of emotions, especially of those "young women, who become involved with married men they desire and who divorce the husbands they no longer love."[25]

This radicality was, according to the Party members speaking at the plenary, contributing to the enemy's cause in the struggle against Western imperialism. As a result, nearly the entire year's production list was shelved and most of the so-called rabbit films were first seen by audiences after the fall of the Wall, at the Berlinale film festival in 1990. The devastation and decades-long reverberation felt by artists and intellectuals was unprecedented:

> The perfectly staged tribunal settled accounts with all progressive tendencies in the arts and the life of the mind, intimidated the protagonists of East German modernity and their allies in the cultural administration for many years to

come, and banned unadulterated reality from official discourse. Whole genres, especially in film and theater, were literally made speechless, and recovered only painfully and laboriously via the detour of detested double-speak and disassociation.[26]

The hysteria and *Schadenfreude* with which the SED deployed its iron fist was fittingly characterized by Brigitte Reiman: "The cat's out of the bag: authors are responsible for the moral depravity of our youth. Destructive works of art, brutal representations, Western influences, sexual orgies, heaven knows what else! And that evil inclination toward doubt. Our writers stand off to the side and complain while our good workers are busy building socialism."[27]

Ulbricht's language, quoted at the beginning of this chapter, is laden with ideological hyperbole: East vs. West, socialism vs. capitalism, revolution vs. counterrevolution, rational (socialist) vs. irrational (bourgeois) liberal democracy. Understandably, much of the discussion regarding the *Kahlschlag*'s effects on the film industry has focused on those films that, according to the SED, fell on the wrong side of the ideological divide and were pulled from or denied distribution. These rabbit films overtly questioned the possibilities for the "all-round development of the socialist personality" in the GDR, thus simultaneously questioning the goals and authority of the state. In doing so, these films have come to be considered the pinnacle of East Germany's New Wave, in which artists saw themselves as participants in the creation of an alternative Marxist society.

Like its contemporaries in both France and West Germany, the East German New Wave equally engaged in both formal and narrative experimentation. Similar to the French example, DEFA films of the early 1960s focused on plots set in the immediate present; privileged the private sphere and domestic life; questioned the notion of the hero by constructing protagonists whose concerns revolved around individual problems and the rejection of institutions; and often depicted everyday life as absurd. The banality and mediocrity of the everyday was also revealed in a growing sense of nihilism, which, in a society based on utopian striving toward communism, had overtly political meanings. And like their West German siblings, East German directors often chose female protagonists to express their political critique in more socially palatable ways. Similar to Kluge's female characters, who seem to fall outside of history because they are "presumably less damaged by the existing power structures," the women of DEFA's New Wave represent both a generational difference in regards to past and present institutions, while serving as safer vessels for channeling political resistance because of their tenuous status as political subjects.[28]

Before the *Kahlschlag* of 1965, this fragile relationship between the feminine and the political enabled female protagonists to emerge, who were not focused on personal issues or romantic concerns. For example, although Konrad Wolf's *Divided Heaven* is presented as a romance between two characters, Rita and Manfred, they function allegorically as representatives of an "Eastern" and "Western" mentality, respectively. The film's formal use of the split screen constantly alludes to this allegorical division, which structures the film's political narrative of socialist *Bildung* [education] or *Erziehung* [coming of age], wherein the young Rita comes to learn that her love for the socialist community is stronger and more meaningful than her love for Manfred, who eventually flees to the West. Her relationship to the community is presented as simultaneously personal and public—she becomes a member of a brigade and learns, through conflict within the group, that she "belongs" because she is personally invested in the utopian striving the East represents, whereas the West is presented as cold, isolating, and impersonal. The film uses Rita's voice-over to privilege female subjectivity, which is structured by a utopian desire to learn from the recent historical trauma of fascism by constructing a community based in a universal love for humanity.[29] Thus, while the romance between Rita and Manfred serves to drive the film's plot, the film's logic is based in what John Urang has called the "New Romanticism" of the *Ankunftsroman* ["novel of arrival"], wherein love functions as a compensatory tool for the problems of social integration and the establishment of affective ties with the East.[30] In particular, the "novel of arrival" attempts to

> reconfigure the East German desiring imagination in line with [a] ... 'neue Romantik' [New Romanticism] ... [that entails] the *abandoning [of] desire altogether*. Indeed according to this model, the demands of desire *can* be met, the clamor of desire stilled, as long as the desiring subject chooses the right object. The "right object" however, is not an object at all, but rather a process: that of production itself.[31]

According to Urang's analysis, the erotic economy of the novel of arrival reveals the limitations of affective ties to production in that it "renders extraproductive ties dispensable or problematic": if work truly "satisfies," then the romantic relationship founders.[32] The novel of arrival ultimately remedies this through a melancholic nostalgia for Stalinist modes of loving and through the proper containment of youthful enthusiasm, each only partially successful attempts to sublimate desire. Thus, *Divided Heaven* uses female desire "properly directed" to sublimate Rita's private love and redirect it into a public love for the collective.

While Rita's desire is ultimately aligned with the GDR's discourse of labor as the ultimate guarantor of socialist subjectivity, Kurt Maetzig's protagonist in *The Rabbit Is Me* serves to further reiterate the fact that women were arriving on the scene as a new form of resistant hero, who was no longer aligned with the utopianism of socialist ideology. As one of only two films that warranted direct critique at the 11th Plenary, *The Rabbit Is Me* uses its young female protagonist, Maria, to directly confront the careerism and opportunism of the state embodied in the figure of her married lover, the lawyer Paul Deister. Drawing overt connections between their illicit affair and the East German legal system, *The Rabbit Is Me* uses female desire to drive the film's critique of socialism as an oppressive state of silence, lies, and punishment.

Interestingly, it is Maria's sexuality that serves to frame the film.[33] In the opening sequence, we discover, via Maria's voice-over, that she had wanted to study Slavic languages and travel the world but was politically stigmatized by her brother's incarceration and has been relegated to serving drinks at a dive bar on Friedrichstrasse. Within seconds of the opening credits, Maria becomes the object of the male gaze as we watch her wittily fend off the advances of the bar's clientele. This is followed shortly thereafter by her first seduction at the hands of her gym teacher, and later by Deister's advances. At the end of the film, Maria finally "makes it": she has successfully advocated for her brother's early release and will try again for admittance to university in Slavic Studies. In the final sequence, we watch Maria prepare for an interview at the university and move out on her own.

After watching her apply make-up and say goodbye to her aunt, we see Maria pulling a cart behind her along a busy street and hear, again in voice-over, her matriculation process. Yet we simultaneously witness her objectification one final time. As the interviewer asks for her citizenship status, she answers "German Democratic Republic." We simultaneously watch as a car with two men in the front seat pull up alongside her and catcall her. This return to Maria's objectification reiterates for the viewer the role that sexuality plays in her agency. Like Leni, she must "act the part" in order to gain access within institutional structures. Although Maria's primary characteristics are truth and rectitude, and her ethical demands for honesty from both the state and Deister anchor her character as a symbol of socialist morality, it is ultimately her sexuality that facilitates her agency: she willingly enters into a sexual relationship with her brother's lawyer, Deister, knowing this will enable her to get closer to him and hopefully aid in her brother's early release. Deister, on the other hand, only discovers who she really is after their sexual relationship has been established. Thus, one of the film's covert critiques is the problem of gender and sexuality in the GDR, reflected in a final shot of Maria being catcalled. The problem of emancipation is simultaneously a public and private affair: Maria's access and agency vis-à-vis the East German legal system—and, as the final shot suggests, within East German society as a whole—remains, in certain ways, contained by the male gaze.

What unites all three New Waves discussed thus far is the use of a female voice—and in Günther's case, a female gaze—that overdetermines the viewer's relationship to the image and to understanding female desire as having the potential for political resistance. While the theory I am applying to these cinematic structures had yet to be formulated at the time, it is clear that concerns regarding woman as object/subject of the gaze and the female voice as a structure for organizing meaning and identification are already being worked through in these early films. Also, given that Mulvey is concerned with classical Hollywood cinema, and the New Waves were, in different ways, attempting to engage and resist traditional Hollywood narrative and cinematic structures, it is fruitful to consider how the gaze and voice function to resist or support the gender ideologies in these modern texts, and to ask how the female protagonists function as a vehicle for political engagement that cannot be reduced to the personal.

In this chapter, I will offer an extended reading of *Lot's Wife*, a film that privileges the female protagonist's desire for self-fulfillment, simultaneously serving as an overt critique of the dominant discourse of socialist marriage. In Günther's film, the female voice is used either to invoke or to problematize personal, romantic desire as a potential site of resistance to the socialist discourse of subjectivity, which is defined primarily through labor. In my analysis, I consider how the film uses Katrin's personal desire for love and self-fulfillment to question the ideological dichotomy of the public/private as manifested in the institutions of marriage and divorce in the GDR. Using film theories of the cinematic gaze and voice, I show how the film attempts to align the spectator with Katrin, thus mapping Katrin's personal desire onto the viewing public, cinematically undercutting the ideological distinction of public/private. Ultimately, I conclude that the residual ideological distinction between public/private actually enabled the film to escape censorship, since it could be seen as an apolitical film about personal desire.

WHOSE GAZE IS IT, ANYWAY?

The Rabbit Is Me, the film from which the so-called rabbit films derive their nickname, focuses on legal corruption and judicial careerism, was considered "counter-revolutionary," and was subsequently banned. However, its contemporary, *Lot's Wife*, also critical of the East German judicial system and released just three months before the 11th Plenary, did not suffer the same fate as its contemporaries. Released in 1965 and directed by Egon Günther, *Lot's Wife* is one of the first East German *Frauenfilme* of the *Alltagsfilm* genre.[34] It tells the story of Katrin Lot, wife of naval officer Richard Lot, whose marriage has become routine. Katrin has a fulfilling career as a teacher and gymnastics coach, and Richard comes home from sea every two weeks. Their two boys welcome him happily, while Katrin awaits each visit with unease, as her marriage lacks one thing: love. Katrin wants a divorce. Richard refuses her one, mostly out of convenience and the desire to avoid blemishes on his Party record. After consulting with a divorce lawyer, who tells her that a loveless marriage is no real reason for divorce, Katrin decides to take things into her own hands: she steals a dress in a department store and refuses to explain why. Because he knows that Katrin will eventually serve a sentence for her theft, Richard chooses to divorce her in order to distance himself from her crimes, citing her "moral weakness" as his grounds. Although she must serve a penal sentence for her crime, Katrin retains custody of their two sons and achieves her divorce. Her penal sentence becomes the path to her freedom.

Lot's Wife is based on the true story of Rothraut Loth who, at the time of filmmaking, was in the seventh year of her criminal sentence at the penal institution in Görlitz.[35] Ms. Loth wrote a letter in 1961 to Kurt Maetzig, director of the banned film *The Rabbit Is Me*, detailing the events of her marriage and divorce.[36] Having found the letter in one of Maetzig's files, Günther decided to make it the basis of his first feature film. The film's critique of bourgeois family values and their persistence in East German law suggests a complex relationship between the film studio and the cultural-political *Kahlschlag* of 1965. While the real Ms. Loth sat incarcerated for her crimes, her story ran successfully in East German movie theaters, promoted via an extensive marketing campaign.

The critical potential of *Lot's Wife* lies in its critique, through the lens of female desire, of the public/private dichotomy in the GDR. Katrin Loth's desire critically engages the failure of the state to truly come to terms with this ideological distinction in spite of its attempt to collectivize all aspects of social life. Specifically, Katrin's desire lays bare the conflicting definitions of marriage as both a private relationship between two people and a public, legal bind recognized by the larger community. Katrin's desire is multiple. On the one hand, she desires love and passion, a desire that is marked throughout the film as particularly feminine and private in that it is unacknowledged, disputed, or outright rejected by each of the male characters and the state in the film. This so-called feminine desire has been heavily debated within feminist film theory with regards to its recuperative impulses, especially within the context of Hollywood melodramas.[37] However, instead of functioning as a vehicle of female sacrifice, the romantic impulse and the desire for mutual love present in *Lot's Wife* functions as a critical tool to resist the narrative recuperation of the female character into a particularly passive role in the love relationship, and to resist the legitimation of marriage as a social institution that is necessary and fulfilling for the female subject.[38] Thus, while at first glance the film might seem to be concerned solely with the residue of bourgeois ideology in the East German institutions of marriage and divorce, through its invocation of this particular ideological split of public/private, the film attempts a larger critique of socialism: namely, the state's inability to recognize when social institutions inhibit, rather than enable, the "self-realization of the socialist personality" and its unwillingness to evolve into a truly democratic republic. It is specifically from Katrin's perspective that the film achieves this critique, and this perspective is already established in the earliest moments of the film. Consider the following sequence:

On screen there is a medium shot of a woman, Katrin, with dark hair and a dark trenchcoat, walking along a stark white hallway. Light floods the hall from large windows. The soundtrack mixes a woman's boppy, jazzy, singing voice-over with the sounds of men talking in the hall. The perspective shifts to that of the woman, in medium close-up, seeing men in conversation, who nod a greeting as she passes. Cut to a close-up of the woman's head, surveying the scene, nodding greetings, as the jazzy singing voice gets louder, drowning out the sounds of the hall. Another cut presents a medium shot of a man (Katrin's colleague) in a dark suit, leaning against the wall, looking longingly, perhaps mischievously, in a diagonal line across and off the screen. The camera cuts to a close-up of Katrin's legs, emerging from the bottom of the trenchcoat, in dark heels, still walking. The soundtrack shifts as the woman's jazzy voice becomes sultrier, parodically echoing the colleague's look. The next cut is to a medium close-up of Katrin, now at home, collecting dishes out of a cabinet, the jazzy voice returning, though less boisterous now. The camera then cuts again to a medium shot of Katrin sitting alone at a dining room table, head in her hands in an expression of fatigue, the jazzy voice playing quietly over the image. The next cut to a medium shot shows her colleague, now dressed as a cowboy, leaning back against the counter in her brightly lit kitchen, then sitting at her kitchen table with arms crossed. The jazzy voice is gone; the sole diegetic sound is her colleague's laid-back whistling. The camera cuts to a medium close-up of Katrin, dressed in a black bodysuit and hair in pigtails with white bows, gathering cups and saucers from the cabinets, then rummaging through the drawers, the sound of silverware clinking together being the solitary sound on the track. Then, looking up, she sees the cowboy standing to her left, leaning once more against the counter—his movement from the table to the counter having been constructed via jump cut. She looks at him quizzically; he then grabs her in his arms and forces himself on her. They struggle and she slaps him, an act presented through overlapping editing, which enables us to see the slap several times. A quiet off-screen cry breaks the silence. The camera then cuts to a medium shot of Katrin covering up one of her sons asleep in bed. Finally, the camera cuts to a close-up of Katrin sitting at the kitchen table—in a sentence she sends her colleague on his way—off-screen we hear several gunshots, signaling his departure. Katrin yawns.

In Kaja Silverman's discussion of the cinema's "scopic and auditory regimes," she expounds on Laura Mulvey's assertion that woman functions as the passive object of the male gaze in classic cinematic texts, arguing that

Figure 1.9. Katrin and the cowboy in her kitchen. *Lot's Wife.* ©DEFA-Stiftung/ Horst Blümel.

[Within Hollywood films, woman's] exclusion from symbolic power . . . is articulated as a passive relation to classic cinema's scopic and auditory regimes—as an incapacity for looking, speaking, or listening authoritatively, on the one hand, and with what might be called a "receptivity" to the male gaze and voice, on the other. Thus the female subject's gaze is depicted as partial, flawed, unreliable, and self-entrapping. She sees things that aren't there, bumps into walls, or loses control at the sight of red. And although her look seldom hits the mark, woman is always on display before the male gaze. . . . Woman's words . . . are scripted for her, extracted from her by an external agency, or uttered by her in a trancelike state. Her voice also reveals a remarkable facility for self-disparagement and self-incrimination.[39]

Elsewhere, Silverman argues similarly that "within dominant narrative cinema the male subject enjoys not only specular but linguistic authority. The female subject, on the contrary, is associated with unreliable, thwarted, or acquiescent speech."[40]

In the sequence described above, two gazes and two voices are constructed that are coded feminine and masculine respectively. The feminine vantage point, marked by the close-ups of Katrin and the shot-counter-shots between her and the colleagues in the hall, as well as by the jazzy voice on the soundtrack, presents a relationship to the world that is nuanced. From Katrin's view one sees the halls and colleagues at eye and shoulder level, which constructs a feeling of Katrin's equality among these male co-workers. The domestic duties are presented as both tiring and meaningful: while Katrin must support her head in her hands at the evening meal, the tenderness with which she cares for her sons reveals that these "duties" are significant. Finally, her attempted yet unsuccessful romantic adventures are reflected in the struggle with the "cowboy" and her final yawn: while she must fight off his aggression, her yawn suggests this failed romance is just one in a longer series of underwhelming sexual experiences. The male perspective, that of her colleague, on the other hand, is much more limited. We see Katrin's legs peeking out from underneath her coat, or we see her as the "scared mouse" backed up against the kitchen counter in surprise. Both images suggest the titillating temptation of a body waiting to be conquered, like the wild West. This clear difference in perspective is further constructed at the level of the soundtrack: the jazzy woman's voice shifts as the scenes change, suggesting an emotional engagement with the image that is not present in the male perspective: the lighthearted "bebop" of the voice in the hall at school is interrupted and subdued by housework and childcare duties and is completely absent in her struggle with her male co-worker, the "cowboy." The sole masculine sounds are those of his whistling and, most important, the gunshots—the acoustic index for phallic failure—to which Katrin's singular response is a disinterested yawn. These looks and voices suggest an altogether different conclusion than that achieved by Mulvey and Silverman when considering classic Hollywood film. Although the male gaze constructs Katrin's "to-be-looked-at-ness"—her legs peeking out from under her coat, for instance—the male gaze is also constructed as "partial" and "flawed." His voice—here represented through the gunshots—is "thwarted," while she enjoys the "last yawn." In *Lot's Wife*, Silverman's idea of the female voice as unreliable, acquiescent, self-incriminating, or nonauthoritative is turned on its head. Rather than serving as the tool of her undoing, the gaze and the voice of the female protagonist structure the narrative's meaning, providing the viewer with identificatory agency that places her (or him) in a position of critique.

As in the previously considered sequence, it is Katrin's gaze—constructed through point-of-view shots and the mise-en-scène—as well as her voice—at the level of the dialogue, in voice-over, and through the soundtrack—that establish her narrative agency. In the next sequence I consider, Katrin voices her main reason for wanting a divorce: the lack of a meaningful and fulfilling love relationship with her husband. Throughout this film, hers is a desire that is articulated as particularly female and private. That is, only men—Katrin's husband, Richard; his friend, Max; and the divorce lawyer—engage Katrin in discussions regarding love, marriage, and divorce. All three of them either do not understand her desire or assert the impracticality of that desire in terms of East German institutions, thus asserting the general infeasibility of her desire. Feminists have debated this so-called feminine desire both with regards to its recuperative and resistant impulses, particularly within the context of the melodrama.[41] Along with others who see the potential political agency therein, I do not read Katrin's desire for mutual love as necessarily sacrificial and containing. Rather, I argue that this desire functions as a critical tool to resist the narrative recuperation of the female character into a particularly passive role in the love relationship, and to resist the legitimation of marriage, and by extension the state, as a necessary and fulfilling institution for the East German female subject.[42]

The opposition in the film between male and female gaze and voice is further developed in the scenes between Katrin and her husband, scenes that focus on her personal reasons for wanting a divorce. Katrin's critical appropriation of the romantic impulse is most clear in her matter-of-fact request for a divorce and in her scathing evaluation of their failed marriage, which is underscored at the level of the image and the soundtrack. Similar to nearly all of the other interactions between Katrin and Richard, this exchange takes place in their bedroom. Here in particular, we are reminded of Gal's discussion of the recalibration of the public/private distinction: not only is the bedroom transformed into a public site for the viewer, but questions regarding the socialist institution of marriage and the legal parameters of divorce in the GDR are overtly discussed in this seemingly private space. Further, the supposedly private dispute in the intimate space of the bedroom calls into question the integrity of an East German icon—in the figure of Richard Lot—and, by extension, the entire paternalist East German state.

Katrin begins by deconstructing her initial "romance" with Richard and by scrutinizing the poverty of their existing marriage. She declares an inherent lack of love, rather than their excessive fighting, Richard's consistent absence from home, or his infidelity as the cause of her discontent. She thus asserts her romantic expectations as a form of resistance to reconciliation, recuperation, and sentimentality. Richard assumes that she is jealous of his affairs and rejects her reasoning; he wants to imagine her as the love-starved, jealous wife. Implicit in his refusal to accept her reasons is also a refusal of implied impotence. That is, he would prefer that she publicly declare, "I must divorce my husband, your honor, because he's such a potent stud and can't stop having affairs!" rather than accept her complete lack of interest in him. As a result, Richard's insistence on their initial romance is met by Katrin with brutal honesty: "Ach, I don't even know any more [that we really] 'loved' [each other]. . . . How was it then? I was pregnant, we didn't want the kid, why be sentimental? For four nights you ran from drugstore to drugstore trying to talk the pharmacist into giving you pills, and I took them all—four pills every few hours, until I was sick! Nothing is more wretched than for us to pretend." Her honesty pushes him to the point of hostility: he shakes her firmly by the shoulders until she stops talking.

The framing, the characters' placement and movement within the mise-en-scène, and the looks exchanged between them underscore the film's alignment with Katrin. Alternately framed in a medium shot on the marital bed and in a medium long shot in front of a dark expanse of curtains that hide their bedroom from the rest of the city, Katrin is presented alone. The mise-en-scène, in particular the looming drapes, reflect a collective desire to hide these problems of socialist marriage, to disavow them as private. In addition, while Katrin is filmed in medium close-up looking directly and intently at Richard, Richard moves distractedly around the room, avoiding eye contact with her. When she asserts her knowledge of his mistresses, he drops his glass of wine in agitation, and she chuckles. Like the gunshots in the initial sequence and Richard's shaking of Katrin, the fumbled glass and Katrin's "last laugh" further underscore the male's loss of specular authority and his "thwarted speech."

The sequence ends with a birds-eye view of the bed that then cuts to a close-up of Richard and Katrin staring up at the ceiling, their heads butting up against one another as they end their conversation. The shift to the bird's-eye view signals Richard's reluctant acquiescence to her erotic and narrative power at the same time that it asserts his social and legal power in real existing socialism, which I will discuss below. Realizing that he cannot convince her of his sexual prowess and her obvious jealousy, he attempts to evoke in her a sense of social and moral responsibility, asking, "Okay, so maybe our love isn't of the 'Monday-evening, made-for-TV movie' variety, but what about our responsibility to society, to the kids?" While she may not love him, he argues, she must be committed to the relationship from a moral and social standpoint. Here, Silverman's arguments regarding the male subject's linguistic authority and the female's subjectivity to the male voice are complicated. The female and male voices compete within the filmic discourse to establish an acceptable notion of marriage. Within that discourse, three possibilities are presented: the version suggested by Richard, a kind of resignation criticized by Katrin as hypocrisy; the one suggested and imagined by

Katrin as "true" or "real"; and the extra-diegetic, generic "great, beaming love of the Monday-night made-for-TV movie" that functions as the ideal romantic narrative through which personal narratives are mediated.[43]

While this third discourse is obviously contradicted by the film's modernist style, Katrin's and Richard's notions of marriage are given different meanings and values in the film. Katrin's is based on socialist ideals of equality and emancipation: at one point she uses the oft-quoted phrase *von der Sowjetunion lernen heißt siegen lernen!* ["to learn from the Soviet Union is to learn to prevail!"] to assert the backwardness of the GDR in achieving this equality. For Katrin, mutual love and respect are key. Richard's definition of marriage, on the other hand, is aligned with the East German legal discourse of the time: until December 1965, divorce was possible in the GDR only if both members agreed to it or if one member could accuse the other of fault (e.g., an extramarital affair or abuse, be it physical, sexual, or emotional). Although Richard is legally at fault—he has had numerous affairs—this is not Katrin's reason for seeking divorce. In fact, several times throughout the film Katrin asserts that she cannot "seek freedom in this way," mostly because she does not want to belittle Richard in the eyes of their children. It is not through accusation or fault, but rather through mutual agreement, that she wants to end her marriage. Thus, although Richard has legally violated the marriage contract, he continues to enjoy a legal right to his marriage because Katrin's reasons for divorce fall outside East German divorce law.

In an ironic twist, Richard equates her personal desire (not his infidelity) with social irresponsibility, and attacks the politics of her family: "You were always against our marriage. I should have known better. Your whole family is like that: two brothers—neither of them comrades, but both divorcés!" In this exchange, the inconsistencies of the public/private distinction in the GDR are made clearer: namely, in the direct correlation made between personal and political life. Here again, Gal's argument regarding the constant recalibration of the ideological distinction of public/private is helpful. Richard transforms Katrin's previously private desire for love into an issue of public propriety. In attacking her and her brothers, he asserts that their insistence on love reveals a lack of marital devotion, which in turn becomes a metaphor for devotion to the Party ("neither of them comrades, but both divorcés!") While the state publically recognizes and protects the relationship between husband and wife to a certain extent, it deems private, and therefore unrecognized and unprotected, other aspects of that same relationship. The legal regulation, ritualization, and institutionalization of marriage unfortunately stops short of intervening on Katrin's behalf.

This contradiction is further complicated and criticized through Richard's implied equation of marital devotion with his own marriage, which is exactly what Katrin has deemed it: hypocrisy. Yet Richard privileges this hypocrisy over and above divorce. His equation of commitment to marriage with commitment to the Party functions as an indirect critique of the Party: that is, his own hypocritical relationship serves as the consummate example of Party membership.[44] Were we to follow Richard's argument, we would have to agree that a failed marriage (to the Party) is better than no marriage (to the Party) at all. One who is willing and able to recognize the hypocrisy and act to change it is, in contrast, "not a comrade." This equation of private with political responsibility reflects Gal's analysis of the public/private distinction in Eastern Europe. While Richard is at once part of the "us" and the "them," it is clear that *Lot's Wife* is attempting to critique what Gal has called the "apparent" hypocrisy of "denunciations of kin, family and friends under socialism, as well as . . . participation in oppositional activities of families and individuals highly placed in the Communist party."[45] As a naval officer and Party member, Richard is able to deny Katrin a divorce, while at the same time being guilty of noncommitment: his affairs underscore the hypocrisy of his denunciation of Katrin for not being a "comrade."

Here, the film constructs two diametrically opposed perspectives: Katrin's and Richard's, one critical and the other resigned. This opposition is constructed visually and aurally as the scene continues. Filmed in a medium shot, Katrin sits on the bed and defends her brother's choices to divorce and not join the Party. Richard enters the frame from the side, but behind her, sits down on the bed behind her and looks hungrily at her hair and shoulders. Impatient with her chatter, he grabs her head from behind and kisses her forcefully on the head and neck. Katrin protests, saying, "I don't like that smell of cigarettes," and their two bodies freeze momentarily in this antagonistic position, with Katrin in the center of the frame. Suddenly, Richard places both arms over and around her, stifling her protests with forceful kisses. The camera cuts to a medium close-up of him pushing her down on the bed while she continues talking in an effort to express her disinterest. He pulls her around on top of him, while her body remains reluctant and unresponsive. The scene ends with a medium close-up of Richard's feet kicking off his shoes with Katrin's limp legs thrown over his. The next scene consists of the following montage: Richard showering (medium shot from waist to head), putting on his shirt (same medium shot), turning on the radio (close-up of his hand turning the dial), buttoning his pants (close-up of his abdominal/crotch area), putting on his jacket (return to previous waist-to-head medium shot), putting money on the nightstand (close-up of his hand with money), putting on his hat and leaving (medium close-up of shoulders/head). During this sequence, Richard's words are limited to banal remarks regarding the temperature of the apartment and getting back to the ship on time. As he places the money on the nightstand, a gesture that is depicted in a close-up of his hand holding the money, the diegetic sound of the radio increases, replacing the sound of his voice though his face is shown as still talking. The final shot is a close-up of Richard putting on his hat, a large smile filling his face.[46]

Günther's use of rapid editing, jump cuts, and nonsynchronous sound in this sequence of shots is telling when considered in the context of Mulvey's analysis in "Visual Pleasure and Narrative Cinema." In her essay, Mulvey develops a binary system of active/male and passive/female narrative and identificatory positions through which she reads the visual and verbal structures of classical narrative film:

> In a world ordered by sexual imbalance, pleasure in looking has been split between active/male and passive/female. The determining gaze projects its fantasy onto the female figure, which is styled accordingly. In their traditional exhibitionist role, women are simultaneously looked at and displayed, with their appearance coded for strong visual and erotic impact so that they can be said to connote *to-be-looked-at-ness*. . . . An active/passive heterosexual division of labour has similarly controlled narrative structure. . . . The man controls the film fantasy and also emerges as the representative of power in a further sense: as the bearer of the look of the spectator. . . . As the spectator identifies with the main male protagonist, he projects his look onto that of his like, his screen surrogate, so that the power of the male protagonist as he controls events coincides with the active power of the erotic look, both giving a satisfying sense of omnipotence.[47]

The verbal and visual structures of power in *Lot's Wife* differ greatly from Mulvey's reading of Hollywood's cinematic codes, revealing again its affinity with other New Wave tendencies at the time. Throughout the sequence described above, the camera does not take the point of view of either character, but rather, functions as a third observer. Yet the visual depiction of marital sex, Richard's "cleansing ritual" and departure, creates a relationship between the viewer and the camera that leads to a privileging of Katrin's narrative perspective. Although the camera's use of point-of-view and shot-counter-shot techniques has likely encouraged same-sex viewer identification up to this point, the camera has constructed Katrin's and Richard's movements and expressions in such a way that an identification on the part of both male and female viewers with Katrin is privileged. Richard's exhibition of masculinity is presented as a grotesque spectacle: his seduction is presented as aggressive and forced; his postcoital behavior as a kind of purification rite that alienates Katrin and the viewer. This postcoital cleansing act is just one of several montages in the film that align the viewer's narrative perspective with Katrin's. In contrast to the typical division of the female body on screen into individual parts, in this montage it is Richard's body that is divided: the medium shot of his naked upper body in the shower, the close-up of his crotch area, the extreme close-up of his hand with the money, and finally the close-up of his silenced talking head turns Richard into a collection of parts, each taking on symbolic character, while Katrin remains off-screen. This division of Richard's body encourages the viewer to see Richard from Katrin's point of view as a collection of parts, specifically those parts that he has just used to enforce her sexual submission. The sexual relationship is constructed through a series of looks as an oppressive and impersonal exchange. Richard's erotic look from the bed at the beginning of the montage is linked to his divided parts, while the viewer and Katrin, united in a shared point of view, have become the victims of his sexual oppression.[48]

While it is clear that Richard may be labeled as the aggressor and therefore the "active" subject in these two scenes, the binaries active/ male and passive/female present in the classical cinema analyzed by Mulvey are altered in *Lot's Wife* through the alignment of the camera with Katrin's voice. Although Katrin does not enjoy linguistic authority within the legal institution of marriage, she does enjoy linguistic and scopic authority within the verbal and visual structures of the film. The diegetic silencing of Richard's voice at the close of the sequence is in stark contrast to Katrin's recurrent voice-over monologues throughout the film and undermines his status as the active subject. Whereas the woman's voice "bebopping" at the beginning of the film signals Katrin's emotional state, the sounds of the radio interrupt and drown out Richard's voice, stripping him of linguistic authority. While Richard might benefit from linguistic authority within external social institutions, within the filmic discourse he functions as the object of Katrin's—and the film's—critique. While Katrin's desire is constructed by the camera as valid and honest, Richard's is constructed as oppressive and illegitimate. Any identification with him, therefore, would have the opposite effect of that described by Mulvey: a necessary recognition of the male's exhibitionism and of his *lack* of erotic and discursive power.

Further, this sequence incorporates a complex yet overt critique of the Party in the figure of Richard Lot, not simply because Richard is an officer, but rather because of the actor playing Richard, Günther Simon. At the time of the film's release, Simon was best known for his popular role as Ernst Thälmann in DEFA classics *Ernst Thälmann: Sohn seiner Klasse* [*Ernst Thälmann: Son of the Working Class*] (dir. Kurt Maetzig, 1954) and *Ernst Thälmann: Führer seiner Klasse* [*Ernst Thälmann: Leader of the Working Class*] (dir. Kurt Maetzig, 1955), in which he embodied East Germany's most important national communist hero. The two-volume film of Ernst Thälmann was a standard part of the school curriculum, and Thälmann was the namesake of vacation homes, inner-city plazas, and memorials, as well as of the Young Pioneers, the state youth organization encompassing grades one through eight. The *Thälmann* films are pure propaganda, constructing Thälmann/Simon as the antifascist German leader who embodies the noble struggle toward international communism. His is a life of personal sacrifice in the name of a greater, utopian good. These films present Thälmann's/Simon's body as a frieze, a statuesque display of heroism. He is the incarnation of the Party, its order and its historical mission. He is the revolutionary instrument of history.

Cast as Richard Lot, however, Simon embodies not a utopian system, but rather one of hierarchy and illogical legality. No longer the "sublime body of the Communist hero," Simon's body has become a simultaneously absurd and oppressively sexual body, a middle-aged, flabby patriarch tied to a stagnating system of Party loyalty.[49] No longer the embodiment of what Kluge and Negt have called the "ideal type of the steel-hard Bolshevik," who inspires heroic struggle, sacrifice, and death, Simon/Lot becomes the ideal turned on its head.[50] The steeled, antifascist body of Ernst Thälmann has become the pathetic, professionalized revisionist, the bourgeois communist careerist, whose partner in the struggle is now a kept woman. The film thus constructs a set of images that ironically underscore Richard's equation of personal duty with political duty. In the alienating construction of Richard's sexual behavior, the Party's alienation from the people is made manifest. Thus, the money Richard places on the table as he leaves for the ship immediately symbolizes the domestic exchange in sexual commodities—clearly an allusion to Engels' critique of marriage as a form of legalized prostitution—while also indirectly alluding to the Party's political and economic exploitation of the people.[51]

Yet the film's critical potential is not restricted to this metacritique of East German foundational myths. Rather, the film's specific engagement with East German divorce law opens up space for the broader reevaluation of the individual's *Glücksanspruch* ["right to happiness"] within the collective. More specifically, Katrin functions as a crystallization of competing public and private needs and desires, giving voice to the gender politics that hinder resolution within her marriage, and to the collective, legal obstacles that thwart individual freedom. This universalization of the film's critique is most strongly developed in the final sequence I will consider: Katrin's meeting with the divorce lawyer.

The sequence begins with Katrin walking to the office. Here, a medium close-up of her stockinged legs reminds the viewer of the "cowboy's" gaze in the school hallway. This is one of the few moments in which we see Katrin outside of the apartment or school. Here, on the public street, she is reduced to parts. Her seductive legs are offset, however, by her voice-over monologue: "Always when I work, I am momentarily, temporarily happy. . . . Perhaps Richard is actually right? Is it better, cleverer, simply to keep on going, eyes closed, playing along, playing it out, gambling away, toying around . . . ?" The juxtaposition of image and

Figure 1.10. Richard as Party patriarch. *Lot's Wife.* ©DEFA-Stiftung/Horst Blümel.

voice-over is an immediate, visceral refutation of women's emancipation. Katrin's words—*mitspielen, weiterspielen, rumspielen*—suggest that her public image, symbolized in her stockinged legs framed by the male gaze, is a continuous obstacle to her emancipation. The "game" she must "play" as an object of male desire, referred to directly in the verb root *spielen,* hinders that emancipation. As long as the law enables her husband to maintain his grip on her, she cannot be fulfilled at work—that fulfillment is only ever "short," "fleeting," and incomplete.

In juxtaposing the gaze on Katrin's legs with Katrin's voice, this scene raises the question of the individual's right to happiness as both a public and private issue. Katrin's voice-over suggests that her professional happiness is offset by her personal misery, that happiness is something that is not wholly resolved or determined by the sphere of work, but rather is also private, and that each form of happiness has a reciprocal effect on the other. In the GDR, work was at the center of social meaning. During the late 1940s and 50s, work became the focus for rebuilding a landscape ravaged by war, functioning at the same time as a public site for working through the mistakes of the fascist past and the crimes against Soviet comrades, as well as for working toward the mutual goal of a utopian society.[52] Work also officially replaced romance and domesticity as the spaces within which women were to achieve self-fulfillment in the GDR, thus reconfiguring woman's identity in the public sphere.[53] This implied that fulfillment in the sphere of work should become women's primary source of individual happiness, and that it was a prerequisite for happiness in personal relationships and in the home.[54] Like its East German literary contemporaries, *Lot's Wife* argues for the recognition of private happiness—specifically within the context of love and marriage—as an important aspect of the social fabric, and problematizes the official assumption that public and private needs have been resolved in the shift from capitalism to socialism.

The film's strongest argument in favor of Katrin's perspective comes in its direct critique of the East German legal system through the figure of the divorce lawyer, who supports Richard's reasons for not granting Katrin a divorce. The film's critique shifts: from one woman's situation to the legal system as a whole, which, the film suggests, has become an institution of repression rather than liberation. When asked why she wants to divorce her husband, Katrin answers, "I don't love my husband." The lawyer's response: "That's no reason! Well, I mean, it is, but actually it isn't." He then searches for "real reasons," asking if Richard has been unfaithful; if he hits her and, if so, how often; and if he is an alcoholic, to

HAPPILY EVER AFTER? 77

which Katrin repeatedly answers no. When she explains her reasons for not wanting to accuse Richard of infidelity—because that will change her sons' perception of their father—the lawyer gives his final verdict: "I'm afraid, my dear, that your case is hopeless. This isn't a case for the courts, it's a case for poets."[55] While the individual's right to happiness is accounted for in the public definition of marriage, Katrin's personal definition of happiness, which includes romantic love, is absent from that public definition. From a legal perspective, lack of love is not a reason for divorce, nor is it necessarily connected to happiness, hence the lawyer's argument that "so many married couples can't stand each other and are still *happily* married; otherwise everyone would get divorced" [my emphasis].

The film's conclusion ultimately reveals the oppressive reality that Katrin faces. Realizing the infrastructural impossibility of her right to happiness, the impossibility of achieving her own happy ending, Katrin is reduced to passive agency. She chooses to act within the constraints of an imperfect system to resolve a problem that officially stands outside of that system: she shoplifts and purposefully gets caught. In doing so, she forces the court to sentence her, which in turn forces Richard to divorce her. Her punishment becomes the means of her emancipation. Yet she is able to achieve her aim only by refusing to participate actively in her legal proceedings. Rather than voice logical reasons for her actions, she chooses *silence* for the remainder of the film. The irony of Katrin's agency—action through inaction—is depicted as a parody of the show trials of the 1950s. Just prior to her trial, Katrin is asked to explain herself during a faculty meeting. However, each time Katrin begins to speak, she is interrupted by her colleagues, who are unable, because they are unwilling, to understand her crime. Rather than offer her a safe space to voice her perspective, the committee meeting deteriorates into a miniature show trial wherein Katrin is interrogated and simultaneously silenced.[56] This public silencing reveals a collective unable to deal constructively with individuals who fall outside of socially accepted behavior, because the collective is unwilling to comprehend the complex contradictions of the public/private dichotomy. In short, to voice the contradictions of real existing socialism is, in itself, a crime. The punishment, which looms over Katrin's offense, is equally reminiscent of the 1950s gulag: as a path to rehabilitation, she is sentenced to hard, physical labor at one of the "large construction sites of socialism." In choosing not to verbally defend her actions, Katrin ultimately refuses to recognize the legitimacy of the system.

THE KAHLSCHLAG AND POLITICAL FILMMAKING

This overt critique of the East German legal system is similar to that of other political films of the 1960s. The question remains, however, why this film, released just months before the 11th plenary, was not banned like many of the other rabbit films. As some critics have argued, films not banned or shelved lacked true political engagement, and the increased focus on everyday problems—here the problems of one woman's marriage—reveals a retreat from social critique into the safety of private, domestic issues. Dagmar Schittly in particular draws this conclusion regarding the *Alltagsfilme* of the 1970s and 80s, those coming after the *Kahlschlag*. She makes a distinction between the political, pre-*Kahlschlag Gegenwartsfilme* of the 1960s and the supposedly apolitical, post-*Kahlschlag Alltagsfilme* of the 1970s and 80s: "Films that had a more socially complete dimension were rarely made. This retreat into private and everyday themes was likewise a result of the political backlash in the mid-1960s. Artists were looking for possibilities to continue working. Very few were willing to continue taking political risks."[57] However, Schittly places *Lot's Wife* in the category of politically engaged, pre-*Kahlschlag* films, while also describing it as a film about women's emancipation that "pleads for individual decisions that do not necessarily serve society, but rather serve self-realization."[58] How does one reconcile this division of political/apolitical, given *Lot's Wife*'s overt emphasis on the interrelated nature of these two "spheres"?

I argue that *Lot's Wife*'s critical potential, as well as its acceptance by the HV Film, lies in its engagement with the contradictory nature of this public/private distinction and the function of woman in that distinction. In the constant recalibration of this distinction, in the inconsistent and contradictory definitions of public/private, "woman" takes on various roles. Gal has suggested such in her analysis of the public/private distinction in the Eastern bloc. On the one hand, state policies instituting "emancipation from above" aligned women with the state: "[W]hile

the standard bourgeois discursive pattern in Europe before the Second
World War associated women with the private and men with the public,
socialism reversed that association in many ways, so that women came
to be seen as allied with the state (public)."[59] Yet the state's assumption
that women had achieved emancipation and, thus, political agency was
often contradicted in the political (public) recalibration of the private
sphere. For instance, within the context of small dissident political or-
ganizations in the private sphere, women's roles as political agents were
also redefined. These dissident groups

> were understood by actors as "politics," and hence public. Once again, the
> private was imagined as subdivided, having a public embedded within it. . . .
> Incidentally, this form of politics was supported by the labor of women who did
> the scrubby work of antipolitics. In the process, they often became invisible as
> political actors exactly because they were understood to be in the private part of
> the private household, not its public part.[60]

Thus, women were seen as both public and private actors, political and
nonpolitical agents, depending on the context and their role in that
context.

Egon Günther's own statements regarding the film's escape from
the *Kahlschlag* and the role of the female protagonist can also be read in
this context. As a young, up-and-coming filmmaker, Günther expressly
wanted to produce films that were oppositional to DEFA tradition at the
time. For members of his generation, deviating from state-sanctioned
socialist realism was an assertion of aesthetic politics. He believes that it
was the film's theme of emancipation that saved it—and him—from being denounced as too "formalist." Offering viewers a larger spectrum of
potential feelings and experiences, female protagonists could represent
"where life happens":

> What saved the film was probably this moment of women's emancipation, which
> was really breaking out at the time. So, a film for women. . . . I find that female
> roles are more prolific, more exciting. . . . If you want to discover what drives us,
> what moves us, where life happens, then I've always felt one is more likely to find
> that with women. . . . Perhaps the female is, for me, really the principal being, the
> essence of human life.[61]

Within this context, woman and her connection to the state, to art, and
to social critique are in flux. Günther seems to be arguing that woman is

both aligned with the state (the emancipation of women is an acceptable theme that draws attention away from the film's problematic aesthetics) and aligned with social resistance and critique (woman represents that which "drives us, moves us . . . is connected to the world," i.e., real existing socialism). Indeed, as Gal has mentioned and I have argued above, the official alignment of woman with the state thus makes her private complaints less overtly political. One can see women aligned with social resistance and critique in numerous films beginning in the 1960s, including the films already discussed in this chapter and in Hermann Zschoche's *Karla* (1965/1966), as well as in later films such as Frank Beyer's *The Hiding Place* (1979), Hermann Zschoche's *On Probation* (1981), Heiner Carow's *The Legend of Paul and Paula* (1973) and *Until Death Do Us Part* (1979), Evelyn Schmidt's *The Bicycle* (1982), as well as Günther's own *Her Third* (1972). Yet one might argue that other female protagonists of the so-called rabbit films focused on corruption in the legal system (*The Rabbit Is Me*) and in the educational system (*Karla*), whereas *Lot's Wife*'s social critique is located within a discourse officially aligned with the state (women's emancipation). Such a reading might then allege the limitations of Katrin's critique, i.e., that it could be construed as strictly having to do with glitches in the system (i.e., the specifics of divorce law), rather than the system as a whole (i.e., the more general contradictions of public/private under socialism, or of a paternalistic system). Once again, the conclusion would be that films focusing less on the overtly political and more on the private as the political, are those that have escaped censorship.

However, political artistic engagement cannot be reduced to complete oppositional critique of the Party line (though it may include this), nor can one assert that the artists' "job from the very beginning was to support the socialist system and to accept the loss of their artistic as well as individual freedom."[62] Given that artists had to navigate the difficult terrain of critiquing socialism while maintaining a socialist perspective, attending to viewer expectations, and competing with Western television and film imports streaming across the Eastern border, this is too simplistic an argument. In fact, one can read the tension between Party control and artistic resistance as two interdependent perspectives that, in any social context, can exist only through their mutually antagonistic relationship. Günther himself states

> The SED leaders always had the feeling of "defend our origins!" These people ... had films in their heads that only the most virtuous artists made. Only the problem was, the films didn't amount to anything. They always imagined the films differently. They had the wish and illusion: Why can't these boys make us a film that would finally help us to govern! And that makes it clear that we live in the best of all possible worlds?—They didn't understand that no one was going to do that, that it just wouldn't work, that art *has* to be subversive.[63]

This interdependence between Party control and artistic resistance can also be seen in the Ministry of Culture's aggressive marketing campaign for the film, clearly an attempt to coopt the film's critical politics. Although *Lot's Wife* was filmed in December of 1964, it was not released for another nine months, just three months before an important political change occurred: the passing of the new *Familiengesetzbuch* [Book of Family Law], which made no-fault divorce legally possible.[64] With the introduction of the new *Familiengesetzbuch*, Katrin Lot's reason for divorce—a lack of love—became legally recognized. Günther may have been right in suggesting that no artist would make a film to "help the Party govern." Yet he could not foresee the Party's ability to manipulate the politics of his critical art, which seems to have happened with *Lot's Wife*. The film's delayed release enabled the Ministry of Culture to construct an extensive marketing campaign that would use the film as a springboard for public discussion of the new *Familiengesetzbuch*. The campaign began five months prior to the film's premier and included a readers' discussion in the women's magazine *Für Dich*, entitled "How can one help Lot's Wife?" wherein Katrin writes for advice about her marriage; a dramatic "reenactment" in the *Neue Berliner Illustrierte* of the court proceedings surrounding Katrin's theft; a series of questions from readers and answers from lawyers on the topic "If I want to get a divorce" in the newspaper *Freie Welt*; a variety of television "info-series" about the new family law; and finally, *Das ganz kleine Ehebuch* [The Very Small Marriage Book], an advertising tool that included an article about marriage, marital crises, and morals, as well as short stories and quotes from famous people about marriage. In achieving an advertising campaign of this magnitude, the Ministry of Culture created a context within which *Lot's Wife* could be read as a moving example of how the East German legal system had failed in the past but had been successfully reformed for the future.

One might argue that the film's overt critique of the East German legal system becomes obsolete through this political maneuvering. However, when considering the true story that serves as the basis for the film, one can argue for the film's muted yet important attempt at critical intervention. In her letter to the filmmaking group *Roter Kreis*, the real Ms. Loth thanks the collective for their work in creating a narrative with a more positive outcome than her own:

> I would like to personally thank you, Mr. Günther, as well as the entire acting collective for the diligence with which you worked on this film. It has been a great satisfaction to me to experience that the director and author and other . . . colleagues have advocated for me with such partiality. At that time—seven years ago—I was not met with any compassion or understanding. . . . Perhaps many, who now seem to understand my situation, would have also thought differently about things seven years ago.

Unfortunately for Rothraut Loth, the success of the film's critique did not correspond to a real revision of her crime and she remained incarcerated. However, the context of *Lot's Wife* suggests a complex relationship between art and cultural policy in the GDR of the mid-1960s. While the film offered resistance to the values and practices of the reigning legal system during its period of production, that resistance was altered through the film's delayed release and the introduction of new laws. One must ask whether the difference between permitted and banned films had to do with the absence or presence of critique per se in the films of the mid-1960s, or if that cultural critique was limited only in its relation to the ever-changing political climate of the GDR.

CONCLUSION

My goal in this chapter has been to question the applicability of gaze and voice, as they have been used within Western feminist film theory, to analyze one of DEFA's uncensored New Wave films in the context of its international contemporaries. While Mulvey and Silvermann suggest that women are assigned a passive position in relation to these cinematic structures and that resistance to the male gaze and women's "thwarted speech" requires an explicitly feminist approach, I argue that this film had begun that work prior to the theory's arrival on the scene. As part of a modernist "counter-cinema," *Lot's Wife* contributes to cinematic history by intervening in traditional narratives that feminist theorists continue to engage with. These foundational theoretical concepts reveal the discursive and political difference of gender in texts produced under real existing socialism, in which certain hierarchies of gender were broken down. While gender in the GDR contained some residue of bourgeois culture, the social and economic context created a new constellation within which gender roles were assigned new and often contradictory meanings, thus enabling gendered desire a different kind of agency. As a desiring, speaking, and therefore demanding subject, Katrin takes a position in this film that from a Western feminist perspective might seem to serve contradictory purposes: while the use of gaze and voice asserts her independence and authority within the visual and linguistic logic of the film narrative, what her voice asserts—namely, a desire for mutual love and passion—seems reactionary and recuperative. I have attempted to show, however, that the category of romantic love and desire as a tool of (negative) critique and (utopian) longing can be understood only within the specific context of gendered relationships in East Germany and within the larger context of the New Waves' discovery of the feminine as a new vessel for political engagement.

2

The Lonely Woman? (Re)production and Feminine Desire in *The Bicycle* and *On Probation*

Socialist ideology, based on a conception of the human being as determined by its place in *production*, [has] not [taken] into consideration this same human being according to its place in *reproduction* . . . [and] in the *symbolic order. . . .* Consequently, the specific character of women could only appear as nonessential or even nonexistent to the totalizing and even totalitarian spirit of this ideology.
 —Julia Kristeva, "Women's Time"

A woman who rejects the trade-off that has been created especially for her sex, who cannot manage to lower her sights and turn her eyes into a piece of sky or water, who doesn't want to be lived, but wants to live: she will experience what it is to be guilty.
 —Christa Wolf, "Selbstversuch: Traktat zu einem Protokoll"

CINEMATIC MOTHERHOOD IN EAST AND WEST

Films about mothers and daughters frequently populated the screens of both the Eastern and Western bloc countries in the 1970s and 80s. E. Ann Kaplan suggests that films about motherhood often function as part of a larger cultural discourse that "emerges to take care of threatening social changes" at particular sociohistorical moments involving shifts in the cultural meanings of gender.[1] In the East as in the West, these cultural meanings of gender were tied up with political and sociohistorical changes such as coming to terms with the fascist and Stalinist pasts, and with the increasingly alienating experience of living under an ideological regime determined by a planned economy and organized around the concept of socialist productivity.

In the context of West Germany, representations of motherhood during this period are closely bound up with the growing second-wave feminist movement, with the 1960s-generation's attempts to come to terms with the fascist past, and with the political and aesthetic reconceptualization of the cinema as a potential site for expanding and democratizing the public sphere. For West German feminist filmmakers, motherhood became a useful terrain for working through intergenerational guilt, responsibility, and loss after fascism and World War II (Helma Sanders-Brahms' *Deutschland, bleiche Mutter* [*Germany, Pale Mother*], 1980; Marianne Rosenbaum's *Peppermint-Frieden* [*Peppermint Peace*], 1983); for depicting and understanding female sexuality during the politically and sexually repressive 1950s (Jutta Brückner's *Hungerjahre in einem reichen Land* [*Years of Hunger*], 1979); and for engaging the material constraints of the divided subject under capital (Helke Sander's *All-Round Reduced Personality—ReDuPers*, 1977).

Actively engaging with the emergent field of feminist theory, West German feminist filmmakers were keen to emphasize that the personal is the political, and were acutely aware of the role film form should play in feminist cinematic practice. Describing the relationship between feminism and film form, Brückner has suggested that feminist filmmaking practices involve "explor[ing] our collective labor of mourning for the cultural paralyzing of our bodies, our eyes, and our space-time relations," with the goal being the recuperation of "the means to reconstruct symbolically."[2] For Brückner, representation is a primary concern. She argues that, while we are confronted with images of women everywhere, "a large part of female reality . . . is not shown. Nor is the way in which we are trained to have an alienated relationship to our body, to ourself."[3] Representing mothers (and daughters) in new contexts, within a range of potential affects, in resistance to the male gaze and through forms other than the melodramatic, became important goals for these West German women filmmakers.

In many of their films, similar to the use of the protocol and the female narrator in the work of Irmtraud Morgner, Maxie Wander, and Christa Wolf in the East, biography and autobiography are used "in a contrapuntal relationship with 'scientific' modes of interpretation . . . [and] provide a figuration and critique of the social realities that structure lived experience."[4] This nonobjective mode of storytelling resists the typical West German postwar scapegoating of mothers as the weak link in the development of the body politic, which ultimately led to fascism.[5] Instead, the highly personalized approach via biography and autobiography in these films privileges the mother-daughter dyad as a site for working through the neglected history of women's wartime experiences, for deconstructing the ideological dichotomy of public/private by overtly politicizing the private sphere, and for resisting a totalizing historical discourse through subjective accounts.[6]

In *Germany, Pale Mother*, Sanders-Brahms approaches history through an autobiographical mode in an attempt to come to terms primarily with her mother's (and secondarily, with her father's) complicity with fascism. She does so by formally complicating the typical maternal melodrama through the use of Brechtian distanciation, offering the viewer a resistant position by interrupting identification with what could otherwise be a seamless, emotionally manipulative cinematic form. Sanders-Brahms' use of an autobiographical female voice-over personalizes the truth of the historical reconstruction of her mother's wartime experience, and the protagonist's retelling of the Grimm fairy tale "The Robber Bridegroom" connects the mother-daughter experience of fascism to a more general history of patriarchal violence. Although aesthetically very different, two aspects of Sanders-Brahms' film are similar to Evelyn Schmidt's *The Bicycle* (1982), which I analyze in this chapter. First, Sanders-Brahms' film emphasizes the mother-daughter dyad as an intensely cathected relationship that serves as the "basis for female authorship and feminist resistance."[7] This resistance moves explicitly from the private into the public with the literal explosion of the domestic space and the resulting transfiguration of the mother and daughter into "vagabonds" and "witches" flying over the rooftops of Berlin as they make their way on foot to distant relatives in the countryside, a move that finds its muted corollary in *The Bicycle*.[8] Second, the mother's narration of "The Robber Bridegroom" in *Germany, Pale Mother* emphasizes the temporal cyclicality of motherhood as the ongoing labor of reproduction and as literal and figurative modes of resistance to patriarchal violence.

Jutta Brückner's autobiographical *Years of Hunger* approaches the problem of maternal complicity from a postwar perspective. Investigating ideals of femininity during the period of the *Wirtschaftswunder* [economic miracle] in 1950s West Germany, Brückner constructs an intergenerational portrait of maternity that interrogates a fractured female identity as a form of historical repression: a commodified body and a consuming/voyeuristic psyche function to disavow guilt, shame, and mourning; consumption-oriented narcissism diverts the women in Brückner's film from coming to terms with the fascist past. Using an autobiographical voice-over, Brückner details the "hysterical symptoms" that serve as the impetus for her film and "shifts the identificatory capacity of women away from a neurotically repetitive, socially conformist commodity orientation and toward an alternative identification" with the repressed histories of their bodies, their selves, and their (national) history.[9] Unlike *Germany, Pale Mother* and *The Bicycle*, however, *Years of Hunger* presents the mother-daughter dyad as "an arrested pre-oedipal bond" that is driven by the mother's neglect of ego boundaries and narcissistic projection of her own desires onto her daughter, a pattern that simply repeats her relationship to her own mother.[10] The cyclicality and repetition presented by maternal femininity in Brückner's film is, thus, conceived as a reactionary rather than a resistant force.

Helke Sander's *ReDuPers*, while aesthetically much different from *The Bicycle* and *On Probation*, offers the most similar West German example of motherhood and reproduction as a site of resistance. Sander's highly autobiographical film grows directly out of the West German feminist movement and the overt politicization of motherhood as both a site of exploitation—domestic labor as unpaid labor—and resistance—as a position from which to question traditional forms of social organization (marriage, family), politics, and scientific modes of thinking.[11] Using the Wall as a symbol of division, Sander reveals how the subject under both Western capitalism and Eastern socialism is equally "reduced"—divided, split, atomized—into a fractured identity that is simultaneously economically and ideologically determined. Foregrounding the protagonist, Edda, as a mother in the first few minutes of the film, Sander explores motherhood as one among many aspects of woman's reduced personality, emphasizing motherhood as both labor and identity. She accomplishes this through what she has called a "feminine aesthetic" and what B. Ruby Rich has termed a "feminist modernism" that positions both the images and narrator's voice dialectically. Rejecting sacrifice as the predominant mode of representing motherhood and speaking the voice-over herself, Sander replaces the authoritative narrator with one who is "demystified [and] intent at working together with the viewer to construct, not merely the film text, but a new vision, a different society, a feminist locus of production and reception."[12] Consequently, motherhood unfolds as an identity that is not inherently, but rather socioeconomically reduced.

In the East European cinema of the 1970s and 80s, motherhood is often the site for exploring issues of loneliness and abandonment in a society whose subjective foundations are rooted in collectivity. This is not just the case for films situated in the contemporary period, but is also true for films dealing with the Stalinist past.[13] In the Hungarian cinema, this is most obvious in Pál Gabor's *Angi Vera* (1978) and in the diary films of Márta Mészáros. In contradistinction to the East German Stalinist mother, who heals the trauma of fascist complicity by forming cathected relationships to "good" Stalinist fathers (simultaneously replacing the "bad" fascist fathers), the Stalinist (step)mother in the Hungarian cinema is a symbol of Soviet occupation and oppression. She is a principled henchwoman, a "vicious communist *apparatchik*," who appears "as a disguised reassertion of patriarchy."[14] In this way, she functions similarly to the East German trope of the postwar mother by translating the historical narrative into a family narrative, but her generally misogynist representation serves to clearly distinguish between the illegitimacy of post-1956 Stalinism and the "nostalgic longing for a lost, mythic homeland" that is embodied by the absent *father*.[15]

Mészáros' films on contemporary Hungarian life, *Eltávozott nap* [*The Girl*] (1968), *Riddance* (1973), and *Örökbefogadás* [*Adoption*] (1975) all reveal motherhood as a primary site of loneliness and loss. *The Girl* centers on an orphan who seeks out her biological mother. Upon finding her—a peasant woman with other children with whom she has a loving and committed relationship—the protagonist experiences yet another moment of abandonment: her mother is reluctant to admit that she ever had a child out of wedlock.[16] Here, motherhood comes to serve as a site of primary, existential loss. *Adoption* is also concerned with abandonment and loneliness.[17] The protagonist, Kata, is a woodworker who lives alone and works in a local factory. Unable to persuade her longtime lover to have a child with her, Kata ends their relationship and, by chance, befriends a young teenager, Anna, who was abandoned by her (still living) parents at the age of six. Anna runs away from the local orphanage and moves in temporarily with Kata. During their brief "adoption" period, Kata and Anna form a strong emotional bond that is aesthetically established through medium shots, tight close-ups and point-of-view shots, and through the obvious exclusion of the male gaze.[18]

In the Polish cinema, single motherhood and poverty is similarly the focus of Agnieska Holland's *Kobieta Samotna* [*A Woman Alone*] (1981). Holland's protagonist, Irene, is the epitome of abjection. A working-class single mother, Irene is a victim of past physical and sexual abuse. Living in abject poverty in a dark, claustrophobic, one-room apartment near the train tracks, Irene suffers brutal economic conditions while attempting to raise her eight-year-old son. Her desperate yet futile desire for mobility is constantly thwarted: her recently deceased aunt leaves her in debt; she loses the opportunity to get a better job; she abandons her son at an orphanage out of desperation; and, as an act of mercy to relieve her suffering, her lover smothers her with a pillow. The film is structured through discomforting close-ups, tight framing, and a sparse soundtrack that "sutures [the viewer] without release," creating a narrative and formal tension "that finds no diegetic resolution between . . . openness and enclosure, mobility and stasis."[19] Irene's desperation is the result of the violent limitations placed on her agency. The film's lack of emotionality, the absence of melancholy or even compassion at both the narrative and aesthetic levels of the film, ultimately leads to the destabilization of the signifiers "woman" and "mother." For Marciniak, this "perspectival truth" of motherhood reveals the near impossibility of mobility at the nexus of class and gender in Poland before the fall of communism.[20]

In the East German cinema, motherhood was a central signifier in the dialectical tension between production and reproduction. In what follows, I use Julia Kristeva's theory of "women's time" to analyze the cinematic construction of motherhood (*reproduction*) as a site of potential resistance and fulfillment in a society founded on labor (*production*). Kristeva's essay, published in 1981, was immediately contemporary to the films under investigation and is useful for articulating the emergence of a particular mode of gendered resistance in the cinema to the socialist discourse of productivity. Kristeva writes from within specific feminist debates emerging in the West at the time. Situating her analysis of the "problematic of women in Europe" within an inquiry on *time*, Kristeva suggests that the time, which "the feminist movement both inherits and modifies," is time "as project, teleology, linear and prospective unfolding, time as departure, progression and arrival ... the time of history."[21] This time is an ideological discourse that asserts mastery and domination as order. She sees the feminist movements as offering an important discursive resistance to this by recognizing the scientific focus on linear temporality as "masculine, civilizational and obsessional."[22]

Kristeva articulates the relationship between gendered discourses of space and time, particularly as they concern the issue of reproduction. She suggests that, while female subjectivity is most often linked to space, the question of time, specifically the temporal modalities of *repetition* and *eternity*, overdetermine women's relationship to space and their access to the symbolic:

> On the one hand, there are cycles, gestation, the eternal recurrence of a biological rhythm which conforms to that of nature and imposes a temporality ... whose regularity and unison with what is experienced as extrasubjective time, cosmic time, occasion vertiginous visions and unnamable *jouissance*. On the other hand, and perhaps as a consequence, there is the massive presence of a monumental temporality, without cleavage or escape, which has so little to do with linear time (*which passes*) that the very word "temporality" hardly fits. ... This repetition and this eternity are found to be the fundamental, if not the sole, conceptions of time in numerous civilizations and experiences, particularly mystical ones.[23]

It is this "eternal recurrence of a biological rhythm," the perpetual cyclical nature of women's material-biological experience in the world that, according to Kristeva, provides a key to understanding women's relationship to space. Women's primary role in Western civilization has been seen as the *reproduction* of a society; *reproduction* is, historically and politically speaking, what binds women to the domestic space.

As was discussed in the introductory chapter, the ideological division of domestic space and the space of (paid) labor, the seeming opposition of private and public, lies at the heart of feminist critiques of socialism. But Kristeva's notion of women's time provides us with a key to understanding the ways in which time functions as an inherent aspect of that ideological division. Socialism, as Buck-Morss has argued, was a modernist project, a utopian conception of society determined by a discourse of linear, progressive time. It was a project of continual striving toward communism, a teleological narrative of history. Kristeva articulates a discourse of time that is antithetical to teleology by way of its endless cyclicality. The temporal chasm of monumental and extra-subjective time makes relative the socialist discourse of temporality, opening up a space for resistance. As "female subjectivity ... gives itself up to intuition, [it] becomes a problem with respect to a certain conception of time: time as *project, teleology, linear* and *prospective unfolding; time as departure, progression* and *arrival*—in other words, *the time of history.* . . . A psychoanalyst would call this 'obsessional time,' *recognizing in the mastery of time the true structure of the slave.*"[24] The refusal to conceive of time in this way is, for Kristeva, a moment of potential liberation from the slavery of teleological time. In resisting the socialist notion of history as progression, focusing instead on cyclical repetition in terms of narrative structure, character development, mise-en-scène and the film's primary metaphor (the bicycle), Schmidt's film posits motherhood and maternal desire, if not overtly then at least unconsciously, as its fundamental critique of socialism.

This resistance to the logical and ontological values of rationality dominant in the nation-state inheres both in the West and East European feminist resistance to a patriarchal society structured around progress, productivity, and rationalism. It is recognizable in works by Sander, Brückner, Sanders-Brahms, Wolf, and Morgner and is also present in the two films by Schmidt and Zschoche that I discuss in this chapter.

Interestingly, these two films—*The Bicycle* (1982) and *On Probation* (1981)—engage the GDR's official discourse of motherhood differently from each other, and also differently from other East and West European films already mentioned. The simultaneous "insertion into history . . .

of the irreducible difference" that each of these films enacts links them, through the figure of the mother, to contemporary works in East and West in their resistance to time as teleology.[25] Yet what distinguishes them is the nature of the resistance. Motherhood is neither a trope through which the second generation comes to terms with parental complicity under fascism—this had already occurred in the films of the late 1940s and 50s—nor is the (step)mother a symbol of the illegitimacy of Stalinism, while the absent father represents our cathected relationship to the (colonized) nation-state. Rather, like their East German literary correlates, *The Bicycle* and *On Probation* enact motherhood as a (potential) site of pleasure precisely because reproduction is linked to the "eternal return," to the extrasubjective, cyclical, and monumental time of which Kristeva speaks.

The Bicycle articulates motherhood as an alternative discourse of subjectivity in the face of a socialist discourse of labor and historical progression. Although the protagonist, Susanne, repeatedly fails to find fulfillment in both her romantic and her professional endeavors, motherhood offers her a respite from her otherwise alienated existence. While the film emphasizes the protagonist's hopelessness as a result of her social and economic limitations, the material experiences of mothering offer her an affective pleasure that serves as the film's only happy end. *On Probation*, however, provides a much bleaker narrative of single motherhood. The film's protagonist, Nina, is able to enjoy motherhood only insofar as she can perform acts of maternal love outside of socialist norms and expectations, and unnoticed by members of her community. As a woman whose maternal abilities are questioned throughout the film, Nina ultimately experiences motherhood as yet another alienating experience to be lived out under the watchful eye of the paternalist state. *On Probation* suggests that woman is bound to her biology through a social discourse that simultaneously assumes her natural inclination to reproduce while also punishing her failure to successfully perform her biological responsibilities in socially acceptable ways. In contrast to the resistant role that motherhood offers Susanne in *The Bicycle*, motherhood for Nina in *On Probation* serves as a form of disciplinary constraint that is inherently linked to her perceived biological essence.

REPRODUCTION AS RESISTANCE

East Germany imagined itself a utopian space for the emancipation of the gentler sex, an emancipation that the state conceived as an integral part of its foundational narrative of socialism. Having been written into the first constitution of the GDR, gender equality was decreed official, and with that official declaration women and men were, at least formally, seen as equals in the eyes of the state. As a result of the demands that had been made by the proletarian women's movement in the decades prior to its founding, the GDR introduced and implemented what was considered a comprehensive *Frauenpolitik* [women's politics] that would finally answer the so-called woman question. With a sociopolitical program that achieved women's legal equality and economic independence through their participation in production, as well as the expansion of social services to assist in the raising and caring for children, and the outsourcing of housework, East Germany considered its gender trouble resolved.[26]

The problem of women's role in the process of *reproduction*, however, remained a thorn in the side of the state insofar as women's bodies could not be emancipated from the material specificity of motherhood (pregnancy, birth, nursing, etc.) The state's attempts to enable and enforce women's equality with men—through their equal access to education and professional training in traditionally masculine fields of labor, as well as through the expansion of social services for the care and raising of children—never fundamentally questioned woman's naturalized role as mother and man's secondary, even cursory, role as father. By the 1970s, the state's primary strategy to reconcile women's careers with motherhood had officially been achieved; the gendered division of labor in the raising of children was naturalized and cemented, and the only question to be answered was how to make paid labor easier for *mothers* (not *parents*).[27]

In arguing that the state did not just see mothers as the ones responsible for the raising and care of children, but rather that women have a natural, biological need to reproduce, Hornig and Steiner uncover the true gender inequality in the GDR: that women, not men, are inherently (i.e., biologically) tied to reproduction.[28] Thus, woman's embodiment as *mother* was seen as *a priori*, a fact of nature. Woman as a site, as the *physical, material* space of biological reproduction, was understood as her primary mode of being in the world. Yet biological reproduction, although necessary for the production process, was absent from the official East German definition of reproduction, as I will explain below. Consequently, the material specificity of woman's experience in the production process as a site of biological reproduction was removed, or at least ignored, in East Germany's idea of a socialist society based on egalitarianism. What Marx postulated as the most basic form of property relations—the division of labor in the nuclear family, the *materiality of gender difference*—stood outside the official East German discourse on women's emancipation.

Kristeva and others have argued, however, that Marx's original notion of historical progress falsely assumes an *a priori* definition of women as *mothers* in that "the daily reproduction of the *species* in the birth of *individuals* is not perceived as an essential dialectical moment of historical progress."[29] This was certainly the case in the GDR, where the official political definition of reproduction included biological reproduction only insofar as it described one aspect of the basis of both the "simple reproduction" and the "extended reproduction" in the production process.

> [Reproduction is] the constant renewal and expansion of social production, *labor power*, the *population*, the mode of production and the people's assets . . . the process of reproduction comprises the phases of production, distribution, circulation and consumption . . . simple reproduction involves the renewal and periodic repetition of the production process to the same extent as before, in which recently produced products replace those that have been consumed . . . extended production is the repetition and continuation of the production process to a greater extent than before. More and better means of production and consumer goods are manufactured than before.[30]

Thus, East German ideology practically ignored the material necessity of *biological* reproduction—the (overdetermining) role of biological reproduction in the economic base—and of women's roles in reproducing the species. By designating (paid) labor in the production process as the foundational moment of socialist subjectivity, "socialist ideology has been compelled . . . to believe that the specific nature of women is unimportant, if not nonexistent."[31]

THE MATERNAL IN SPACE AND TIME—*THE BICYCLE*

Evelyn Schmidt's 1982 film, *The Bicycle,* tells the story of Susanne, a young single mother living on the brink of poverty with her kindergarten-aged daughter, Jenny. Susanne works as an unskilled laborer in a sheet-metal factory while her daughter spends long days at kindergarten and evenings in daycare. Susanne struggles to manage her everyday expenses— lunch money for Jenny, insurance fees, rent, and groceries—while her sole outlet is bar-hopping with drunken friends. The monotony of her job leads her to quit without any other immediate prospects, and her status as an unskilled laborer limits her job opportunities and threatens her financial stability. Desperate for cash when Jenny becomes ill, Susanne commits insurance fraud, reporting her bicycle as stolen. She meets Thomas, a young, recently promoted engineer, who shows interest in her and who, upon discovering she is out of work, offers her a new job. As their romance develops, Susanne and Jenny move in with Thomas and enjoy the comforts and security of middle-class domesticity. Upon discovering Susanne's crime, however, Thomas distances himself from her emotionally and they separate. Although Susanne returns to living hand-to-mouth, the film suggests that she is happier alone with Jenny. The film ends with Jenny learning to ride Susanne's bike in the cul-de-sac of their urban neighborhood as Susanne looks on happily.

In the previous chapter, I investigated the critical potential of female desire within the context of the East German New Wave film. While Schmidt's *The Bicycle* certainly foregrounds romantic desire as an important aspect of its narrative structure, I argue that it is actually maternal desire, and not romantic desire, that serves as the central signifier of the film's libidinal economy of resistance. In fact, it is the tension between the two forms of desire and their relationship to both narrative development and discourses of time that reveal their importance for the film's critique. While the story of Susanne's romance with Thomas plays an important role in driving the narrative forward, it is the cyclical return to the mother-daughter dyad throughout the film that serves as the narrative's foundational discourse of happiness and fulfillment, ultimately anchoring the film in a resistant discourse of time.

To begin, let us return to Feinstein's articulation of the difference between the *Gegenwartsfilm* and the *Alltagsfilm*. In his analysis, Feinstein argues that unlike the *Gegenwartsfilm*, the *Alltagsfilm* resists the historical progression so strongly emphasized by official East German ideology in narrating the shift from socialism to communism. In resisting the GDR's utopian discourse of progress, the *Alltagsfilm* focused instead on the halted, stagnant nature of life under real existing socialism, revealing a more skeptical, even cynical relationship to East German reality.

Interestingly, the studio documents reveal anxiety about Susanne's relationship to narrative time as progress, an anxiety that is then disavowed by situating the narrative's cyclicality as generational, individual, and particularly gendered. The official acceptance documents begin by suggesting that Susanne's situation is "characteristic of many people" and should be interpreted as the "amplification of a typical case."[32] Susanne's failure "to progress" is then couched as being typical of a younger generation of East German *women*, in particular, who are always ready "to break off ties" with the men in their lives. General Director Mäde of the DEFA Studio supported the project by explaining the narrative's cyclicality as an emancipatory "reflex of our newly developed social conditions that enable women to live independently," (e.g., East German women can freely leave unsatisfying relationships because they are financially emancipated).[33] Yet the Head of Artistic Production saw Susanne's return to single motherhood as the film's ideological failure, as indicative of her *personal* unwillingness to grow, learn, and progress.[34]

Schmidt's film certainly falls into the *Alltagsfilm* genre and accomplishes its resistance to the GDR's progressive discourse at the level of the story; through the development (or lack thereof) of the protagonist, Susanne; through the mise-en-scène; and through the film's primary metaphor, the bicycle. The film's focus on Susanne's poverty, on the dead-end jobs she takes, on her drinking binges with friends at the local pub, and the prevalence of domestic labor in the depiction of her everyday existence (the tedium of washing clothes by hand, heating water on the stove to bathe, and grocery shopping on a nearly nonexistent budget) reveals a never-ending cycle of living hand-to-mouth. For Susanne, therefore, the East German slogan "wie wir heute arbeiten werden wir morgen leben" ["how we work today is how we will live tomorrow"] means nothing more than the endless repetition of *lack* of progress.

The film begins and ends with an emphasis on the mother-child dyad and the banal routine of everyday life. The opening sequence in particular foregrounds various points of tension that the film will investigate: the tension between romantic and maternal desire, between the public and the private, as well as between progress and repetition. Opening with a slow pan of an urban landscape under construction in the darkness of the early morning, the film's opening credits are introduced with the title song:

> Love doesn't leave love / Even if it has to broaden its scope . . .
> Must love escape the world? / Love . . . love . . . love stops short at love . . .
> Shouldn't we call each other bride and groom?
> When you prick me in the heart / Love . . . love . . . love doesn't leave love.

As the female voice-over sings, the camera cuts from a pan of the urban landscape to a high-angle shot of Susanne entering the courtyard of her apartment building with her bicycle. The shift in color is notable: the previous shot of the city is presented in various shades of grays, blues, and blacks, while Susanne is shown emerging from a warmly lit hallway, the golden light spilling onto the brick courtyard and illuminating her frame against the darkness. The first shot of her red bicycle, the first splash of color on the screen, is followed by Jenny emerging from the doorway in a bright yellow raincoat. As Susanne lifts Jenny onto the bicycle, the voice-over sings "Love, love, love remains with love." As Jenny and Susanne emerge through two warmly lit halls into the dark street, the colors shift again to shades of gray and blue. The camera holds a long shot as Susanne and Jenny bike out of the frame, and the song comes to an end.

The film's opening sequence articulates the tensions mentioned above through a structural tension between the aural and the visual, as well as between different aspects of the visual within the frame. In regards to the former, the romantic desire expressed in the love song is reconfigured in the depiction of Susanne and Jenny on the bicycle. While the film's theme song suggests a romantic narrative of love, the images suggest a very different love narrative: that between a mother and her daughter. In fact, the film's narrative trajectory is revealed during the first

performance of the refrain, "love, love, love remains with love": while the
film purports to be about Susanne finding (and perhaps losing) love with
Thomas, the love that will remain is that between Susanne and Jenny.
This is then further emphasized through the long take of Susanne and
Jenny as they depart from their apartment and disappear into the gray urban space. Although the aural cues emphasize romantic love (the female
voice-over sings of a bride and groom), the visual cues suggest that the
future of this love lies in the mother-daughter relationship. Hence, what
might have been an image of two lovers disappearing out of the frame
into their mutual romantic future becomes the first of many recurring
images of the mother-daughter dyad.

Further, visual tension is created within the frame through the use
of color. While the urban space is depicted as gray and dismal, the use
of bright primary colors for the bicycle and Jenny's raincoat, as well as
the golden glow of light emerging from the domestic space, suggests
that the happiness to be found in this film might be located only in the
intimacy of the mother-daughter dyad. The scene immediately following
the opening sequence affirms this: while waiting in traffic for the light to
change, a large transport truck dumps rainwater from its roof down onto
Susanne and Jenny on their bicycle, solidifying the cruelty of the public
space in contrast to the warmth of the private sphere.

The visual/aural distinction in the opening sequence between romantic vs. maternal desire and public vs. private space foregrounds the
banality inherent in the *Alltagsfilm*, its generic refusal to engage a progressive socialist discourse and to focus instead on the perpetual, repetitive, and perhaps, therefore, unresolvable problems of everyday life. As I
will argue, it is this problem of *time*—repetition and perpetuity—in conjunction with *space*—private versus public—that lends Schmidt's *The
Bicycle* its critical potential. Although the film's opening sequence aurally
and visually emphasizes narrative as departure and teleology—both in
terms of the progressive nature of the song (moving from falling in love
to marriage) and of the image (biking out of the frame as the launching
moment of the narrative trajectory)—one can argue that, for Susanne,
time actually functions cyclically. While the opening sequence suggests
that time is something that passes and unfolds, leading to development,
I argue that *The Bicycle* is actually a cyclical narrative that posits the

pleasure of maternal identity as a form of repetition in contrast to other positionalities that adhere to a teleological notion of time under socialism (narratives of romance, labor, etc.)

The Bicycle resists the progressive mode of temporality both in terms of its narrative structure and in terms of the development of its characters. To begin, the film's plot consists of narrative conflicts and resolutions that are cyclical in nature. The first sequence following the opening credits reveals Susanne and Jenny in a never-ending cycle of living hand-to-mouth: as she drops Jenny off at school, Susanne is approached by the kindergarten teacher for having missed Jenny's lunch payment again. Susanne's inability to pay is met with contempt. When Susanne is finally able to pay, the relief is apparent, but the monotony of her job leads to frustration and to her quitting, putting the family in financial jeopardy again. When Jenny falls ill, the situation becomes precarious. Unable to pay for the necessary medication, Susanne commits insurance fraud. The 450 Marks from the insurance enable Susanne to obtain the medicine and for a while they live more comfortably. After spending a good deal of time seeking work that is both stimulating and doesn't require her to work nights, Susanne is hired for a position as clerk at a travel agency, which offers the potential for traveling abroad. This is the first moment in the film in which labor is presented as potentially pleasurable, and Susanne is visibly excited about her new prospects. However, Jenny's recurring sickness causes Susanne to have to stay home with her, and she loses her position because she fails to inform her new employer of her circumstances. She finds more alienating work at a brewery and the cycle begins again. Moments of private happiness—a brief romance with Thomas, dancing in the courtyard with neighborhood children, biking with Jenny into the city, a picnic in the park—are interrupted by the discovery of her fraud and she must seek Thomas' help. Although the brigade and the conflict commission are able to mediate her case, her relationship with Thomas crumbles. By the end of the film, Susanne has returned to her sparse apartment, where the only real change is the discovery that their previous roommate, an elderly woman, is no longer living there (and is, presumably, dead). Susanne spends the last minutes of the film happily watching Jenny learn to ride her bike in the roundabout outside their apartment building.

The film's narrative trajectory is not one of progress, therefore, but rather one of repetition and recurrence. By having its protagonist begin and end in the same (narrative and physical) space without any overt development, the film eschews a teleological trajectory. Although Susanne and Jenny have had to traverse various obstacles and have experienced various resolutions over the course of the film, the end of the film presents progress or achievement solely in Jenny's learning to ride her mother's bicycle: she literally steps into her mother's footsteps, reiterating that the cycle is intergenerational, perpetual. Further, while the opening sequence has the mother and daughter riding off into the gray, urban landscape (literally escaping out of the frame and into another, suggesting a linear structure), the film ends with Jenny taking her mother's place and riding in one long, repetitive circle as her mother also turns in place, exclaiming with joy, as she watches her daughter move concentrically. The movement of the camera in a steady 360-degree pan, alternating between the subjective perspectives of Susanne and Jenny, reinforces this cyclical (non)ending.

While the cyclical experience of labor is presented as monotony, the film's representation of the mother-daughter dyad is the clearest positing of a cyclical structure of resistance to socialist teleology. The friction between Susanne's role in the reproduction process and her role in the production process offers the viewer both an overt critique of real, existing socialism, while also positing an alternative narrative of pleasure and fulfillment. Susanne's role in the production process is overdetermined by her reproductive role: as a poor, single mother with few credentials, she must maintain gainful employment for her and her daughter's survival, but is limited by her narrow skill set and the shift system that relegates much unskilled labor to the night shift. Yet her ability to successfully perform her role in the reproduction process is strained by her limited access to the production process: as a single mother, she cannot spare time pursuing advanced qualifications that would place her in a better position, which leaves her financially, professionally, and emotionally starved. The cyclical nature of her lack of access, her inability to gain a solid foothold in the production process, is inextricably linked to her role in the process of reproduction as a single mother.

An emphasis on the cyclical nature of Susanne's experience of the production process is also emphasized in Schmidt's cinematic choices. After dropping Jenny off at kindergarten, the camera cuts to a long shot of Susanne working in her first job at a metal factory. The left and right thirds of the frame are dominated by large, gray, pock-marked blocks of concrete—the door frame to Susanne's production space. In the center third of the frame, Susanne can be seen as only one third of the center of the frame, sitting with her back to the camera as she punches metal at a machine. The machine is twice as big as she is; her stool is easily three times too big, big enough for a giant, which serves to dwarf her figure further. Although side and key lighting illuminate her frame against the massive machine, the gray and slate blue of her clothing cause her to blend into her surroundings. The steady whir of the industrial machinery is only disrupted by the hard, repetitive punching sound of Susanne's own machine. The camera then cuts to a medium shot of Susanne straight on. Although she now takes up one third of the frame, the massive gray machine at which she sits now dominates the right third of the frame, and her clothing, in similar shades of gray, black, and blue, as well as her lack of expression and repetitive movement, give the impression that she is physically connected to the machine, a kind of human outgrowth of the mechanization process. Finally, the camera racks focus and we see, in an extreme long shot, two other women in the deep space of the background, dressed similarly in blue and gray, sitting at identical machines and performing the same repetitive movements as Susanne.

In this first depiction of production in the film, repetition and recurrence are overtly used as a form of critique. The actors' gestures, the camera framing, the use of a slate blue palette, and the placement of bodies in relation to the machines within the mise-en-scène suggest not progress, but rather a kind of static repetition or repetition of stasis. The repetition within the mise-en-scène functions to emphasize the halted, stagnant experience of alienated labor under real existing socialism. In this sequence, the teleological narrative of socialism as utopian striving grinds to a halt, and the socialist slogan "the way we work today is how we will live tomorrow" takes on dystopian overtones. Less than ten minutes later, the second representation of Susanne at work reaffirms this. She has, as Marx noted of the mechanized worker, become absorbed by

Figure 2.1. Punching metal. *Das Fahrrad (The Bicycle)*. Dir. Evelyn Schmidt, DEFA, 1982. ©DEFA-Stiftung/Dietram Kleist.

the machine.[35] The space of production in *The Bicycle* is presented as a never-ending experience of alienation, devoid of humanity, destined to repeat itself infinitely.

This vicious cycle is countered in the film only by Susanne's personal experiences as a romantic subject and as a mother. Unlike the depiction of repetition and recurrence in production, the depiction of reproduction, particularly in the mother-daughter dyad, foregrounds the potentially liberating aspects of cyclicality as the film's primary mode of representing maternal desire. While repetition within the sphere of labor is experienced by Susanne and the viewer as oppressive and alienating, within the sphere of motherhood it is experienced as a meaningful, often pleasurable respite from the world outside. Although her class and her gender limit her access to progressive time/labor under socialism, they offer her access instead to a cyclical experience of time that privileges maternal desire as pleasure.

This becomes most obvious in the brief oases of maternal intimacy in the film: lying in bed and spinning tales, dancing in the courtyard with Jenny and the neighborhood kids, taking an afternoon bike ride and picnicking, and teaching Jenny to ride her bicycle. In the first example we find one of the most overt instances of cyclicality and maternity as resistance. The sequence comes just after Susanne has quit her job punching metal. In the dark of the apartment, Jenny frantically leaps out of bed, insisting that they get up. Susanne, surprised out of sleep, jumps to attention and then realizes that they don't have to get up yet, since, she says, "today we're not going to work." Instead, she suggests that Jenny climb into bed and snuggle with her. The camera cuts to a medium close-up of the two in bed—the only bed scene in the entire film—as Jenny asks Susanne to tell her the story about the king. Patches of light and dark fall on their heads as they lie in bed and Susanne strokes Jenny's arm. Susanne, whose face is nearly indistinguishable behind her tousled hair, is wearing pajamas with miniature pastel swans, and the pillowcases are covered in a delicate floral pattern. Susanne has to be coaxed into telling this story yet again, and Jenny begins telling the story through a big smile: "Once upon a time there was a king, who rode out in his carriage to search for a queen. And a queen came along just then who was going to her wedding. The king said, 'You wanna get married?' And they both said, 'yes!' And then they all went with the king back to his palace." Susanne turns to face Jenny, stroking her arm all the while, and takes over the storytelling: "In the palace a big wedding banquet had been prepared, with lots and lots of music. And the king and queen danced all night long. And the next morning they fell into bed completely exhausted. And the king said, because you danced so well, I will grant you one wish." And Jenny says, "I wish for a doll!" Susanne smiles and the camera cuts to them walking along the street together, carrying groceries and eating pastries.

This scene reveals mothering as a particular form of *production*—as *creation*—within the sphere of *reproduction*. The spinning of a fairy tale, which Jenny can reproduce in full, reveals the act of storytelling as a form of *maternal production*. The cut to Susanne and Jenny walking down the street eating pastries thus becomes a momentary happy ending to the fairy tale. In this choice, Schmidt provides us with a metacommentary on the ideological function of the fairy tale. Susanne's discursive role as storyteller emphasizes the mother's importance in introducing and reinforcing the ideological primacy of romantic love in the development of female subjectivity. In narrating the romantic fairy tale with its obligatory happily-ever-after ending, Susanne speaks from within the discourse

Figure 2.2. Susanne and Jenny spinning fairy tales. *The Bicycle.* ©DEFA-Stiftung/Dietram Kleist.

that the mother-daughter dyad ultimately resists: the discourse of romantic desire constructed as teleological narrative. This disjuncture is obvious to the viewer because Susanne herself has few positive interactions with men in the film and because the story she narrates develops in contradiction to her own.[36] The fairy tale functions, in fact, within the film's cyclical discourse of resistance. While the narrative structure of the fairy tale itself is romantic and teleological, the social function of the fairy tale—its material iteration—is cyclical: as oral transmission, it recurs and is recycled through the creative labor of the mother as storyteller and the daughter as audience and future storyteller. As such, the fairy tale further serves to illustrate Kristeva's understanding of female subjectivity being linked to the temporal modalities of both *repetition* and *eternity*, and as a form of maternal labor that "becomes *creation* [production] in the strong sense of the term."[37] Ultimately, the resolution of the sequence (Susanne and Jenny shopping and eating pastries) serves to undermine the teleological discourse of the fairy tale: the real happy ending is to be found in the eternal return to the mother-daughter dyad, and not in marrying the fairy-tale prince.[38]

The sequence following Susanne's receipt of the insurance money also reveals how maternal desire functions as Susanne's respite from the tedious and precarious void of the everyday of socialism. Having submitted her falsified insurance claim, Susanne picks up her money from the clerk and rushes out the door, stopping on the stairs in a low, medium close-up to frantically count the 450 marks, afraid to believe that she made it out of the agency without getting caught. Dropping Jenny off at school, Susanne then rushes off to her new job at the travel agency. There she discovers that, because she did not notify her new employer of the reason for her absence (Jenny's recurring illness), the job has been given to someone else. Shot at a low angle, out of focus, we see Susanne's skirted legs walk toward us, aurally emphasized by the stark sound of her heels clicking on the floor. In a voice-over, we hear her potential employer explaining to her why she lost the job: she didn't show up, she didn't call to explain herself, and the job was given to someone else; what did she expect? The scene ends with Susanne walking into a focused, close-up shot of her profile from outside of the frame, swallowing hard at this setback, which will return her to living hand-to-mouth.

The next scene begins with a panning medium shot of Susanne in a familiar space: the cavelike bar where she regularly drinks away her worries. Shot with minimal fill light, the bar is mostly dark, with single hanging lights placed directly over the individual tables, which dot the vast yet sparsely populated space. The lights create stark spotlights over tables cluttered with empty bottles and gray clouds emanating from the smokers assembled around them. The camera slowly pans to the left and finally rests on Susanne in profile again, sitting alone at a table, arms stretched out stiffly in front of her, hands pressed flat to the table, looking as if she is literally trying to get a grip. Staring at the numerous empty glasses scattered about the table, motionless, head tilted down, Susanne is the picture of defeat. The near silence of the bar, broken only occasionally with the sound of bartenders collecting and cleaning glasses, is then exploded by a cut to the sound and close-up shot of thousands of empty beer bottles moving along a conveyor belt. The camera pans up, the bottles stop briefly, the camera racks focus, and we see the back of a woman in the deep space of the background inspecting the bottles as they move along the conveyor. The camera then moves one last time in the sequence, panning left to rest on Susanne's profile once more, this time barely visible in the sea of bottles that move past (figure 2.3). Again,

Figure 2.3. Susanne working the line at the brewery. *The Bicycle.* ©DEFA-Stiftung/Dietram Kleist.

her face is empty and motionless. The final scene in the sequence begins with a well-lit close-up of a grocery cart, in which we see a bag of milk and bottle of yogurt. The camera then cuts to a brightly colored pyramid of canned pineapple. We see Susanne's arm reach out and turn the can around. Her hand then stops, withdraws, and the fingers twitch. Finally, her hand puts the can into the cart. The camera slowly pans from the cart up to Susanne's face, sighing and looking around, her blank stare barely scanning the space around her with a distant look. The camera then cuts to a long shot of her turning away and dragging the nearly empty cart behind her toward the check-out registers.

Similar to the early shots of Susanne working as a metal puncher, these scenes use mise-en-scène, color, lighting, camera distance, and movement to reveal Susanne's alienated existence in the socialist public sphere. Her obvious fear of being caught for submitting a fraudulent claim is made manifest in the low, claustrophobic shot of her on the agency stairs, where the colors are primarily browns and grays. The out-of-focus camera, the distinct sound of heels, and her deliberate steps at the travel agency reveal a moment of vertigo: she is about to fall into the abyss again, with no hope of lucrative or fulfilling work prospects.

The cavernous shots inside the bar emphasize a spatial void with little lighting and a palette of black, gray, brown, and blue. Susanne's placement in the first half of the frame, dominated in the other half by empty bottles and sparse lights, also isolates her from the others in the bar and emphasizes her marginality (the only other populated table is filled by a circle of friends). The penultimate scene in the sequence, dominated by the jarring sounds of clattering glass, is a vast sea of grays, blacks, opaque glass, and muted whites. Not even the bluish-gray of the women's work shirts stand out in the blank space of the brewery, where Susanne has finally found work again, and Susanne's minimal movements within the frame give her presence there a moribund quality. Finally, while the pineapple on the grocery shelf is brightly displayed in cans of green, pink, and yellow and are surrounded by other colorful commodities, Susanne's physical hesitation (the unsure hand movements, revealed in medium close-up) and her retreat from the grocery aisle is presented as a kind of flight. Further, the visible price tag on the pyramid of cans in concert with her nearly empty cart suggest that her hesitation is materially motivated: because pineapples were a luxury fruit in the GDR, they were likely not in Susanne's grocery budget. The momentary happiness expressed in the bedroom scene with Jenny pales in comparison to the steady stream of images and sounds announcing Susanne's marginal, precarious existence, and the eternal return of impending defeat is offset only by brief escapes with Jenny or Thomas.

The film's most blissful moment of mothering is also the sequence that transports the mother-daughter intimacy from the private into the public space: the bike ride and picnic. It is one of the few moments in the film not plagued with anxiety, tension, emptiness, or sadness. Opening with the boisterous sounds of children playing and an extreme low shot of the bright blue sky above the apartment courtyard, we soon see Susanne dancing with jacket in hand like a matador, as various small children run at her like bulls. Suddenly Susanne and Jenny, dressed in mint green and turquoise, hop on the bicycle and ride through the city streets where lush green trees form the backdrop for a bike ride. Already, the mise-en-scène suggests a less burdened and more fulfilling existence: the bricks of the apartment building have a warm red tone, and the children are dressed in bright hues of blue, lavender, green, and yellow. The sounds are full of life and contrast starkly with the jarring sounds of glass and machinery in the previous sequence, wherein we see Susanne at her second dead-end job at a brewery.

When we next see the two of them, it is from a bird's-eye-view. Susanne, lying outstretched on a large patch of green grass, and Jenny, sitting at the edge of steps near water, are nearly dwarfed by their natural surroundings. The leafy crown of a tree dominates the left third of the frame, Susanne is placed directly in the center third of the frame, and Jenny is sitting in the upper part of the right third of the frame. Arranged in an upwardly moving diagonal from left to right, their bodies are presented as small in terms of their context, yet harmonious within the dynamic movement of the frame. The camera then cuts to a medium shot of Jenny throwing stones into the water. She is framed in the bottom left-hand corner with grass and in the top right-hand corner with blue-green water. Susanne calls her over to eat and, positioned in the center of the frame, Jenny snuggles on her mother's lap. In the penultimate shot, we see Susanne holding the bicycle steady as Jenny begins to learn to ride, coaxing her along. Finally, the camera cuts to a low straight-on shot of Jenny in the foreground, picking dandelions and making daisy chains, while Susanne dozes, her head decorated with a dandelion crown.

In this sequence the camera work, sound, color palette, and narrative development work in concert to construct the mother-daughter dyad as an enclave resistant to the progressive discourse of East German socialism. The warm, bright colors and sound tones of the courtyard are expanded into the lush green that surrounds the city. The sounds of birds chirping and water lapping, and the bright greens, blues, and yellows in the costuming and mise-en-scène in conjunction with the natural light creates a warmth that exists nowhere else in the film. Although Susanne and Jenny are made miniscule by their natural surroundings, their contentment is visible and contrasts greatly with the minimization of Susanne's body and her obvious discontent in the metal-punching facility and in the brewery. Further, the nature of their actions reveal once again the way in which cyclicality offers resistance in the film: dozing on the grass, making daisy chains, riding the bicycle in an infinite circle, Susanne and Jenny are not producing anything; rather, they are idling. Furthermore, in moving the mother-daughter dyad outside the

Figure 2.4. Susanne and Jenny at the park. *The Bicycle.* ©DEFA-Stiftung/Dietram Kleist.

domestic sphere into a natural environment that seems to envelop the urban space, Schmidt pushes the cyclicality of motherhood into a natural space that overwhelms a strictly politico-economic understanding of the public sphere. The lush landscape visually and aurally emphasizes the "eternal recurrence of a biological rhythm which conforms to that of nature and imposes a temporality . . . whose regularity and unison with what is experienced as extrasubjective time, cosmic time, occasions vertiginous visions and unnamable *jouissance*."[39] In this sequence, nature is given a monumental presence—in terms of its scale within the image— "without cleavage or escape."[40] In resituating the mother-daughter dyad within monumental nature, Schmidt reveals the potential "natural" resistance offered by maternal desire and *jouissance* to a socialist discourse of subjectivity defined solely through labor and production.

The happiness depicted in the maternal-oriented sequences never quite finds its equal in scenes depicting the romantic relationship between Susanne and Thomas. While Susanne finds pleasure in mothering, the happiness she finds in her romantic relationship takes a cinematic backseat. As noted above, the romantic narrative per se carries with it a progressive kernel: two people meet, fall in love, marry, and live (happily) ever after. The teleological movement of the romantic narrative stands in stark contrast to the cyclical narrative of motherhood. In what might be the closest the film comes to the visual portrayal of romantic pursuit, Susanne and Thomas are depicted on a boat on their first (and only) date. Shot in medium close-up with a diffusion filter and soft, natural lighting, Susanne and Thomas are presented on opposite sides of a table, where they take turns speaking in voice-over monologues about their feelings and anxieties. Turned directly toward the camera while Thomas sits in profile, Susanne states, "If you stayed, I'd have a place to crawl into. . . . Then I could talk to you, and it wouldn't be so quiet. . . . I can't just say, 'I love you.'" The sentiment of the scene is romantic and tender and, thus, we expect some display of physical intimacy. The next shot—a medium close-up of Susanne in profile—satisfies that expectation but does so in an unexpected way (figures 2.5 and 2.6). Susanne's profile presents itself as an impressionist painting: the sun shines in from the window, illuminating the crown of her head and highlighting the loose hairs that have fallen out of her relaxed bun. Then, from the left-hand side of the frame, a small hand emerges and strokes the side of Susanne's hair. Suddenly Susanne is transformed: she closes her eyes and leans her head back to meet the caressing hand. Turning and looking with half-closed eyes, Susanne turns not to Thomas but to Jenny, smiling

Figure 2.5. Romantic boat ride with Thomas and Jenny. *The Bicycle.* ©DEFA-Stiftung/ Dietram Kleist.

Figure 2.6. Romantic boat ride with Thomas and Jenny. *The Bicycle.* ©DEFA-Stiftung/ Dietram Kleist.

blissfully (eyes still closed, head tilted toward Jenny's hand) and laying her hand on top of Jenny's as it rests on her shoulder. The scene ends shortly thereafter without any comparable tenderness exhibited between Susanne and Thomas. The romantic boat ride in which the two potential lovers express their feelings for each other (albeit hidden from the other through nondiegetic voice-over) is resolved with a loving caress between mother and daughter, rather than between the two lovers.

Schmidt's privileging of the mother-daughter relationship and lack of investment in the romantic plot is also revealed in the speed with which the romance develops, if one can even use the word "develop" to describe the plot movement. In the span of only a few minutes, we see Thomas and Susanne courting in Thomas' kitchen, Thomas suggesting that they move in together, Thomas and Susanne carrying luggage and potted plants down a flight of stairs, followed by a culminating shot of Thomas' living room, where we discover that she has indeed moved in with him. The speed with which the relationship is established and the manner in which it manifests speak volumes regarding the secondary role the romance plays in establishing Susanne as a resistant East German mother. Most overt is the lack of romantic or erotic development. Brief moments of physical intimacy—kissing on the bed, embracing

during the move, a kiss after Susanne has discovered the bathtub—
function more as a substitute for eroticism than true erotic attachment.
Their embrace while moving, including heavy breathing between gasps
for air, functions as an *ersatz*-post-coital scene, and Thomas' embrace of
Susanne's naked torso in the bathroom is both chaste and complicated
by Susanne's ambiguous declaration of love: "Now push a button so that
everything stays just the way it is.... I could stay with you forever." While
her happiness seems to be connected to his presence, it is also clearly
motivated by the pleasure she gains from the *space* he inhabits. No longer sharing a cramped one-room apartment with Jenny where she must
cook bathwater on the stove and share her sleeping space, Susanne has
suddenly been lifted out of her poverty-stricken existence and can now
enjoy the many comforts of a middle-class home.[41]

In fact, what comes across in each of the scenes is the film's investment less in a romantic or erotic economy, and more in an economy of
class. Susanne's relationship with Thomas is primarily presented as a
move up the social ladder.[42] The film takes great pains throughout to
illustrate their class differences, beginning immediately with the introduction of Thomas' character: in Susanne's first trip to her regular pub,
which is housed in the basement of a modern *Plattenbau*, she must first
walk through a party on the ground floor where Thomas is celebrating
his promotion to departmental manager in a factory. The obvious visual
differences in the two spaces—Susanne's dark and smoky grotto-like
bar and the bright, modernist space of Thomas' party, populated with
well-dressed "suits"—immediately establish their class differences. The
fact that Thomas has a car and not just a bicycle at his disposal indi-
cates his substantial disposable income, which stands in stark contrast
to Susanne's attempt to find space in her budget for bicycle insurance
and Jenny's medication. But it is Thomas' domestic space that is given
the spotlight in this sequence, and Susanne's slow, careful investigation of each room with its modern décor, bright lighting, and multiple
rooms separated by doors culminates in the bath scene. Her wide smile
upon closing the door and her imploring request to "push a button so
that everything stays just the way it is" serve as an *ersatz*-eroticism. The
warm embrace of a *Neubau*-apartment is the closest Susanne comes
to ecstasy, a cinematic choice that again relegates the romance to a

secondary role and emphasizes the role of space in (over)determining female subjectivity.

Susanne's experience of domestic bliss with Thomas is short-lived, however, as Thomas eventually discovers that Susanne has been accused of fraud. Fearing that he will be implicated in her crime, he calls her a troublemaker and worries aloud what the company will think of him once they discover her situation. They argue, she becomes hysterical, and he smacks her. After enlisting the help of the brigade, Susanne's case is eventually resolved, but their relationship falls apart. However, what truly causes the relationship to fail is Thomas' view of motherhood. While discussing the domestic abuse of a female colleague, Susanne suggests that the woman hasn't left because she fears having to raise three children on the pittance she earns at the factory. Thomas refutes her hardship: "She may be scared, but she's not broke! She gets financial support—she's got three lucrative kids!" suggesting that she is *kinderreich* [rich with children]; i.e., she is rich because her children support her through their eligibility for state welfare money.[43] Thomas sees this welfare mom as living high on the socialist hog, while he has to work hard for his middle-class wages.

His nonacknowledgment of motherhood as labor becomes most obvious when he complains to Susanne that he is unable to make the changes at the factory that he was hired to engineer. He is distraught and rants at Susanne about his having to work so hard for nothing. When she suggests he be happy that he has such a well-paying job, he responds, "What have *you* done? What kind of work have *you* accomplished?" She responds: "I've raised Jenny." He retorts, "Yeah, who will also end up stealing one day." Thomas' accusation is twofold. Not only does he suggest that Susanne is a bad mother—by defrauding the state, Susanne is teaching Jenny to steal—but, ultimately, he questions motherhood as a form of labor per se. In asking, "What have *you* done? What kind of *work* have *you* accomplished?" he asserts that Susanne's domestic labor—including her acts of mothering—is not labor at all. In defining labor as waged-based *productivity*, Thomas reveals his primary subjective identification as a model socialist, that is, as one who labors. As before, the question of class enters into the film's deployment of motherhood as a form of critical resistance to socialism's discourse of progress: Thomas' disappointment at work is largely the result of his having "grown up in that factory," his having been "encouraged to study" so that he could "change things." His disappointment is based on an unfulfilled promise: that he would be the engineer to make the factory bigger, better, and more productive. Yet his complaints come across as selfish and naïve in the context of his class position and in contrast to Susanne's experiences as a single mother living a desperate, poverty-stricken existence. Thomas' overt alignment with a progress-oriented discourse of production serves as the film's final positioning of masculinity as inseparable from teleological time, while motherhood—as *reproductive labor*—is used to resist teleology, both in terms of the romantic narrative and the socialist narrative of production-oriented subjectivity.

Schmidt concludes her film with the closest thing to a happy ending one could imagine for Susanne and Jenny: Jenny successfully learns to ride her mother's bike in the small roundabout of their urban neighborhood. Beginning with a medium long-shot of Susanne physically and verbally supporting Jenny on the bike, we watch as the camera follows the mother and daughter moving in a perpetual circle. As Jenny picks up speed, Susanne must let go, a moment that is represented with an overlapping edit, purposefully lengthening the moment for the viewer through repetition of the image. Now occupying the frame alone, Susanne watches Jenny, who is off-screen, with excitement, repeatedly encouraging her with the exclamation, "Yes! Good!" The use of a shot/counter-shot structure of close-ups of Susanne's face as she watches, and long shots of Jenny as she cycles around her mother, reveals Susanne's joy. Thomas' approach from a side street spatially marginalizes him—he remains outside of the film's "true" love story. Completely immersed in the fulfilling experience of motherhood, Susanne does not notice his presence, instead registering intense excitement over Jenny's success. All the while, the camera remains fixed on Susanne, resting in a long shot of her laughing heartily for the first time in the entire film.

The film ends, therefore, by representing Susanne's subjective fulfillment as that which is bound by *cyclicality*: having initially carried the two protagonists out of the frame into a dark, unwelcoming city, the bicycle now eternally returns in the bright afternoon. This return to the mother-daughter dyad, and to the primary metaphor of the bicycle, privileges

Figure 2.7. Motherhood as cyclicality. *The Bicycle.* ©DEFA-Stiftung/Dietram Kleist.

motherhood as that which offers Susanne the possibility of happiness outside the alienating experience of subjectivity defined through labor. The eternal repetition of the mother-daughter dyad—symbolized in the image of Jenny "stepping into her mother's shoes" on the bicycle—offers the viewer a resistance to the teleology of socialist progress through an alternative discourse of self-fufillment. Susanne's final words, "Good, good! Keep going! Keep looking forward!", suggest that progress is a notion that might be more productively understood within a discourse of time that resists teleology and instead embraces the eternal repetition of maternal desire.

DOMESTICATING THE MATERNAL—*ON PROBATION*

Hermann Zschoche's 1981 release, *On Probation*, creates a picture of single motherhood in the GDR that is rather bleak in comparison to Schmidt's film. Unlike Susanne, Nina is only marginally able to enjoy motherhood; that is, she experiences moments of maternal abandon only outside socialist norms and expectations. Nina's maternal abilities are questioned throughout the film, creating a tension between her *a priori* nature according to socialist ideology—as a woman, she will *naturally* also be or become a *mother*—and her material experience of motherhood as socially alienating, an experience observed and regulated by the paternalist state. *On Probation* suggests that woman is bound to her biology through a social discourse that simultaneously assumes her natural inclination to reproduce while also punishing her failure to successfully perform her biological responsibilities in socially acceptable ways. In contrast to the resistant role that motherhood offers Susanne in *The Bicycle*, motherhood for Nina serves as a form of disciplinary constraint that is inherently linked to her perceived biological essence.

The paternalistic discourse of gender that assumes woman's natural mode of being in the world is as a mother, and which overdetermines Nina's experience of motherhood as constraint, reveals itself throughout the film as the result of the contradictory ideology of the public/private distinction in the GDR. As I have already argued, because women's embodiment as mothers was an *a priori* and women's bodies could not be emancipated from the material specificity of motherhood, *reproduction* was seen as woman's (not man's) primary *private* responsibility at the same time that it was only cursorily accounted for in the Marxist-Leninist understanding of a socialist *public* sphere founded on *production*. Therefore, although the East German government made attempts to improve the gendered division of labor in the home through various PR campaigns, laws, and public policies, parenting was—at least practically speaking—subsumed under the category of mothering, which in turn was seen as a private concern insofar as the goal was to make mothering and paid labor two shifts (one private, one public) that women (not men) could easily manage.

This *Muttipolitik* resulted in a living contradiction for East German women, who had been interpolated into a sociopolitical ideology that assumed their social equality, regardless of their gender. The guarantee that "in East German socialist society, woman can develop her personality *for the benefit of society and of her own use*" reveals this inherent contradiction, in that it assumes the commensurability of the public and the private in the development of the personality.[44] But personality as such was defined in strictly public terms that did not take the private into account:

> "Personality" encompasses ... above all the conscious person actively engaged in the production process and in society, which means in the process of history, an historical process that is characterized by a particular productive, political, culturally-inflected state of mind, moral conduct and qualities, that enable him to take this active role. ... Just as man's being is not an abstract concept, nor an eternal or unchanging condition, but rather the "ensemble of social conditions," so too can each personality be understood only within the context of the socio-economic, political, intellectual and cultural conditions under which it develops.[45]

Conspicuously absent from the "socio-economic, political, intellectual and cultural conditions" that overdetermine the development of the socialist personality are the private concerns of romantic and maternal *desire*, of individual happiness. In her foreword to Wander's collection, *Guten Morgen, du Schöne*, Christa Wolf addresses the growing awareness among East German women that these "socio-economic, political, intellectual and cultural conditions" are only the preconditions of women's (and men's) actual emancipation:

> They are beginning to think about what their lives have made of them, what they have made of their lives. ... Women, maturing through their struggles with real and significant experiences, signal a radical claim: *to live as a whole person, to be able to make use of all their wishes and abilities.* This claim is a great provocation for a society that ... consciously or not, awoke this claim in them; responding to these women solely with financial support, with day care spots and child subsidies is not enough ... we must get used to the fact that women will no longer be satisfied with equality, but rather, that *they are searching for new ways of living. They offer up reason, sensuality, and a longing for happiness as their resistance to utility-based thought and pragmatism—the so-called "pure reason" that lies to itself.*[46]

Thus, political, economic and intellectual emancipation was only the necessary precursor for a much more fundamental interrogation of the meanings of and possibilities for emancipation. In problematizing the Enlightenment discourse of "pure reason," these women were in search of "new forms of life" that would privilege (or at least validate) sensuality and their yearning for happiness in opposition to the rationalist discourse of utility-based thought [*Nützlichkeitsdenken*] and pragmatism. In questioning the dominant discourse of the all-round developed socialist personality, they had begun to make the radical demand "to live as a whole person, to make use of all of one's senses and abilities."

In her work on the maternal melodrama, Kaplan emphasizes melodrama's social function in "articulating what has been repressed."[47] Although the melodrama was not a genre produced in the GDR, the DEFA women's film served a similar function as "a sense-making system which man has elaborated to recuperate meanings in the world."[48] There are, in fact, many affinities between what Kaplan calls the "resisting maternal women's film" and DEFA films about mothers. As a resistant alternative to the melodrama, the "maternal women's film . . . assumes a feminine desire, even if its expression is constantly repressed or thwarted . . . [and] open[s] up space for theories of the female subject complete in herself, with her own desire; or at least with contradictory desires."[49] Demanding the fulfillment of what Kaplan calls "non-substitutional desires," the mother in the maternal women's film asserts the absolute commensurability of love (either within or outside of marriage) and career in her search for an existence "beyond and outside the discourse of the male."[50] By demanding that their desires not be substituted, that they should be able "to live as a whole person, to be able to make use of all their wishes and abilities," Susanne and Nina reflect the tendencies Kaplan describes, and also mirror their correlates in both Eastern and Western bloc cinematic and literary texts of the period.[51]

One of the functions of the maternal women's film is its attempt to articulate what has been repressed; in *On Probation* it is *feminine desire*. Returning briefly to Urang's notion of the "new Romanticism" of the early 1960s, we may remind ourselves of the ideological imperative of early East German narratives to quell desire absolutely through production. By disembodying desire—making its object not a *body*, but rather a *process*—socialism attempted to reconfigure desire through labor as complete sublimation.[52] Ultimately, Urang argues, the "deeper fantasy, the second layer of the 'neue Romantik,' would posit a subject without desire—one who has no *need* for romantic love in the first place."[53] By recuperating meanings and values that are aligned with women's repressed desire, the maternal women's film opens up a public space of resistance against a discourse of subjectivity founded solely on labor.

While Schmidt's *The Bicycle* posits maternal desire as a form of re- sistance to the productionist logic of socialism and to romantic desire through its emphasis on cyclical rather than progressive time, Zschoche's *On Probation* suggests that neither romantic nor maternal desire can withstand the oppressive regimentation of socialist everyday life. The film's protagonist, Nina Kern, is a twenty-seven year-old divorced mother of three children who are living in a state-run orphanage due to Nina's "willful neglect." Faced with the possibility of being fully deprived of her custody rights, Nina argues at her final hearing for the chance to prove she can be a responsible mother. Although she has failed to change her lifestyle in the past, she is placed on probation and two of her jurors, a civil engineer and a teacher, assume responsibility over her bond. Nina works hard during the day, cleaning subway cars—a menial and exhaust- ing job—and locks herself into her apartment at night to keep from going out with her delinquent friends. She struggles to be a good mother to her three children, the oldest of whom, Jacqueline, is emotionally dis- turbed. She must manage the economic irresponsibility of her alcoholic ex-husband, whom she fears; evade the groping and sexual blackmail of her neighbor, whose wife cares for her children; and invent reasons to avoid intercourse with her dependable yet boring partner, Werner. Her attempts to improve her mothering are not made any easier by the surrounding community: she is berated when her children are too loud in the hallway; she is met with contempt when arguing for the needs of her youngest daughter, Mireille, in kindergarten; and her free-spirited maternal indulgences are visually and verbally reproached. On a whim, she becomes involved with a handsome stranger at a party and is crushed when he loses interest. In sacrificing her stable relationship for momen- tary pleasure, Nina ends up alone. Ultimately, however, her probation ends, and she retains custody of her children. Yet Nina finds the burden of raising her three children alone too much to bear. She resigns her cus- tody rights for Jacqueline, with whom she is unable to come to terms, and the film ends with their parting at the door of the state-run orphanage.

In the most detailed analysis of the film to date, Marc Silberman has suggested that we read Nina Kern as a character whose femininity embodies a kind of childlike maternity that must be disciplined and contained: Nina's femininity, he argues, "derives from a subjective pleni-tude or wholeness related to her maternal role, but one that she must demonstrate to the authorities."[54] He contrasts her feminine "vitality," "dynamism," "interiority," "wholeness," "childlike spontaneity," and "subjective plenitude" with the rational, efficient, principled, disciplined, and inflexible behavior of the men and the state institutions in the film.[55] Nina's femininity, Silberman argues, is constructed by the film "as the interiority that promises emotional intensity and plenitude (to men). At the same time, however, this interiority is premised on [romantic/erotic] dependency and loss of self, the foundation for the very power relations that contain the interiority in the name of stability and the maternal function."[56] Nina's desire for a fulfilling domestic life in which both her romantic and maternal desires can be fulfilled is denied; her professional life consists of washing subway cars and is, thus, completely unfulfilling. Silberman argues that, although the film emphasizes soci-ety's need "to learn to tolerate the emancipatory power of desire, even when it undermines society's rules," Nina's transgression of boundaries must ultimately be domesticated according to the film's logic: becom-ing a mother means "learning to respect limits, to accept responsibility, and to deny the self. . . . By the end of the narrative, however, Nina has failed. . . . [She] surrenders, abandoning the dream of a family and resign-ing herself to isolation."[57]

I would like to suggest an alternate reading of Nina's "dream of a family" and of her "failure," however, by answering the following ques-tions: How is Nina's dream of a family, her desire for both romantic and maternal fulfillment, presented as both socially constructed and refused? More specifically, does the film suggest that Nina's contradic-tory nature is commensurate with, perhaps even the necessary result of, the contradictions of real existing socialism? That is, does the film posit, if only ambiguously, Nina's failure as the result of the unresolved public/private distinction under socialism, a failure that has its roots beyond the maternal (i.e., the private sphere)? And, in so doing, does it move beyond the question of femininity as motherhood to an articulation of femininity as "otherness" that has not and cannot be incorporated into a progressive teleological discourse because its desires stand outside those discursive parameters?[58] Finally, how does Nina's experience reveal an experience of the cyclicality of motherhood that is different from the one represented in *The Bicycle* and that moves beyond Kristeva's own naturalization of motherhood as the feminine position *par excellence*?

Archival documents suggest that these are not unproductive questions. The film's ambiguous assignment of responsibility, e.g., whether Nina's probation is the result of a public or a private failure, was clearly a point of concern for DEFA and Central Committee authorities. The official meeting minutes from an evaluative discussion of the film by the Department for Science and Information in January 1983 reveals institutional anxiety about this very ambiguity, which DEFA, in an attempt to calm potential Party protest, posits as the film's critical provocation of the spectator and thus a sign of the film's "high artistic quality":

> The author correctly opines that the intensification of contradictions between the individual and her environment, the individual's claim to self-realization, etc., often remains unconnected to the question of the individual's responsibility (for herself and for society). Therein lies the new quality of the cinematic work of *On Probation*. [This is] a film that motivates the viewer to reflect on the meaning and demands of life in terms of the individual's responsibility.[59]

This anxiety is also present in the HV Film approval documents, which argue that, while the film's conflict revolves around public and private responsibility, Nina's failure as a mother is a public problem because of private failures: "society must repair . . . what is often neglected in the parental home."[60] Ultimately, Nina's failure is seen as personal, a result of the "contradictions between *wanting* and *being able to*, between social norms and individual abilities," and of the "intersection and interplay between social responsibility and individual action."[61]

The film foregrounds these contradictions already in its opening sequence. Beginning with a nearly continuous long take of a conference room, the viewer sees various members of a probation committee—juvenile authorities, citizen representatives, consultants, and social workers—scrutinizing Nina's case file. Using slow back-and-forth panning with minimal reframing and zoom, the camera gives the viewers the sense of being a fly on the wall of the committee meeting. The sequence is aurally directed by the male committee chair, who opens the proceedings by saying, "The case of Nina Kern: rather hopeless, I'm afraid. Looks like we'll have to deprive her of custody. We had to put her children in a home four months ago: extreme neglect of the children, antisocial behavior, etc." Each authority is the given the opportunity to speak, and we discover that the eldest child, Jacqueline, "should be introduced to a child psychologist" since she is "difficult"; that the apartment during the last visit was tidy but that "the children's room was cold and unattractive"; and that Nina is working and has no problems with alcohol. The use of direct sound and an unobtrusive, almost observational camera creates a documentary feel that asserts itself as journalistic reportage.[62] As someone leaves to fetch Nina, the camera slowly zooms to a female adoption consultant who asserts that "adoption would be rather difficult for the two older ones. Still, I think she should be deprived of custody." Her decision is seconded by the male social worker, who has deemed Jacqueline difficult, saying "It's much better to grow up in an orphanage than between dirty glasses and drunken men."

The authorities' assessment of Nina's inadequate mothering is then more fully developed once Nina enters the room. Silent and obviously fearful, Nina enters and sits without saying anything. She is accompanied by her neighbor, Mrs. Braun, who is there to provide Nina with support and to answer questions posed by the committee. As Nina's case is read aloud, the camera slowly zooms from a medium shot that includes Mrs. Braun in the frame to a medium close-up of Nina. Through the off-screen voice of the female social worker, we discover Nina's age and address; that she is a divorced mother of three children; that the children's father, her ex-husband, is an alcoholic who regularly beat Nina; that the social welfare agency learned of the children's neglect two and a half years earlier through neighbors, whom the children had begged for food; that the Brauns regularly cared for the children while "the mother ran around with numerous men"; that the two eldest children often arrived at school hungry and with too little sleep; that Jacqueline failed a grade because of poor performance and shows signs of emotional disturbance; that René, her son, is "at risk of delinquency"; that house visits revealed dirty dishes, beds without sheets, and windows without curtains; and that four months prior, the authorities were informed that the children had been left alone without supervision in the apartment for two days in a row, resulting in their being institutionalized for their own protection.

The narrative constructed by the authorities is one in which Nina plays the role of a deadbeat mom who does not provide her children with a comforting and inviting home and who spends so much time "running around with men" that she cannot remember to feed her children, clean up after them, or prevent them from following in her own delinquent footsteps. Nina's responses to these accusations ultimately support them: fluctuating between a distant stare, downcast eyes, embarrassed looks from side to side, and heavy sighs, Nina responds in such a way as to encourage the viewer's identification with the authoritative female voice as it tells us how to correctly interpret Nina as a failed mother.

Silberman's analysis of the opening sequence rightly focuses on the issue of voice and enunciation, arguing that

> Nina is mute.... The authority's voice meanwhile is both the point of discursive origin, relating Nina's history for her, and inaccessible, spoken from a vantage point that is invisible and apparently omniscient. The disjuncture between the off-voice, invested with the authority to summarize this woman's life as an inadequate mother, and the image of the woman forced to listen to this voice, situates the narrative problematic from the outset within the context of female voicelessness in the regime of power relations and maternity.... Nina is inarticulate.... Nina lacks a voice in a society that identifies speech with paternalistic authority and mastery.[63]

Much like Katrin Lot during her trial in *Lot's Wife*, Nina is reduced to silence, while the authoritative voice informs us of her nature as a mother. In terms of the enunciation of which Kaplan speaks, the voice of the institution serves as the discursive authority, while Nina is *spoken about*. Yet, over the course of the film, the viewer will come to identify Nina and femininity with this discourse—even if it is primarily a discourse of silence—because, as Silberman has argued, she is the "human" in the text over and against which the increasingly inflexible bureaucracy stands.[64]

Silberman argues that Nina resists and disrupts the authoritative voice through the feminine characteristics mentioned earlier—vitality, naiveté, emotional spontaneity—and that Zschoche's observational style creates the possibility for ambiguity in judging both her and the state.[65] The construction of Nina as the embodiment of silence, interiority, emotional excess, indulgence, spontaneity, and the private sphere in opposition to the masculine characteristics of the state, he argues, is what gives the film its critical potential, inviting the spectator to "imagine other possibilities beyond . . . the state's paternalistic sovereignty [and] the hierarchy of public and private concerns."[66] Further, Nina's "will to revise the past" and "regain her children because she has truly understood the importance of this family bond" are what position the spectator, Silberman argues, to identify with Nina and not with the paternalistic state.[67]

Yet I would argue that the opening sequence raises a potential question for the viewer that proves more provocative: Does Nina really *want* her children back? If so, why, and what is the nature of her desire? What does mothering mean for Nina, and are those meanings the same for the institutions that see her as a subject in need of discipline? Her first speech acts in the film actually suggest a rather ambiguous reading of her feelings about motherhood. When the committee chair asks her to respond to the allegations about the neglect of her children, her first answer is, "The orphanage, that was a real shock for me. I only just realized that I can't live without my children." This initial response suggests a very ego-oriented relationship to motherhood: the orphanage is a shock *to her*. Now that her children have suddenly been taken from her, she "only just realized" that *she* cannot live without *them*. This is a far stretch from Kristeva's utopian imagining of motherhood, in which, "the arrival of the child . . . leads the mother into the labyrinths of an experience . . . [of] love for an other. Not for herself, nor for an identical being, and still less for another person with whom "I" fuse (love or sexual passion). But the slow, difficult, and delightful apprenticeship in attentiveness, gentleness, forgetting oneself."[68] In contrast to our initial image of Susanne, Nina is presented by the authoritative off-voice as a narcissistic subject, whose children seem to occupy a position of fulfillment for Nina but not the other way around. Nina's own speech then verifies this interpretation of her.

Nina's ego-oriented response complicates Kristeva's theory of motherhood, which, as Judith Butler has argued, tends to naturalize maternity and mothering in the face of the paternal, symbolic law:

> Kristeva understands the desire to give birth as species-desire, part of a collective and archaic female libidinal drive that constitutes an ever-recurring metaphysical reality. . . . Insofar as Kristeva conceptualizes this maternal instinct as having an ontological status prior to the paternal law, she fails to consider the way in which that very law might well be the *cause* of the very desire it is said to *repress*.[69]

What emerges as Nina's voice in her first speech act is a refutation—or at least a complication—of motherhood and maternal desire as an *a priori*, biological essence of the feminine. In the first part of the opening sequence, we are led by both the authoritative voices and by Nina's own voice to perceive her desire as selfish, not as selfless. While one certainly would not argue that Nina does not love her children—her effort to win them back from the state and her obvious concern for their well-being refutes such a reading—the film does provide moments in which Nina's *desire* to be a mother is ambiguous and complex. What the film does successfully is to present its audience with a female protagonist who embodies the contradictions of gender under the conditions of real existing socialism. For Susanne in *The Bicycle*, maternal desire is the *irrepressible desire* that serves as an overt critique of the socialist imperative to *produce*. Susanne finds pleasure strictly in *reproduction* and this maternal desire usurps any romantic desire that the film proposes to establish as the center of the film's conflict. In *On Probation*, however, the nature and domestication of Nina's desire and the question of whether any desire remains in the end create the tension at the heart of the film. By the end of the film, one has the sense that both Nina's maternal and romantic desires have been fully contained or, as Silberman articulates, disciplined, and that neither *production* nor *reproduction* offer her any hope of self-fulfillment.

Interestingly, Nina's initial speech act is not completely heard by the committee, and she is asked to speak up. This creates a gap between what the institution knows of Nina and what the viewer has just witnessed. In answer to the institution, she states emphatically, "I want my children back . . . I miss my children so much. . . . I promise, I'll do everything for them. . . . The children will be ruined [in the orphanage]!" Nina vociferously asserts her desire to have her children back and overtly suggests that the institution cannot be a sufficient substitute, even for her. She is then reprimanded by the committee chair, who refutes the idea that Nina would be a better choice than the institution. This verbal disciplining puts Nina back into the position of defending herself against the authoritarian voice and also serves to remind the viewer that Nina's primary concern should not be her *self* but, rather, her *children*. Further, once Nina asserts that her apartment is now clean and tidy, her boss is happy with her work, she no longer parties all night with her group of friends, and her new boyfriend is responsible and loves the children, the committee chair provides Nina with the correct wording for her request to retain custody: "You have decided to change your former way of life because you have, as a result of the institutionalization of your three children, fully realized what responsibilities you have as a mother, and what your children need from you. Correct?" By rewording Nina's request for her, the committee chair asserts a dominant narrative of motherhood, articulating for Nina the proper reasons for wanting one's children back. However, rather than assent to this interpretation of her request, which maintains the ambiguity of her maternal desire, Nina asks if they might just give her the youngest daughter, Mireille, to take home in order to prove herself. Refusing either to agree or disagree with the chair's reasoning, Nina maintains an ambiguous position, and the viewer is left contemplating what Nina's desires really are.

This opening sequence also indirectly critiques the naturalization of motherhood in the GDR through absence of discourse: namely, through its lack of engagement with *paternity*. Although Nina was married and has been divorced for three years, her husband seems to have no parenting responsibilities to fulfill beyond paying child support (which he does only later, once he is confronted by Irmgard Behrend, one of Nina's citizen representatives). Despite the state's knowledge of his abuse of her, no mention is made of any counseling or therapy she might have received as a result, nor is there any discussion of state assistance in caring for her children after the abuse and the subsequent divorce. The insistent authoritative voice reprimands Nina's "unnatural" relationship to her children while remaining silent regarding Nina's own experience of abuse and the paternal responsibilities that have so obviously been neglected. In so doing, the sequence suggests a very different discourse of motherhood than that offered in *The Bicycle*. The unspoken discourse of fatherhood in *On Probation* reveals that Nina is tied to reproduction because the state has failed to eradicate the public/private distinction and the gendered division of domestic labor. The opening sequence obliquely reveals the state's essentialist discourse of motherhood: biology binds woman to reproduction, from which man remains exempt. While Susanne finds respite in mothering, Nina finds a burden—as a result of having multiple children (Susanne has only one); of having children with behavioral issues (both Mireille and Jacqueline have difficulty adjusting to the institution that contains them); and of dealing with an absent father, who neither shares, nor is officially expected to share, her burden. While mothering offers Susanne a cyclical discourse of pleasure and fulfillment, for Nina mothering is a cyclical discourse of social control and discipline that is based in the naturalization of motherhood as the core of her personhood.

In fact, Kristeva's theory of women's time can only be read within the context of *On Probation* as wholly contained within a paternalistic discourse of domestication. This is evident in the cyclical recurrence of certain images and events in the film, most notably Nina's ritual of locking herself into her apartment each evening and the tedious washing of subway cars. The viewer witnesses the former immediately following the opening credits. The scene opens with a close-up of Nina's hand turning the lock, followed by a long shot of Nina walking from the front door of her apartment, face blank, to her kitchen, where she opens the door and lowers the keys to her downstairs neighbor, Mrs. Braun. The camera then cuts to a medium shot of Mrs. Braun, looking up to Nina's balcony, saying, "Nina? It'll all work out. You'll see." The camera then cuts to a medium shot of Nina, head resting on the balcony railing, staring blankly out in front of herself, answering, "Ah, now the whole damn shit is starting all over again. 'Night." The camera follows her in a medium shot as she walks back into the apartment and over to the empty crib, then over to a small shelf holding a few dolls and other toys. Finally, the camera cuts to a close-up of Nina's face as she lies alone in bed, the light illuminating her blank stare for an extended shot, before she closes her eyes. The shots of the keys locking the door and being lowered down to Mrs. Braun are then repeated eight minutes later, assuring the viewer that repetition is indicative of Nina's disciplining.

Similar to the repetitive scenes of Nina washing subway cars—long and medium shots of Nina working, sometimes alone, sometimes with a co-worker, scrubbing surfaces and wiping sweat from her brow in the dark, dank station—the camera reveals the way in which cyclicality exists primarily as a form of social containment rather than liberation for Nina. Repeatedly locking herself in the apartment, endlessly scrubbing

Figure 2.8. Repetition as discipline. *On Probation*. Dir. Hermann Zschoche, DEFA, 1981. ©DEFA-Stiftung/Waltraut Pathenheimer.

dirt from the subway cars, and scrambling to make her apartment cozy and inviting for the juvenile authorities illustrate that both the private and the public sphere are experienced by Nina as sites of discipline and restraint.[70] The moment when Nina watches as the social worker checks her armoire for enough sheets, towels, and jackets for the children illustrates the extent of her domestication at the hands of the state. For Nina, the only repetition is that of alienation, similar to Susanne's experiences of labor in *The Bicycle*. At various moments in the film, motherhood offers Nina the potential for escaping from the discipline of labor and domestic lockdown. However, these moments are always re-inscribed in the

Figure 2.9. Repetition as containment. *On Probation.* ©DEFA-Stiftung/Waltraut Pathenheimer.

discourse of discipline and containment through the watchful eye of state institutions, through the actions of neighbors, or through the public reproaches of strangers on the street.

Nina resists this containment primarily through impulsivity, which comes to the fore in various scenes. It is expressed in her desire to eat out, although the fridge is stocked and she has no money; in her decision to buy Mireille an expensive baby-doll buggy simply because Mireille wants it; in her decision to give Mireille bread and butter for lunch rather than a more nutritious meal; in painting her children's room without time for things to dry; in begging her neighbors for coffee and coal that she forgot to order before the winter set in; in glueing and nailing up curtains that she never got around to sewing; and in her decision to have an affair with a handsome stranger at Werner's expense. While these examples reveal Nina's "lack of control," they also suggest that we read the complaints lodged by the juvenile authorities in the context of Nina's personality (spontaneity, naiveté, and warmth) rather than as indicative of her "failure" to mother her children successfully.[71] Yet the authoritative voice of the institution continues to insert itself into the narrative, reinforcing Nina's ambiguous status as a mother: upon leaving the apartment after their final home visit before returning Mireille, both the social worker and Mr. Müller reflect on her nature as an inconsistent, tricky *"Räuberbraut"* [hussy], whom they will have to "keep an eye on."

While Nina's impulsivity clearly serves as her most resistant characteristic, it is one that sometimes makes her character most ambiguous and difficult to identify with, particularly in relation to her romantic desires. Interestingly, Nina's desire for a fulfilling sexual and romantic relationship is in direct contrast to her experiences with men both represented and articulated in the film, and it is also inextricably linked to her experience of alienation as a single mother. In preparation for Nina's probation, Ms. Behrend and Mr. Müller visit Nina's neighbors, the Brauns, who summarize Nina's failed attempts at constructing a dependable, fulfilling domestic life: as a child, Nina grew up in an unhappy home with a father who was often sick and a mother who was left

Figure 2.10. *Räuberbraut*/Hussy. *On Probation.* ©DEFA-Stiftung/Waltraut Pathenheimer.

alone with four children; Nina married early because her first baby was on the way; Nina's second child was an attempt to save her marriage with her alcoholic husband; Nina's third child was an accident that she noticed too late and that led to her husband's departure; Werner's arrival, at least, provides hope for stability. This description alone, considered in concert with the opening sequence, reveals a good deal of Nina's ambivalence about motherhood: her own mother was abandoned and overburdened; her first marriage was forced; and additional children led to its final collapse. Nina's current relationship with Werner, while stable, functions solely as a support for her mothering; Werner is a reliable partner but an uninspiring lover whom Nina avoids through verbal contortions and physical evasion. Her sole fulfilling romantic and sexual experience is presented as a result of her impulsivity and is, itself, only fleeting: after throwing herself into a passionate affair after a party, Nina discovers her lover on the subway with another woman. Hence, even in terms of romantic desire, Nina must be disciplined: romantic love exists in the monotony of domesticity, contained by a partnership built of repetition and predictability (Werner); is hampered by an uninvolved, irresponsible patriarch (her ex-husband); or is impermanent and disappointing (the one-night stand with the handsome stranger). Each of these options reveals the incommensurability of romantic and maternal happiness for Nina, and none are able to relieve her of her naturalized role as mother, a role increasingly revealed to be the result of the gendered division of labor based in the state's naturalization of motherhood (not fatherhood).

Yet Nina's impulsivity is simultaneously her most productively resistant characteristic—and her most endearing—because it is most obvious during her moments of maternal abandon, which, I argue, have less to do with mothering than with Nina's egocentric desire for happiness and fulfillment. Although DEFA films about mothers lack the melodramatic excess formally present in the films that Kaplan discusses, *On Probation* allows for excess to be expressed through the protagonist herself. It is Nina's excessive, impulsive emotionality, which Marc Silberman calls her "subjective plenitude," that stands at the heart of her romantic and maternal desires, determining her narrative potential as a tool of critique because it is the focus of the institutional control exerted over her.[72] In these moments, Nina completely disregards the institutional attempts to discipline her, relying on her "subjective plenitude" to forge a strong emotional bond between herself and her children. Like the representation of maternal fulfillment presented in *The Bicycle*, these moments are sparse, yet they reveal motherhood as Nina's sole site of potential pleasure and resistance. At various points in the film, we watch Nina find in motherhood a potential escape from the state's watchful eye: she happily coaxes Mireille through a long walk home from the store by jumping over shadows; she disregards her newly established monthly budget to give Mireille a baby buggy that resembles one at Mr. Müller's house; and she excitedly accompanies Mireille—both of them in rollerskates—down the stairs of their apartment building and into the front door of her primary school, despite the disapproving stares and complaints of neighbors, who are shocked to see this mother enabling such chaotic behavior in her own child. In the most touching scene of all, we witness Mireille's homecoming. In a medium shot, we see Mireille climb out of Mr. Müller's car and turn around. The camera cuts to a medium long shot of Nina walking out of the building, then cuts to zoom from a medium to a close-up shot of Mireille who asks, rather than declares, "Mommy?" The camera then cuts to a medium shot of Nina as she walks up to Mireille, kneels and embraces her with great emotion. Putting her head against Mireille's chest as Mireille wraps her arms around her, Nina exclaims with relief, "I thought you weren't coming . . . everything is all right now," before resting her head against Mireille's chest.

This scene, like the others, suggests that her "subjective plenitude" is connected to a childlike state, that Nina, particularly in her relationship to her youngest child, is living out desires first experienced in her own troubled childhood within a patriarchal state that has deemed her incapable of mothering. Her words reveal fear of abandonment—"I thought you weren't coming!"—rather than maternal reassurance. Her "subjective plenitude" is what enables her to disregard order and structure, to live and love spontaneously, to connect with Mireille in ways that her other caregivers—the kindergarten teacher and Mrs. Behrend, in particular—are unable to.[73] It is what causes Nina to seek out romantic fulfillment and to perform her motherhood without restrictions, yet it is also what must be controlled and domesticated: Nina, not "naturally" suited for motherhood, must be *erzogen* [reared].

Zschoche shows the viewer, however, that this domesticating impulse is *socially* determined. Motherhood, as it is articulated through Nina's experience, is thus presented not as an *a priori*, but rather as the symptom of a paternalist discourse of femininity. This is most obvious in relation to the articulation of masculinity in the film.[74] Zschoche asserts through Werner's rational responses to Nina's desires ("Why eat a hamburger out when there is food in the fridge?!"), Mr. Müller's principled mastery of problems (as an engineer, he approaches Nina and her issues with calculation and precision), and the social structure that enables her ex-husband's lack of interest in the children (his only obligation as a father is to pay child support), that society must "learn to tolerate the emancipatory power of desire" represented in Nina's "subjective plenitude."[75]

Motherhood as a socializing (rather than a natural) process is also indirectly expanded upon through the other female character in the film, Irmtraud Behrend. Irmtraud Behrend is not a mother, is unmarried, and is in her late 40s. As a piano teacher, she deals daily with young children, yet a professional distance separates her from her students and is reflected in the shots of her teaching: she is often looking away, arms folded, lost in thought and unable to connect with them in a caring and meaningful way. Irmtraud's lack of maternal instincts is also mirrored in her difficulties managing Mireille, Nina's least difficult child, on a single afternoon while Nina has to be in court. Grocery shopping with a tired six-year-old, struggling to escape the overcrowded streetcar, and dragging the child along so as not to be late for work, Irmtraud experiences firsthand that motherhood is not something she is innately prepared for or for which she has great reserves of patience. Thus, her experience serves to underscore that of Nina's, offering viewers another example within the film of Butler's refutation of the maternal as having an ontological status prior to the paternal law. Further, given that Irmtraud is the only member of the community who actually confronts Nina's ex-husband—insisting that he leave Nina alone and start making his child-support payments in full and on time—she also serves to overtly question the paternal law as an ideological *a priori* for the naturalization of motherhood under real existing socialism.

By the end of *On Probation*, Nina has become properly socialized as a mother: she has learned "to respect limits, to accept responsibility, and to deny the self."[76] Only in slight contrast to Nina's voicelessness in the opening sequence does the final sequence reveal Nina's resignation through her own articulation of defeat, followed by a return to voicelessness. Nina stops by Irmtraud's neighborhood to catch up with her, and Irmtraud asks how things are going now that the two older children will be returned to her. Sitting on a park bench, with an absent gaze that reminds the viewer of her first night on probation without the children in the apartment, Nina answers: "It's working out quite well. Almost like a real family . . . only without a man in the house." As Mireille brings her something to look at, she beams back at her. But once Mireille leaves the frame, her face falls again, revealing her desolation. Irmtraud is so moved by this, she gasps and embraces Nina, while Nina continues staring nowhere in particular, unresponsive. She then admits that she'll be giving Jacqueline up for adoption, since she "just can't manage everything by [her]self." In the final tracking shot, we follow Nina as she walks with all three children to the orphanage, where she drops René and Jacqueline off again. The gulf that separates her from Jacqueline, who asks, "You'll come and get us out of here soon, won't you?" reveals the gulf between Nina's personal desires and the enforcement of her role as mother. In a final shot-reverse shot, we see Nina looking down—not at Jacqueline, but at the ground—as she nods her head. Off-screen, we hear Jacqueline and René say, "Bye-bye, Mama." Nina raises her head to watch them go, and the frame freezes on a close-up of her empty gaze.

With this freeze frame, *On Probation* reiterates Nina's containment. Her assertion that they are *"almost* a real family" reveals the bitterness of motherhood as it is experienced within a paternalistic system that both relies on and disavows the public/private distinction. By naturalizing motherhood, East German socialist discourse relegates it to a position outside the production process, while also punishing those women who fail to perform their maternal duties in socially acceptable ways. Despite the insistence that women's emancipation was guaranteed by the "socio-economic, political, intellectual and cultural conditions" that would enable the complete development of the "socialist personality," Nina and Susanne reveal the discursive absence of the private—concerns of romantic and maternal desire, of individual happiness—the *lack* in the patriarchal discourse of East German socialism.

In concert with female protagonists in both East and West, and in collusion with their East German female viewership, Susanne and Nina are "no longer . . . satisfied with equality, but rather . . . they are searching for new ways of living."[77] Yet while Susanne provides the viewer with hope for the resistant potential of sensuality and desire for personal happiness, Nina reveals their discursive impossibility. Whereas the cyclicality of motherhood provides viewers of *The Bicycle* with a respite from the teleology of socialist progress, *On Probation* asserts that resistance, while possible, can end only in resignation and defeat.

As I argued at the beginning of this chapter, both *The Bicycle* and *On Probation* engage in larger cinematic debates regarding feminist aesthetic politics. Using both narrative time and reproduction as modes of political resistance, these films privilege the mother-daughter dyad as a site for working through the neglected history of women's experience, for deconstructing the ideological dichotomy of public/private, and for resisting a totalizing historical discourse through subjective accounts. Like her East German counterparts Susanne and Nina, Edda, the protagonist in Helke Sander's West German *ReDuPers*, begins and ends the film struggling to balance her role as mother with that of her various other social roles—photographer, lover, friend, colleague. The film's title, which refers to "the all-round reduced personality," emphasizes this splintering of the subject according to a division of labor that relegates some aspects of personhood to the private (mother, lover) and others (photographer, colleague) to the public sphere. As an ironic inversion of the socialist slogan, the "all-round developed personality," *ReDuPers* points to the reduction of the subject—its social, economic, and political division and atomization—under both capitalism and socialism. Sanders uses the contradictions between these nodal points of subjectivity as the dialectical tension that drives the narrative. The viewer watches Edda navigate these contradictions in various contexts: while scanning photos for the perfect aesthetic composition, Edda's voice-over simultaneously describes the material costs of survival; while lying with her lover in bed, Edda's voice-over expresses her lack of interest and her worry that her daughter will be hurt most if she breaks things off; while working on a photography project with a female collective, Edda is confronted with

her feminist colleague's masculinist assumptions about juggling motherhood with professional work; while developing large-format photos of
spaces that reveal "what is similar in East and West" and "where . . . there
[are] holes in the Wall," Edda struggles alone with the cumbersome developing apparatus and listens to an East German broadcast celebrating
the "collective revolution of gender roles" on International Women's Day.
In doing so, Sander, like her East German colleagues, portrays femininity as the example *par excellence* of subjective alienation.

By foregrounding Edda as a mother in both the opening and closing sequences of the film, Sander explores motherhood as one among
many aspects of woman's reduced personality, emphasizing reproduction
as an inherent and necessary aspect of the production process, while also
emphasizing the ways in which motherhood, linked to cyclicality, is "reduced" and restricted through the division of labor under capitalism. In
the opening sequence, we see Edda in a medium shot in the foyer of her
apartment, her daughter Dorothea's legs around her waist and a tight grip
around Edda's neck. Dorothea is refusing to let Edda leave for work, saying
she doesn't care that Edda needs to leave, she won't let her. Edda tries to
untangle Dorothea's legs from her waist, promising her a trip to the swimming pool and ice cream the next day. Dorothea intensifies her grip and
her verbal resistance. Edda reasons with her, to no avail, as her daughter
incessantly barks in monotone "No. No. No." Frustrated, Edda asks her
not to do this every time she has to leave, trying to pry her legs and arms
from her body. Finally, Edda grins and shouts for her roommate, Carla, to
"come get this child off my neck!" Both women struggle to peel Dorothea
off of Edda's body, and the mother finally escapes only by relinquishing
her scarf, which the daughter has in her grip again (figure 2.11).

The following sequence gives us our first glimpse of Edda at work.
The viewer watches Edda, standing with two other photographers in
the wet cold of a Berlin winter, waiting. As we, too, wait, we hear Sander
in voice-over: "Edda Chiemnyjevsky, photo journalist, is waiting for an
event worthy of publication." This scene is followed by one of a freelance
gig, with Edda snapping photos for an annual conference on divided
Germany, wherein the voice-over again emphasizes labor, production,
as inextricably tied to the reproduction of everyday life:

> The job: two photos at 45 marks each. She must earn at least 3,000 marks a
> month to live modestly. Her expenses: rent, 550 marks. Telephone, about 200.

Figure 2.11. "Carla! Come get this child off my neck!" *The All-Round Reduced Personality* (*ReDuPers*). Dir. Helke Sander, West Germany, 1977.

Health insurance, 197. Pension contribution, 40. Electricity and water, 150. Car, 300. Miscellaneous expenses, 45. Office materials, 70. Photographic equipment, about 500. Taxes, 120. Total, 2,172 marks. Last holiday, over two years ago. Sick pay, none.

Like her role as photographer, motherhood functions as one aspect of Edda's "divided personality" that is socially, politically and economically overdetermined by alienated labor and the time of progression, the teleology of capitalism. Yet, similar to those of her East German counterparts Susanne and Nina, Edda's role as a mother points the viewer toward an alternate understanding of subjective experience that does not conform to a linear conception of time. Like Susanne and Nina, Edda shares her final frame with her daughter (figure 2.12). On the corner of a West Berlin street, Edda and Dorothea cross paths on their way to school and from work, respectively. Like the final frames of *The Bicycle* and *On Probation*, the last shot in *ReDuPers* does not offer the

Figure 2.12. Arrival and departure as "eternal return." *ReDuPers.*

viewer a sense of narrative culmination. The only "progress" of *ReDuP-ers'* narrative is located in Edda's dialectical engagement with the material conditions of production and reproduction. In this final frame, however, the cyclicality of women's time is reiterated in this passing gesture—literally, the moment of mother and daughter passing each other on the street—representing visually what Kristeva has called the "eternal recurrence of a biological rhythm," the perpetual cyclical nature of women's material-biological experience in the world.[78] The brief, routine encounter of mother and daughter on the corner, of greetings and farewells that will be repeated with each new day, makes manifest the non-finality of the film's narrative. Instead, these passing gestures articulate "arrival" and "departure"—the teleology of progressive time—as no more than brief recurrences in the cyclicality of their lives. Like the "eternal return" in *The Bicycle* and *On Probabtion, ReDuPers* attempts to imagine and enact a discursive shift in which *reproduction* might be conceived as the basis of an emancipated, all-round developed society.

3

Pleasure in Seeing Ourselves? *All My Girls*

The people don't want to see themselves ... they'll turn the channel! My God, brigades! Always brigades! What do I know about them?! And even worse—they're women!
—Ralf Peschke, documentary film student, *All My Girls*

The determining gaze projects its fantasy onto the female figure, which is styled accordingly. In their traditional exhibitionist role, women are simultaneously looked at and displayed, with their appearance coded for strong visual and erotic impact so that they can be said to connote *to-be-looked-at-ness*.
—Laura Mulvey, "Visual Pleasure and Narrative Cinema"

The term *lesbian continuum* ... include[s] a range—through each woman's life and throughout history—of woman-identified experience.... If we expand it to embrace many more forms of primary intensity between and among women, including the sharing of a rich inner life, the bonding against male tyranny, the giving and receiving of practical and political support ... we begin to grasp breadths of female history and psychology that have lain out of reach.
—Adrienne Rich, "Compulsory Heterosexuality and Lesbian Existence"

WOMEN'S WORK AND FEMALE COLLECTIVITY IN EAST AND WEST

During the 1970s and 80s, women's work, women's emancipation, and female collectivity became a central concern for East and West European cinemas. With the increased entry of women into the workplace—as a result of the women's movement in the West and state-instituted emancipation "from above" in the East—women entered into the cultural

imaginations of the first and second worlds as individual laboring subjects and as a new collective subject.

Similar to films about motherhood, West German films about labor and collectivity were closely bound up with the various goals of the
women's movement. Based primarily in a Marxist politics of anti-authoritarianism and leftist humanism, the West German feminist movement
approached women's labor and collectivity in ways that moved beyond
campaigns for equal rights. Overt resistance to the patriarchal institution of the nuclear family, demands for access to birth control and the
decriminalization of abortion, as well as critiques of the exploitation of
women at work and in the home (including the "wages for housework"
movement) manifested in forms of collectivity that included women's
separatism, radical lesbianism, collectivity centered around motherhood (for example, the *Kinderladenbewegung* [child care movement]),
an emphasis on collective, participatory forms of organization, and the
establishment of communal households.[1]

This emphasis on collectivity and non-hierarchical organization
also revealed itself in the growth of a feminist film culture, which included the establishment of film collectives, women's cinemas, and film
groups that screened films by women for all-women audiences.[2] Similar
to, though perhaps more radical than, their male colleagues of the New
German Cinema, these female filmmakers also expressed an emphasis
on collective gestures as a path toward developing a truly democratic
public sphere. To that end, feminist films also needed to resist ghettoiza-
tion and assert the primacy of women's experience for a more general
social revolution:

> Feminist films are not something that women could or would want to make only
> for themselves, they are not films for limited audiences or minorities. . . . [They]
> seek to redefine history. . . . Capitalism [is] the mortal enemy of art as well as
> woman (Ernst Bloch). . . . We find in the cinema a space to wish for our own im-
> ages, our own experience of lost speech and lacking images, because increasingly
> we are made into images instead of having one of our own.[3]

Brückner's assertion that feminist films are an attempt to "redefine history" as a space for wishing for and constructing images of women's
selves and voices that have been absent (and excluded), reiterates the
critiques of narrative form, film aesthetics, and film content that feminist

theorists like Mary Ann Doane, Jane Gaines, Molly Haskell, Laura Mulvey, and B. Ruby Rich, as well as the French feminists Luce Irigaray and Julia Kristeva produced in the 1970s and 80s. Here there is also a strong affinity to Sander's emphasis on expanding the public sphere through the foregrounding of women's experiences that have been traditionally defined as private.[4] As Knight has argued, these films function as collective gestures in the double sense that they implicitly explore women's collective experiences and collective experience generally, constructing women as protagonists with whom both women and men are led to identify.[5]

Women within collectives and collective female subjects were, thus, a recurring focus of West German feminist films, and constructing films with a "feminine aesthetic" became a shared goal. While many films focused on women's struggles in the workplace, several films considered the collective in the larger sense of an alternative community.[6] The work of Helke Sander in particular reveals a complex and differentiated understanding of female collectivity. In *ReDuPers*, Sander emphasizes collectivity in a variety of ways. The photography collective, of which her protagonist, Edda, is a part, emphasizes the collectivity of labor in terms of production and division of labor. This is most obvious when the female artists bring the photography work they have done individually together to discuss how and in what space(s) their project should be constructed. Through a collective process of discussion and interpretation, they determine the collective meaning of their work: an interrogation of the "holes" in the Berlin Wall and its insignificance as a barrier compared to the barriers produced by Western capital. Sander's voice-over in advance of the female artists' discussion simultaneously produces another layer of collectivity, namely, of collective exploitation: before the women meet to discuss their photo project, Sander's voice explains that the female collective was awarded the project by the city government partly because it was in the local government's interest to prove that they were interested in women's issues but also because the female collective proposed to complete the project for about half the cost of what other (male) groups had proposed. In this respect, collective labor equals collective political and economic exploitation. Sander also engages collectivity and/as motherhood by foregrounding not only Edda's own role as a mother

living in a collective household, but also by foregrounding the ways in
which women must "reduce" and divide their subjectivity into mother-
hood/artist: during the sequence wherein the female collective carries
their photos around town to test their potential effects in public spaces,
another member of the collective says that she will need to pick her son
up and bring him along for most of the day. This attempt to assert the
nonreducibility of the subject mother-artist into mother/artist is met
with mixed feelings; while Edda expresses solidarity with the mother-
artist, another woman in the collective (who is not a mother), complains
that children tagging along disrupts their work. The problem of collective responsibility for children as a "woman's concern" thus becomes
another potential space of the film's critique. Finally, Sander's incorpo-
ration, in the middle of the film, of a split screen of four contemporary
films by women is introduced with the voice-over "how other women
see the world." Films by Yvonne Rainer and Valie Export are included,
juxtaposed with newspaper clippings about the arms race, and accompanied by Sander's voice-over reading from an "aunt's" letters about the
banalities of everyday life. With the split screen and voice-over, Sander
emphasizes her participation in the construction of a collective feminist
cinema that privileges "female gazes and voices" in women's attempts to
enter history—writ both large and small—through the cinematic form.

In *Der subjektive Faktor* [*The Subjective Factor*] (1981), Sander continues to use an autobiographical approach to expand on the problem
of collectivity for women. Her protagonist, Anni, is actively engaged in
the student movement and lives collectively with other members of the
student Left. A single mother, Anni is the only member of the household
with a child. Participating in the theoretical and political debates in the
context of this alternative family, Anni comes into consciousness and
realizes the limits of a co-ed collective. Faced with the residue of patriarchal structures inherent in the Western Left—most notably her male
colleagues' continued dependence on the gendered division of labor in
the household—Anni must seek out the companionship of other women
involved in the women's movement in order to realize the potentials (and
failures) of collectivity.

In the former East, collectivity carried rather different discursive meanings. As a result of industrial growth in the postwar period,

particularly in the late 1950s and 60s—what is referred to as the *Aufbau* period—significant numbers of women entered the workforce, and many of them began working in traditionally masculine fields, including manufacturing and heavy industry. While this development enabled many women to acquire new professional skills and achieve a certain amount of economic independence, numerous problems stood in the way of gender equality. Because socialist collectivity, like women's emancipation, was state-instituted "from above," the experience of collectivity was stripped of its radical potential. Instead of becoming an outlet for subjective emancipation, as it was imagined and implemented through grassroots movements in the West, socialist collectivity became a mode of enforcing what Engler has called the "arbeiterliche Gesellschaft," an officially sanctioned "reducing" of the "all-round developed (socialist) personality" to a subject defined strictly as laborer.

Thus, in the East European cinema, collectivity is often depicted as a form of confinement and alienation. For instance, Miloš Forman's *Lásky jedné plavovlásky* [*Loves of a Blonde*] (Czechoslovakia, 1965) offers a darkly humorous depiction of the "mating crisis" in the Czechoslovakian provinces. As a result of the rapid industrial growth in the 1950s and 60s, prefabricated towns throughout the Eastern provinces were constructed around newly built factories.[7] Because of the gendered division of labor in manufacturing that persisted under socialism, some of these towns were populated solely with young, female laborers, who had moved there for the purpose of finding work and were living in dormitories. Forman's film reveals the frantic loneliness of young women who defect from their jobs after months of same-sex confinement because they have no romantic or sexual prospects in the vicinity. Similarly, though much less humorous, Márta Mészáros' *Riddance* (Hungary, 1973) is set in an all-female factory dormitory and depicts women's attempts to find "rooms of their own" amid the cramped confines of communal living and alienated work. Moments of individuality are often presented as possible only in isolation: in the shower or on a walk in the woods. Other films that focus on the individual's attempt to free herself from communal confinement and the desperate desire for privacy in a society constructed around collectivity include János Rózsa's *Vasárnapi szülöki* [*Sunday Daughters*] (Hungary, 1979); Wiesław Saniewski's *Nadzor* [*Surveillance*] (Poland,

1985); Barbara Sass' *Bez milosci* [*Without Love*] (Poland, 1980); Péter Gothár's *Ajándék ez a nap* [*A Priceless Day*] (Hungary, 1979); and István Szabó's *Édes Emma, drága Böbe—vázlatok, aktok* [*Dear Emma, Sweet Böbe*] (Hungary, 1992).[8]

An interesting response to the tensions between enforced collectivity and individual desire is Věra Chytilová's *Sedmikrásky* [*Daisies*] (Czechoslovakia, 1966). While the film does not overtly address collectivity, the playfully destructive behavior of the two protagonists, manifested through the recurring game *Vadí? Nevadí!* ["Does it matter? It doesn't matter!"], becomes the medium through which the primacy of the collective is nullified. In the film's prologue, Marie I and Marie II reason that, since "everything in the world is spoiled," they will be spoiled too. Having thus determined their "narrative trajectory," the two young women, mirror opposites of each other, move through a farcical, fragmented text that incorporates a wide range of visual and audio experimentation and is loosely held together by philosophical ruminations on death, meaning, and sexuality. The film's only consistent focus is on consumption: the two Maries "take advantage" of older men by accompanying the men to dinner, where they gorge themselves on inordinate amounts of food and then gleefully trick the men into departing via train without them; they sit in their bedroom and feast on eggs and phallic objects—bananas, pickles, sausages, baguettes—which they merrily cut into pieces with large shears and devour; and, in a final sequence lasting fifteen minutes and accompanied by the score from Richard Wagner's *Twilight of the Gods*, the two Maries indulge themselves in a feeding frenzy when they discover a banquet room set for over fifty guests who have not yet arrived on the scene.

The two Maries' seemingly nihilistic individualism, presented in a fanciful display of color—filters in blue, red, and sepia recur throughout the film—and amid a constantly shifting, often fantastical mise-en-scène—a stylized "garden of earthly delights," a swimming pool, a cabaret, public bathrooms, and a bedroom that resembles a collage installation, wherein the girls wield their shears—creates a montage aesthetic that feels more like a rhythmic "happening" than a traditional narrative. The culmination of this collage/montage farce, a fifteen-minute orgy of consumption that Peter Hames has described as

Figure 3.1. Consumption as resistance. *Daisies*. Dir. Vera Chytilová, Czechoslovakia, 1966.

"an attack on established order, opulence, good taste and good manners" is, I argue, a covert attack on the notion of collectivity in the former Eastern bloc.[9] This attack on socialist collectivity is embedded in the films' emphasis on consumption as the primary source of both the girls' identity and their "destructive" pleasure.

Similar to the use of reproduction as gendered resistance to pro-ductivity and progress discussed in the previous chapter, the girls' or-giastic consumption resists productivity as the foundation of socialist subjectivity. Chytilová's emphasis on consumption in a society of lack is itself "opulent" and "attacks the established order" not simply in terms of "good taste and manners," but rather is a willful resistance to that lack and to the collective for whom the food is intended—the large, opulent banquet, the viewer must assume, is laid out for a large P/party.[10] Further, it can be argued that Marie I and Marie II function as an alternative community—a philosophically reflective, feminist-inflected example of female separatism—that resists a patriarchal discourse of the female body as re/productive through its embodiment of the all-consuming female. Consumption here becomes a playful, critically creative inversion of the *vagina dentata* in its emphasis not on consuming the male but, rather, on using the male as access to consumption (e.g., in the restaurant scenes) or foregoing any relation to the male altogether (e.g., in the final orgy sequence). The inclusion of a "fashion show" without an audience during this final sequence further underlines the female body as site of resistant pleasure in and for itself, as the girls participate in a massive food fight that begins, like other resistant acts in the film, with a return to the game *Vadí? Nevadí!*.

The film's "moralistic" ending is highly stylized, introduced with the sounds and font of a typewriter superimposed on the image of the girls, who, "like witches . . . are subjected to ritual dunking on the end of oars"[11]: "It had to end like this. Is there any way to mend things?" The girls assert that they "don't want to be bad," and the typewriter responds with "If they had the chance [to fix things], it would probably look like this." The use of the typewriter is a direct allusion to socialist bureaucracy and official discourse; thus, "fixing things" is perceived by the viewer as being imposed from above. The final scene of the girls "fixing things," further supports this reading. Dressed in catsuits made of newspaper clippings, the girls reenter the banquet hall, whispering repetitively, "When we're hardworking and good, we'll be happy . . . we'll be happy because we're hardworking." This whispered voice-over paired with the girls' attempts to "clean up" their mess ends in absolute destruction: the chandelier from which they were previously swinging falls on them in slow motion, and there is a cut to an atomic explosion. This ending emphasizes the inherently destructive discourse of "when we're hardworking and good, we'll be happy" and insists that we perceive the girls' "destructive" consumption as the only critically "productive" resistance to the socialist ideology of productivity and progress.

In *Daisies*, the orgiastic nature of the two Maries' consumption anchors their collective resistance in pleasure: pleasure in and of the female body that is oppositional to production. While the film's aesthetics place it in a more avant-garde, experimental category, the emphasis on female pleasure as the mode through which the primacy of the collective is questioned places Chytilová's film on the radical end of a cinematic continuum that emphasizes femininity as a resistant subject position within the progressive, productionist discourse of socialism. Radically provocative in both form and content, the orgy in *Daisies* finds its tamer, more subdued progeny in a brief "orgy" scene in the 1979 DEFA film *All My Girls*, the subject of this chapter, a film that also emphasizes collective femininity as resistance. While *Daisies* resists the primacy of collectivity per se, *All My Girls* suggests an alternate meaning of collectivity that falls somewhere between the radical separatism of West German female collectivity and East European cinematic constructions of collectivity as alienation and confinement.

In *All My Girls*, the female collective is imagined as an emancipatory response to the patriarchal division of labor and overtly engages contemporary feminist discourses of how to represent women's experiences as collective experiences. The film presents the issue of female collectivity primarily as a problem of reception. This reflects broader feminist debates of the time regarding the need to use the cinema to redefine history as a space for constructing images of women's selves and voices that have been absent (and excluded). In emphasizing the double "problem" of representing collectives and, more important, female collectives, *All My Girls* participates in cross-cultural feminist debates to expand the public sphere through the foregrounding of women's experiences, contributing from a second-world perspective to what Knight has called feminist "collective gestures."[12]

"GREAT DIRECTORS" AND THEIR SPECTATORS

All My Girls is the story of an all-female brigade in the Berlin light bulb factory NARVA, which is the subject of a television documentary by a young male film student, Ralf Peschke. Yet the film's opening sequence reveals that it is simultaneously a film about making film or, rather, the problem of making popular films about collectives, in particular, female collectives, for a socialist audience. The film's framing story is the story of Ralf, whose thesis film will be aired on television. Upon discovering what his assignment is, his initial reaction is one of annoyance and frustration with an object that presents itself as both unpalatable and unknowable: "The people don't want to see themselves . . . they'll turn the channel! My God, brigades! Always brigades! What do I know about them?! And even worse—they're women!" These few sentences over-determine the film's meaning from the very opening scene. The scene begins with a close-up of a Charlie Chaplin poster swinging on the wall of Ralf's office. As the camera pulls back from a close-up to a medium shot of the room, the viewer sees posters of Federico Fellini and Mikhail Romm hanging next to Chaplin. This opening shot provides the viewer with a complex contextual frame for the film's story. First, it asserts, in contrast to his complaint, what Ralf actually does know: the feature films of great directors like Chaplin, Fellini, and Romm. The opening shot's focus on the looming images of these directors can be read in several ways. First, it can be read as an homage to "great men" who were also "great directors": Chaplin, considered by Germans on both sides of the Wall to be a comic genius skilled in the art of lighthearted social critique; Fellini, whose early neorealist films made him a model for DEFA direc-tors in the 1950s and 60s; and Romm, the Soviet filmmaker whose thesis "the individual is complex" became the slogan for *Alltagsfilm*-directors in the 1970s, and under whom *All My Girls*'s director, Iris Gusner, studied at the Moscow Film School. These visual references to cinematic history place Ralf in the company of such "great directors," suggesting that he shares and draws on their visions of cinema, while also asserting his failure: the television studio rejected his own feature film proposal and imposed on him, instead, an *Auftragsfilm* [contractually commissioned film] made for television.

Further, Ralf's complaint, voiced under the watchful eyes of Chap-lin, Fellini, and Romm, directs the viewer to the film's multivalent cri-tique. First, it addresses the contradictions of popular filmmaking and state ideology. In comparison to these "great directors," DEFA directors notoriously had difficulty creating films that could bring in large num-bers of viewers. Second, it asserts that "these people" do not want to see themselves represented, which is inherently related to the first level of critique: they don't want to see *themselves*; they want to experience works of "cinematic genius," or at least they want to be entertained and distracted from the monotony of their own lives. Ralf's complaint sug-gests that his object of study is both something he has seen over and over again—"My God, brigades! Always brigades!"—and still knows nothing about—"What do I know about them?"—intimating that, although DEFA produced an inordinate number of films about labor, their own directors could neither stomach nor remember much about this overemphasized subject, nor did they have any relationship to the leagues of workers they were depicting. Finally, and most important for feminist film scholars, Ralf's assertion, "And even worse—they're women!" suggests that women exponentially increase the problem of making popular films about "the people."

DEFA's awareness of its viewing public—the people who apparently do not want to see themselves represented—is a critical aspect of understanding DEFA and its reception in the GDR. *Das Kinosterben* [the death of cinema] became an everyday word in DEFA studios as a result of the significant decrease in the number of moviegoers in the 1950s, a problem that persisted until the 1980s.[13] This was a result of the increasing availability of televisions, on which East Germans could view both East and West German programming; the increasing lack of intelligent, interesting, and critically engaged East German films (as a result of the *Kahlschlag* in 1965); and the increase in foreign imports from Hollywood, Western Europe, and various socialist countries.[14] Clearly, the *Kahlschlag* did nothing to sedate the public's desire to view entertaining and artful films; if anything, it exacerbated their already tenuous reception of domestic films. Ralf's own dismissal of representing the working masses overtly acknowledges that inundating the public with brigade films leads viewers to simply turn the channel. DEFA's increased awareness of viewers' desires and expectations, as well as its well-documented attempt to meet those desires at various levels, is more than playfully critiqued here.[15] Whether or not Ralf's television documentary will meet viewers' expectations, enabling them to enjoy and identify with the characters on screen, remains to be seen. If we assume Bisky and Wiedemann's list of spectators' "basic expectations"—entertainment, good artistic realization, and a realistic portrayal of life—then Ralf's complaint, amid the backdrop of cinematic greats Chaplin, Fellini, and Romm, unequivocally asserts the filmmaker's awareness that creating a popular, artistically savvy socialist cinema is a perplexing, perhaps even impossible, endeavor.

With regard to viewers' expectations, Ralf's complaint contains yet another layer of complexity. First, his assertion that "the people" do not want to see themselves portrayed on screen is interesting, since *All My Girls* enjoyed a great deal of critical acclaim from viewers, as well as from East and West German critics.[16] In fact, positive viewer responses to the film were focused primarily around the very issues that Bisky and Wiedemann lay out in their study of viewer expectations: entertainment, character identification, plot, and narrative structure. Viewers mentioned the importance of the humorous and entertaining moments in the film, while also emphasizing that the film didn't have a "false happy ending" or "false pathos." They praised the film for its ability to "help the viewer find the strength to solve problems in his own life on his own" and for not offering "pat answers to difficult questions." Most important, however, is the assertion from several viewers that "the characters are likeable women and girls just like us; not heroes, but with individual characteristics, different opinions and temperaments."

Second, Ralf's assertion leads the viewer to ask who these people are, these brigades, who apparently "don't want to see themselves." For the most part, these "unknown/unknowable" brigades are made up of women. That is, women—not men—made up the largest percentage of unskilled, assembly-line workers in the GDR, meaning that female viewers made up the majority of "the people" who, in this instance, supposedly didn't want to see themselves on screen.[17] Given the fact that *All My Girls* is one of the few DEFA films that creates a group portrait of women working on the line, its overwhelmingly positive reception suggests that Ralf's complaint is doubly complicated: while it seemingly suggests that the "brigade theme" is overused to the point of exhaustion—imagine years upon years of television documentaries depicting "our comrades at work!"—what it really asserts is a general failure on the part of DEFA to represent "the people" in a way that truly interests (and entertains) the people.

Further, the film's overt intertextual reference to an earlier, well-known and celebrated documentary about female laborers adds another layer of complexity to Ralf's complaint. The subject matter and location of *All My Girls* directly alludes to Jürgen Böttcher's *Stars* (1963), one of DEFA's most critically acclaimed documentaries about women laborers at the NARVA light bulb factory in Berlin. The title of Böttcher's film, *Stars*, functions as a metaphor for the women in his plant (they are the stars of his film), while the light bulbs they produce are a metaphor for the filmmaking process (Lights! Camera! Action!) and for stardom (the spotlights in both Böttcher's and Gusner's films are on the female laborers). As the workers who make this artificial light source, they also make filmmaking possible. In invoking this DEFA documentary classic, *All My Girls* complicates the film's social critique by emphasizing class difference and anxieties about that difference that are an inherent part of the division of labor in the filmmaking process. As the women who produce the light source, they are an indispensable part of the film production process. Yet, as manual laborers—the socialist cinematic subject *par excellence*—they are also inherently undesirable as objects of the spectatorial gaze. As my reading of *All My Girls* will attest, the problem of (not) wanting to see the materiality of this (and other) difference is one of several social problems the film foregrounds.

VIEWER PLEASURE AND FEMINIST FILM THEORY

In accentuating the desire (not) to see difference, *All My Girls* reveals that the problem of representing "the people" (who do not want to see themselves represented) simultaneously involves questions about representing women on film, about the possibilities of viewer pleasure, and about identification with women protagonists. As my reading of the opening sequence attests, the question of viewing pleasure is a primary issue at the heart of *All My Girls*. Ralf's final words of complaint, "And even worse—they're women!" suggests that women further complicate the already difficult job of filming the masses; that women represent something unknown, unpalatable, or frustrating; or that women are characters with whom viewers have trouble identifying. Viewing pleasure was the focus of many debates in film theory in the 1970s and 80s. In the works of Mulvey, Silverman, and Doane, viewing pleasure has been theorized around the concepts of voyeurism and masochism, in which the positions for female viewers have largely been understood as positions of silence and absence vis-à-vis women on screen.[18] One blind spot of these theoretical perspectives is their inability to imagine an emancipatory position for women within the realm of pleasure, which led some feminist theorists to demand the destruction of narrative pleasure. Yet, as some critics have pointed out, such demands require the viewing public's awareness of and willingness to forego pleasure and engage with a political and aesthetic cinematic avant-garde. As Jane Gaines and E. Ann Kaplan have argued, these demands involve a certain level of intellectual rigor and/or academic specialization (i.e., cultural privilege) on the part of viewers even to comprehend and "enjoy" such an aesthetic.[19] Given the resistance on the part of the SED and the HV Film to any kind of aesthetic "formalism," the imperative to assert a national cinema that could compete in an international market, and the need for films to satisfy viewer expectations, the destruction of narrative pleasure was never a goal of DEFA filmmakers.[20]

In spite of DEFA's awareness of and concern for viewer pleasure, its lack of a theory of viewer pleasure informed by gender difference is disappointing. Although Bisky and Wiedemann allude to the likelihood of gendered differences in reception, identification, and engagement with film narrative, there remained a lack of research and rigorous theoretical engagement with those differences.[21] Given the focus in *All My Girls* on working women protagonists as the those who "don't want to see themselves" on screen, it is helpful to revisit moments in Western feminist film theory contemporary to the production of *All My Girls* that emphasize gendered spectatorship vis-à-vis women on screen, while also asserting the critical potential of women's pleasurable viewing. In the context of Hollywood cinema and the demands of feminist theory, Jane Gaines has argued for the imperative of "investigating women's pleasure as counter-pleasure."[22] For Gaines, the most important questions that remain to be answered are "Is the spectator restricted to viewing the female body on the screen from the male point of view? Is narrative pleasure always male pleasure?"[23] *All My Girls* raises questions about the nature of pleasure evoked through the representation of women's bodies on screen and about who experiences that pleasure. I argue that the film constructs an alternative narrative space that resists the hegemony of both the dominant Hollywood cinema of the period and DEFA's labor narratives by asserting the primacy of a female gaze and of female pleasure. This alternative narrative space privileges a feminine/female

viewer perspective—regardless of the viewer's gender—because it encourages both enjoyment of and identification with the various positions
of the women on screen. The construction of a feminine narrative space
necessarily involves different notions of "pleasure" which results in a different positioning of the women characters within the narrative, and of
both the men and women spectators vis-à-vis the text.[24] This is a result
of textual strategies that are most commonly associated with feminist
filmmaking practices from the period: the contextualization of women's
bodies and voices within the spaces of the film and in relation to the camera; the overt emphasis on filmmaking as a process of meaning-making;
the representation of difference as it crosses both class and gender lines;
and the attempt to get closer to "real women," both as protagonists and
as spectators.

An investigation of the textual strategies that create spaces for
female pleasure thus also involves an attempt to historicize the term
pleasure and to suggest that the assigning of pleasure solely to a male
subject—as was being debated by Mulvey, Silverman, and Gaines at
the time—is limited, at least to some extent, to the heteronormative
discourse that predominated in Hollywood and was then translated into
other cinematic landscapes. Thus, I will point to the role of pleasure in
same-sex relationships, specifically in the *zwischenmenschliche Beziehungen* [interpersonal relationships] between the women in the film, as a
way of rethinking the meaning of *pleasure* when the male subject is either
absent or, in the case of *All My Girls*, plays a marginal role. Here I draw
on another theoretical model contemporary to the film's production,
Adrienne Rich's notion of the *lesbian continuum*. For Rich, the lesbian
continuum must be understood as "a range—through each woman's
life and throughout history—of woman-identified experience."[25] Rather
than emphasize the sexual and erotic aspects of love between women,
Rich broadens the notion of *lesbian* to mean a "primary intensity between and among women, including the sharing of a rich inner life, the
bonding against male tyranny, [and] the giving and receiving of practical
and political support."[26] This expansion of the term *lesbian*, she argues,
enables us to "grasp breadths of female history and psychology that have
lain out of reach" because of the social, medical and legal marginalization of lesbian experience in Western culture.[27]

The marginalization of gays and lesbians was not limited to the West, however. Although male homosexuality was decriminalized in the GDR by 1968, lesbian and gay experience remained excluded from dominant discourses in the GDR until 1985, when the East German government tentatively introduced a more open and accepting, albeit official and state-regulated, discussion of homosexuality through the mainstream media, and through one feature and one documentary film, *Coming Out* (dir. Heiner Carow, 1989) and *The Other Love* (1988), respectively.[28] Yet, while hundreds of articles about male homosexuality were published in literary, scientific, and political journals in the 1980s, lesbianism continued to be marginalized.[29] Further, despite a thriving movement of gay and lesbian activism beginning in the early 1970s, popular homophobia remained widespread until the fall of the Wall, and the SED never took a clear, official position on homosexuality, which enabled homosexuality's continued marginalization from dominant discourses of socialist subjectivity.[30]

Given social taboos surrounding homosexuality in the GDR, it is impossible to point to an explicitly gay or lesbian aesthetic in DEFA films. However, if we focus on Rich's notion of the lesbian continuum as a "primary intensity between and among women," "woman-identified experience," or "the sharing of a rich inner life, the bonding against male tyranny, [and] the giving and receiving of practical and political support," then uncovering an explicit (erotically based) lesbianism at the heart of the film is only of secondary importance. Instead, drawing on queer theory, we can begin to understand the pleasure produced in and by the text as one that resists absolute categorization. In her book, *The Queer German Cinema*, Alice Kuzniar defines *queer* as a term that

> signals difference, but not in the binary difference of masculine men/feminine women, homo/hetero, normal/pathologizing, or even gay/lesbian.... Insofar as it represents a deferral of decision regarding such alternatives, it participates in the dynamism of Derridean *différance*. In other words, queerness destabilizes identifications that would adhere to one pole of the binary and acknowledges that individuals often experience their subjectivity hybridly, contingently, and sequentially.[31]

Thus, although we may—indeed, must—assume the structural impossibility of overt representations of lesbianism in *All My Girls*, we can uncover moments of pleasure among women that the film privileges as potentially "queer" if we adhere to Kuzniar's emphasis on the destabilization of binaries and to Rich's notion of a lesbian continuum.

Finally, questions regarding female pleasure also necessarily involve important questions about genre. As I have stated before, the introduction of "woman" as the new socialist subject in many of the *Alltagsfilme* suggests that the genre of the so-called "women's film" should be read as a "mass" genre, rather than as a feminized niche product in the GDR. As I have already argued, "woman" becomes the central signifier for the "socialist personality" in the mid- to late-1960s because she is assumed to be closer to the everyday, which makes her emotionality, her hopes, and her troubles "near to life." Further, the immediate social context of these films also suggests a reading of "woman" as the "mass subject." Given the high percentage of women who made up the masses of unskilled and semiskilled laborers in the GDR, "woman" can be read quite literally as this "mass subject," and certainly as the intended "mass audience" implied by Ralf's complaint. In *All My Girls*, "woman" as the "mass subject" also becomes an issue of film content, as Gusner's film constructs the group, rather than the individual, as its protagonist. Further, this female group portrait is not structured by romance, maternity, sacrifice, or other generic codes that discursively order the traditional "women's film," but rather by the women's interpersonal relationships with each other, which function as meaningful alternatives to the monotony of their labor.

The term *zwischenmenschlich* [interpersonal] is also critical for understanding "woman" as the new "mass subject." Gusner uses the phrases *zwischenmenschliche Beziehungen* [interpersonal relationships] and *die Beziehungen zwischen den Frauen* [the relationships between the women] interchangeably to describe the film's core relationships. I suggest that we consider the possible emancipatory agency located in the equation of "woman" with *Mensch* [man/person] in the term *zwischenmenschlich*. This interchangeability enables woman to become the subject/being of reference in the term, and the masculine noun *Mensch* can thus be read as taking on feminine characteristics. In making woman the subject of reference in her film, Gusner achieves a common feminist goal of representing the hybridity of subjectivity, and like her West and East European colleagues, of "redefin[ing] history . . . [and making] a space to wish for our own images, our own experience of lost speech and lacking images."[32] Finally, it is in the simultaneity and intersection of their class, gender, and sexual differences that the women in *All My Girls* reiterate their "near[ness] to life."

Gusner achieves this emphasis on difference in several ways. First, because the women in the film function as representatives of unskilled labor per se, spectatorial pleasure is predominantly located in identifying with their social roles as members of the working class. These women replace the men who made up the majority of manual labor protagonists in East German films.[33] Consequently, these women laborers invite the identification of those men in the audience who would normally be represented by their same-sex surrogates on screen. This possibility for non-gender specific identification, or "trans-sex identification," as Doane has called it, further supports a reading of *Mensch* as "woman," and therefore of "woman" as the "mass subject."

Second, while the space of the factory plays an important role in creating the possibility for this trans-sex identification and pleasure, it is especially important for establishing an explicit connection between class and gender difference, and for foregrounding the problems of why "the people don't want to see themselves" on screen.[34] And while the portrayal of manual labor is nothing new for DEFA, the depiction of the workers themselves as almost exclusively women and of the labor performed as unskilled is much less common in DEFA films.[35] In fact, after the release of *All My Girls*, women were increasingly used as protagonists in films that depicted unskilled labor as tedious, monotonous, and alienating. More important, however, is the way in which these differences are emphasized through the characters of Ralf and the members of the all-female brigade. The choice to foreground the power hierarchies in the GDR in terms of gender and class are exemplified in the choice of a male actor to play the diegetic filmmaker and in the choice of an all-female brigade. As a member of the intellectual class, Ralf embodies the discursive and political power of art, and his gender difference from his filmic object overtly marks his social and political difference from them. In choosing to represent a female labor force, to use women as representatives of the "worker's and peasants' state," the *Gruppe Berlin* foregrounds both the nature of "women's work" in the GDR as primarily unskilled or semiskilled, and the power hierarchy embedded in the documentary process between the "subjects" and "objects" of the film. Given that the production group, *Gruppe Berlin*, was almost solely female, we may further consider these gender and class differences as part of a metacommentary on the practical absence of a female vision at DEFA.

In chapter one, I argued that feminine desire in the context of domesticity could be used to critique the residual ideological distinction of public/private under socialism and its ultimate promise to enable the full development of the "socialist personality." In this chapter, I show how women's bodies and women's voices are constructed within the space of the factory—as opposed to the private space of domesticity— to construct an alternative representation of women on the screen. This representation achieves two things. First, it enables new forms of women's viewing pleasure at the same time that it encourages male viewer identification with women on screen. Second, this "trans-sexual"/non-gender-specific identification enables the critique of a second ideological distinction under real existing socialism, namely the "us"/"them" dichotomy. As in Gal's discussion of the "us"/"them" distinction under socialism, *All My Girls* reveals the constant and often contradictory recalibration of who belongs to "us"—alternately presented in the film as "laborers," "women," and "non-members of the state apparatus"— and "them"—alternately presented as "intellectuals and artists," "men," "members of the managerial class," and "the Party." Within this fractal distinction, both "woman" and "labor" become especially contested categories. As in my discussion of *Lot's Wife*, "woman" fluctuates between the various recalibrations of "us"/"them," sometimes aligned with labor, sometimes with the intellectual elite, and sometimes with the state. "Labor," as we shall see, is revealed to be equally contradictory: on the one hand, it is aligned with "us" and is constructed as a semiprivate space within which the women in the film establish their feelings of community; on the other hand, it can also be aligned with "them," and can be construed as a public space that the state uses to manipulate and punish the individual. In identifying with the various women on screen, the viewer is encouraged to consider the numerous possible meanings of this distinction and his or her own shifting location amid such categories.

The viewer first encounters the women on the assembly line, and the first factory scene begins without an establishing shot. The sound of machinery is nearly deafening, and although they are only separated by about three feet of assembly line, the women must shout in order to converse. Each of them is shown one at a time in a medium shot wearing an apron, partially obscured by the glass bulbs in the foreground of the frame. They are young, perhaps mid-twenties. They speak in a thick Berlin dialect with an air of cheekiness:

> ANITA. [sarcastically] "Look at that suit, eh! That one's got fat cash, huh?!"
> SUSI. "And me, silly goose! I ran to the hairdresser for *that*?!"
> [Both laugh; cut to Marie walking briskly in front of Ralf; Marie introduces him as the visiting filmmaker.]
> SUSI. [whistles, then yells]: "Hey! There's room between us!"
> [Both women laugh robustly; cut to Ralf, making an obviously uncomfortable face, who moves around the machinery. Cut to medium shot of Ella on the left of the screen, Ralf on the right, with a large machine separating them.]
> RALF. "Bulbs."
> ELLA. "Yep. Bulbs."
> RALF. "Light bulbs."
> ELLA. "Uh-huh. Light bulbs."
> RALF. "Aha. I think I can move on."
> [Ella laughs in his direction; Ralf makes an uncomfortable face. Cut to Ralf approaching Gertrud from behind, who is screwing bulbs into a tester.]
> RALF. "Hot in here, huh?"
> [Gertrud turns around and gives him a funny look, then looks in the direction of the other women and laughs.]
> RALF. "How can you all stand the heat?"
> [Gertrud laughs again, now somewhat uncomfortable. Cut to a medium shot of Ralf standing in front of a machine, Susi sitting on the line diagonally behind him with a machine separating them.]
> SUSI. "Man, you've got it easy: standing around watching while other people work!"

In this initial scene, the women's relationships to each other are established through the mise-en-scène and through a constellation of looks. Susi and Anita are positioned on stools on either side of the line. As they talk, they lean across the sea of bulbs to get closer to one another, suggesting an intimacy with each other and with their work, since they rarely have to look down at the bulbs to continue working, keeping their eyes fixed on each other or in the direction of Marie and Ralf. Ella's

Figure 3.2. Susi: "Man, you've got it easy: standing around watching while other people work!" *All My Girls.* Dir. Iris Gusner, DEFA, 1980. ©DEFA-Stiftung/Wolfgang Ebert.

gum-chewing grin and hearty laugh suggests a control of and comfort in her space; her looks toward the other women establish a visual marker of belonging for the viewer. Gertrud's easy laugh in the other women's direction and uneasy visual contact with Ralf suggests an unfamiliarity that marks a divide between her space as part of the women's brigade and Ralf's intrusion into that space. The mise-en-scène and exchange of looks between the women and Ralf suggest that, at least at the NARVA factory, the space of manual labor is a feminine space and a working-class space.

Through both the constellation of looks and the dialogue, this scene immediately establishes a clear division between "us" and "them," "collective" and "outsider," "working class" and "intellectual." Ralf is positioned as an outsider who does not feel comfortable in the presence of these assembly-line workers, having no understanding of the work, the machinery, or the tasks at hand. Their brusque and forward banter also marks them as members of a class below him. In each shot, the women's work—the bulbs, the large machines, and the noises produced by them—foregrounds the very material divide that separates them from Ralf. Ralf's exchange with Ella ("Bulbs. Light bulbs. I guess I can move on") reveals the monotony of the women's task at the same time that it emphasizes Ralf's not knowing where to begin with these women, his lack of knowledge and insecurity in their presence and in the factory space. Anita and Susi's laughing about there being a "seat left" for him on the line and Susi's comment that his work is not really "work" but rather "watching other people work" immediately question Ralf's position in the worker's and peasants' state as an equal among them. Ralf's sensitivity to the heat is a marker of his position as a socially privileged artist, who is not subject to physical strain or discomfort for most of the workday. Marie's reluctance to let Ralf work on the line is also a marker of his lack of "worker" status, his membership in a different class of so-called workers. In answer to his request to work alongside the women on the line, Marie points to the awards they have won for production, saying, "Man, we make 10,000 per shift! You don't get that handed to you!" Marie eventually caves and allows him to pack bulbs into boxes. At the break, however, she reminds us again of Ralf's special status, telling him, "And when you get tired, then go home. You're not used to this kind of work!" Again, Ralf's level of discomfort with the physical activity and the long hours is emphasized. Although the traditional image of the worker propagated in the GDR has been theorized at times as overtly masculinized and at others, gender-neutral, in Marie's eyes, it is the man here, not the women, who cannot take the hard labor.[36] Ralf's position as an artist is thus immediately problematized, revealing the *Gruppe Berlin*'s self-reflexivity in understanding their own roles as laborers in the so-called worker's and peasants' state, a self-reflexivity that will resurface throughout the film and to which I will return at the end of the chapter.

By clearly positioning women and men along distinctly different class lines, this first scene of the female collective results in a structuring of spectatorship that encourages viewer identification with the women on screen. Because the women are clearly constructed as the dominant subjects of the narrative whose status as workers (and thus, as social agents) goes unquestioned, they represent the agents of history in *All My Girls*. To identify with Ralf at this point in the narrative is to identify with a member of society whose status as worker and agent is not only questioned, but overtly (if playfully) mocked. The result is the creation of a female viewing perspective—a female gaze that privileges the enjoyment of and identification with the female looks constructed in the film, regardless of the viewer's gender.

Yet this seamless alignment of gender and class is immediately complicated in the character of Kerstin, reminding us of the constant recalibration of distinctions, here of the "us"/"them" established in the brigade's distinction from Ralf. As the viewer will soon discover, Kerstin works on the assembly line as a form of punishment: having finished her *Abitur* [diploma], she should be studying at the university, but instead she is working on the line. The apparently clear distinction of "us"/"them," workers/intellectuals, women/men is redrawn in the figure of Kerstin, who becomes aligned both with "us" and "them." Kerstin's isolation—packing a box of bulbs rather than working directly on the line—immediately suggests her outsider status, and is later confirmed and reiterated throughout the film by Anita. Anita first tells Ralf to pay no attention to Kerstin, since she is not part of the brigade. Later, in the scene in the break room, the class tensions between Ralf and the brigade are shown to have existed already within the brigade itself, between Kerstin and Anita.

This is most obvious during the "comma argument." In this scene, the camera cuts from a shot of Ralf and the brigade eating lunch to a medium shot of Anita from behind; she is painting a poster encouraging other brigades to participate in a volunteer project. Anita turns to look tentatively behind herself, and the counter-shot reveals Kerstin sitting and eating. Kerstin looks up and catches Anita looking at her (established through a final counter-shot). The camera follows Kerstin as she puts down her food, gets up, walks over to Anita, and stands behind her. Anita, still bent over her work, looks around again tentatively, then, seeing that Kerstin has gotten up in response to her wary looks, says in her thick Berlin dialect, "Why are you standing around here? Can't you see the place needs cleaning?" As Kerstin walks away out of the frame, Anita follows tentatively with her eyes. The camera cuts to a medium shot of Anita from the front with Kerstin sweeping the floor behind her. In answer to Anita's unasked question, Kerstin says, "The comma is missing." Anita straightens up, looks at her work, then behind herself at Kerstin, then back to her work, and asks, annoyed, "What comma? Oh right, you have an *Abitur*! Why don't you just worry about the floor that

needs sweeping?!" Anita calls Ralf over to mediate their "comma argument," his answer being "it depends on what it's about." When he then
asks, "what's it about?" (meaning not the placement and meaning of the
comma but, rather, the obvious tensions between Kerstin and Anita),
Anita answers "It's about the comma." Ralf answers "ah, right," with a
look of half-understanding and returns to the break table (in the background), leaving Anita and Kerstin to continue staring at each other.

This important sequence is framed by looks between Anita and Kerstin that reveal both tension and longing inherent in their relationship,
which also functions as a metaphor for the relationship between workers
and intellectuals in the GDR. Anita's anger and resentment toward Kerstin is simultaneously a kind of fascination with and interest in Kerstin as
an educated woman being punished by the state—later in the film we are
told that Kerstin is on probation, though it is unclear why.[37] Anita's look
toward Kerstin is curious and desiring at the same time that it is cautious
and jealous. Kerstin's look toward Anita carries both a recognition of
Anita's desire as well as her own desire to get closer to Anita. By taking
up the broom and suggesting that Anita add a comma, Kerstin attempts
to approach Anita, who functions in the film as the socialist subject
par excellence: she is the brigade leader, morale builder, and conflict re-
solver. At the same time, Kerstin also clearly recognizes that Anita, the
exemplary socialist worker, holds more social power than Kerstin, the
Abiturientin [graduate] on probation, does. At this moment, the viewer
becomes fully aware of the class distinctions that establish and maintain
Kerstin's outsider status. The broom serves to visually mark her demo-
tion as an intellectual and her simultaneous attempt to fall in line, to gain
the brigade's acceptance and Anita's especially, whose initial look invited
Kerstin's attempt at camaraderie.

Here, the film's emphasis on interpersonal relationships within the
brigade begins to underscore the contradictory nature of the ideological
distinction "us"/"them." The seemingly obvious division of characters
along the lines of gender and class, established in the opening sequence
and on the assembly line, is recalibrated, revealing another layer of the
film's critique: namely, the contradictory definitions of labor as both
a site of emancipation and political suppression in the GDR. Kerstin's
position outside the brigade seems to mark her as part of "them" in the

sense that she is not a "real" worker, and is thus more similar to Ralf than she is to the other women in the factory. Yet her presence in the factory is a direct result of her being denied and punished by "them," in this case the state, making her a part of the "us" described by Gal.[38]

In *All My Girls*, the tensions between Kerstin and Anita, more so than between Kerstin and any other of the women in the brigade, serve to confront the viewers' own experiences with those members of society who work among them as a form of punishment.[39] As both the viewers' responses and the studies by Bisky and Wiedemann attest, the ability on the part of the spectator to identify with and enjoy the characters on screen is closely linked to the viewers' ability to make connections between the narrative on screen and their own everyday experiences. What makes this especially important for both male and female viewers is that both the outsider and the exemplary socialist worker are women. While very few of the viewers will be able to identify with Ralf as a result of his status as artist, most viewers will be able to identify either with Anita, the less educated worker, or with Kerstin, the demoted member of the intelligentsia. Viewer pleasure—a combination of identification with and/or desire for the character, as well as engagement with the narrative—is structured by the pleasure and antagonism constructed through looks between the two women, who represent social types that the viewers themselves are either representative of or understand from personal experience.

Yet as my analysis of the looks between Kerstin and Anita suggests, there is more to their relationship than meets the eye. Returning to Rich, if we understand the "primary intensity" between them as an antagonism, that is, as something built out of both curiosity and jealousy, we can see their relationship as being overdetermined by the contradictory nature of desire. This makes sense given that the significant moment of loss at the end of the film is one between Kerstin and Anita: Kerstin departs abruptly as a result of Anita's accusation that Kerstin stole money from the brigade. Upon discovering that she was wrong, Anita is distraught and racked with guilt.

This antagonism between the individual and the collective is most evident in the scene in which the other women find out that Marie, their manager, has been recording the times when they cheat the clock by

taking breaks, arriving late, leaving early, and not showing up for work
at all. The scene begins with a medium shot from behind Ralf's shoulder
as he interviews Anita on camera, asking what she wants to be doing in
twenty years. Her reaction is one of discomfort: she sits up straight, then
squirms in her seat, looking around at the others as if not knowing how
to answer the question. The camera then cuts to a close-up of Susi, who
exclaims, "In twenty years we'll be grandmas!" and laughs. The camera
then cuts to a medium shot of Marie behind her desk as she picks up the
uncomfortable question, answering: "Whaddaya think was going on
here thirty years ago? When I started out, I didn't wanna stay a single
day. . . . I'm gonna say it like this: you have to stick together on the line.
Work on the line is community work. Ya have to be able to depend on
each other, more than in other places. When someone's missing [looks at
Susi] or doesn't pull her weight, the whole thing comes crashing down."

Marie's monologue asserts the brigade's primary role as
community—"work on the line is primarily communal work." While the
occasional "girl" may want to escape, as Marie did when she first arrived,
the important thing is to "stick together" and "rely on others." The question of what the women want to be doing in twenty years is not a question of work, but rather a question of community, since the labor they
perform is, based on Marie's evaluation, monotonous and unfulfilling:
"I didn't want to stay for a single day!" Labor as alienating, rather than
emancipatory, is particularly evident in Marie's evaluation. This is also
emphasized in Susi's answer—"In 20 years we'll be grandmas!" Unlike
in the socialist realist classics, where work is the tool through which the
socialist individual can fully realize herself, work has brought the women
in the brigade together, but work itself is not what binds them. It is not
the labor, but rather the camaraderie, that determines their interpersonal
relationships.[40] Taken in concert with the antagonistic "primary intensity" between Kerstin and Anita, this scene emphasizes the alienation of
socialist labor itself, while reiterating the film's assertion that the brigade,
as a community of women, is all these "girls" have to hold on to.

The women's communal enclave is then overtly threatened, however, by the "us"/"them" distinction when Ralf asks what will happen to
the brigade while a new line is being installed. Marie's first reaction is
to tell him that she would have rather discussed it *"unter uns,"* ["among

ourselves"] rather than have it brought up by an outsider (Ralf). Marie
then shifts gears and embodies the managerial position as she announces
what will happen during the restructuring of the assembly lines: the
women will be split up onto other assembly lines for the next six months.
Marie asserts that "*they* decided that; *we* should consider it." Ella responds, asking "Why are *we* just learning about this now?" and Susi asserts "Don't make *us* any promises. Even Ralf knows about it. The whole
world knows about it . . . only once again, *we* didn't know!" Finally, Susi
draws a clear line between Marie as manager and the other women as
workers: "Marie, *you* wheel and deal and always fall into line! Behind
our backs! Sure! I can hear her now, 'Comrade Lauterbach—always prepared!' *You* can forget about greasing the wheels at *our* expense, it's like
you don't know *whose* camp you're in!" Realizing that the other women
have constructed a clear distinction between her and themselves, Marie
takes on the position of "them" as a way of asserting her power, complaining that the other women come late and don't work as hard as they
should. Pulling a small diary out of her desk, she recites the number of
missed shifts, late arrivals, and early departures listed under each of their
names, ending with, "*We* could think about that, now couldn't *we*?" The
women, shocked that she has recorded their failures in such great detail,
are spoken for by Susi: "Did *you* write down everything *we've* said as well?
And then you go and tell your bosses, right?!" The camera cuts to a close-
up of Marie's distraught face. As she moves to the closet to get her coat,
Kerstin steps in front of the camera and covers the lens with her hand.

    In this scene the ideological distinction "us"/"them" is more explic-
itly brought to the fore than during the "comma argument." Marie begins
by including herself in the "us." In using phrases such as "discuss among
ourselves," "*we* will be divided up," "*we* should consider *their* suggestion,"
and "that's what *they* decided" she asserts herself as part of the collective and sets herself apart from "them," the men from "*da oben*" ["on
high"] who make decisions that the brigade is expected to accept. But the
women immediately call her use of "us" into question, revising their definition of "us" and assigning Marie a position as one of "them." Whereas
Marie and Ralf are in the know, Susi asserts that "*we've* been kept in the
dark yet again," accusing Marie of "wheeling and dealing behind *our*
backs" and "greasing the wheels at *our* expense." Thus, Marie's failure to

discuss with them decisions being made about the brigade reveals the contradictions inherent in her own ideal of the collective, of "sticking together" and "relying on others." In recognizing that the other women have separated her out of the "us," she immediately repositions herself as management, using an I/you distinction. Suddenly, it is no longer about sticking together but about the other women's failure to live up to Marie's (and by default, the factory's) work standards. Marie's assertions—"if *I* weren't on *your* backs" and "which of *you* even know what real work is?! None of *you*!"—position her as an authority figure with membership in a group that knows the value, importance, and meaning of labor. Yet the most insidious recalibration of the "us"/"them" is illustrated in Marie's final defiant rebuttal of her exclusion. In secretly keeping a log of each girl's failures on the job, she confronts them with her true power as one of "them," that is, in her intersecting position as brigade leader and member of the state apparatus. Her final comment—"Sixteen missed shifts in two years. *We* should think about that, don't you think?"—in combination with the triumphant lighting of a cigarette, vehemently asserts that management and the Party, not the workers, ultimately determine where lines are to be drawn and crossed.

This scene opens up complex questions of socialist democracy and the role of the working-class individual in the space of labor managed by the state. The women's indignation toward Marie reveals class-based feelings of disenfranchisement at the hands of the state and reminds us of Gal's description of how the "us"/"them" distinction is constantly recalibrated under real existing socialism. Gusner emphasizes this contradiction in her interview with *Sonntag*. The interviewer praises her for asserting with her film that "the individual's claims to self-realization are not addressed to society as if to a credit institute," but rather, the individual is reminded in the film of "his responsibilities to society." The interviewer uses a typical division of individual/society in order to deflect social responsibilities of the state (them) onto the masses (us). Gusner's reaction, however, is a contradiction of this simplistic allocation of responsibility to the individual, by reminding the interviewer that the "society" is nothing other than "all of us as individuals, of course." She argues:

> This has to do with the lovely term "socialist democracy," with which we concern
> ourselves in this film. When the girls defend themselves against decisions from
> above, decisions that come to them as givens or facts, that is democratic. We
> have the right, the obligation even, to defend ourselves against the formalization
> of ideas like "socialist society" or "socialist democracy".[41]

Thus, both Marie's idealistic image of collectivity and her failure to resist the "orders from above" are revealed as a social problem that the entire collective must solve. The brigade's struggle to assert its power in what should be the democratic process of socialism reveals the reification of the ideals of socialist democracy: the so-called workers' and peasants' state is not run by the workers and peasants, but by managers, who dictate their orders from above. While Marie emphasizes the pleasure of the collective as a substitute for the pleasure of labor, that *ersatz* pleasure is threatened by the conflict between the "individual" and the "socialist democracy" that is supposedly representative of the working masses.

The possibilities for viewer identification and critical engagement with the narrative are numerous here, and are intensified particularly through the women's articulation of the "us"/"them" divide. The women's resistance to authoritarianism in the workplace makes them believable, and the use of nonprofessional actors in the film adds to the realistic quality of their critical resistance. As such, they embody what one viewer described in his response to the film: "The characters are women and girls from our midst, not heroes, but they have their own character traits, differing opinions and temperaments. In terms of the film's truthfulness, I would say that I could identify in particular with the critical traits [of these girls]."[42] Thus, the women's critical resistance can be understood as foundational for constructing a feeling of authenticity for some viewers.

Important also is the absence of Ralf from the scene. While he is visible at the moment that he asks the provocative question, the camera immediately shifts from the perspective of the filmmaker to the perspective of the women during the contentious argument. This emphasis on the differences among the women as brigade members and supervisor creates disparate positions with which the viewers, regardless of gender, can identify. The contested issues of labor and management are not framed as "women's issues"; that is, they are not framed in terms of combining work and romance or work and motherhood. Rather, they are framed as questions of the individual and the collective, and the problems that arise are issues with which all viewers can identify.

The overt antagonisms inherent in the ideological division "us"/"them" are temporarily interrupted during the film's cinematic climax. In this sequence, all divisions between the characters—worker/intellectual, female/male—break down, and a neutral space is created that is at once liberating and fantastical. While the public space of the factory serves as a site of homosocial intimacy between the women, it also contains divisive elements. In contrast, the private space of a bed and breakfast serves as an emancipatory and Dionysian escape, in which erotic pleasure displaces all previous divisions, most notably those having to do with labor, class, and political and intellectual power. In what I will call the "orgy" sequence, erotic pleasure is framed as a "private" enclave of resistance that is both freeing and fleeting.[43]

In this sequence, the women have traveled to the countryside to visit Marie, who is convalescing after a nervous breakdown that was brought on, it is assumed, by the argument about the potential splitting up of the brigade across various assembly lines and the discovery of Marie's little black book. In the space of the bed and breakfast, the women reflect on the brigade's role in their lives as an *ersatz* family and on their guilt for having driven Marie to a breakdown. Rich's notion of the lesbian continuum is most clearly illustrated in this sequence as we watch the women experience the "primary intensity" of their "woman-identified experience." Rich emphasizes "woman-identified experience" as fluid and continuous, as a spectrum of relationships that are distinct from the limited "clinical associations [of *lesbian*] in its patriarchal definition," arguing that

> female friendship and comradeship have been set apart from the erotic, thus limiting the erotic itself. But as we deepen and broaden the range of what we define as lesbian existence, as we delineate a lesbian continuum, we begin to discover the erotic in female terms: as that which is *unconfined to any single part of the body or solely to the body itself, as an energy not only diffuse but,* as Audre Lorde has described it, *omnipresent in "the sharing of joy, whether physical, emotional, [or] psychic."*[44]

The continuum Rich describes here emphasizes the diffuse nature of women's desire for other women, or "the erotic in female terms." In my analysis of the orgy scene, I focus on this dispersion of female desire as illustrative of Rich's analysis of the diversity of feeling that the lesbian continuum encompasses. Further, it enables us to read the cinematic construction of the sequence as being overdetermined by the heteronormative discourse of socialist ideology, and the discursive taboo against homoerotic relations. Regardless of whether we actually see the women engaging in sex acts together (we do not), we can assume Ralf's role in the scene to be that of prop or catalyst, since all of the following are true: five of the six sexual actors in the room are women, and Ralf cannot possibly satisfy them all at once; sexual acts do occur, albeit off-screen; the sexual gestures presented on screen occur almost exclusively between female bodies; all sexual acts will be construed within the context of East Germany's official and unofficial discourses on hetero- and homosexuality, meaning that homoerotic relations *must be hidden from view*, even if they are assumed through narrative development, cinematography, editing, and sound techniques.

The sequence begins with a medium shot of Ralf entering a room in the bed and breakfast from a point of view within the room, requiring a counter-shot for the viewer to know whose perspective we are taking. Ralf's face shows surprise at what he has discovered there, and there is a cut to a medium shot (Ralf's perspective) of Susi and Anita lying in the bed with only their heads and their bare feet poking out from under the comforter. They giggle, and the camera cuts to a medium shot of Ralf through the mirror (i.e., a shot of his reflection from a point of view other than that of Ralf and the women), as he closes the door and stands at the foot of the bed. The shot is held steady as Ralf proceeds to undress, during which the spectator hears the women giggling, one of them eventually saying in a surprised tone mixed with humor, "Ah, lovely!" As Ralf reaches a point of near nakedness in his red briefs, he reaches down and rips the comforter off the bed. There is a quick cut to his point of view of the women lying completely dressed in the bed, roaring with laughter (figure 3.3). The camera then cuts to the women's point of view, during which Ralf demands in a playful tone that they also undress. Cutting back to Ralf's point of view, the camera presents the women, giggling and undressing on the bed. Suddenly there is a sound from the door and the women look in that direction. The camera cuts to a close-up of

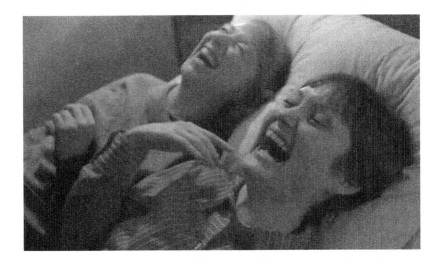

Figure 3.3. Susi and Anita "exposed." *All My Girls*. ©DEFA-Stiftung/Wolfgang Ebert.

Kerstin standing dumbfounded in the doorway, with an immediate cut to her point of view looking at the women in bed and Ralf standing next to them, all in their underwear. Susi looks at each of them and bursts out laughing, pulling Anita on top of her and Ralf down onto the bed. The camera cuts to a point of view from the bed in which Ella and Gertrud arrive at the door, behind Kerstin, with a bottle of wine and a glass. As the two see what is transpiring, they laugh robustly and push their way into the room with Kerstin in front of them.

At this point the diegetic sound is replaced by an extra-diegetic soundtrack in which a woman's voice sings happy notes with the nonsense words "la-la-la-la" and "do-do-do-do," the same melody that is used during the film's opening and closing credits. The camera cuts to a close-up of Ralf as he pours wine into the glass and hands it to Kerstin. Kerstin drinks, smiles, and then holds it for him to drink. She then hands the glass to Gertrud, who drinks, smiles, and passes it on to Ella, who does the same. The camera cuts to an extreme close-up of Susi laughing. Ralf enters the frame, kissing her cheek and mussing her hair. The camera cuts to an extreme close-up of two women's upper torsos, one facing the screen, the other from the side. With only an arm and a hand visible, the hand proceeds to caress the other woman's arm, framed by a breast in a see-through bra. The camera cuts to a direct medium shot of Anita's head and shoulders as she lies at the end of the bed. Ralf enters the frame and whispers something funny in her ear; she laughs. The camera then cuts to a medium close-up from behind a woman wearing a bra, with another woman's naked torso behind it. As the naked woman raises her glass of wine, the bra strap on the other woman's back falls. The camera cuts to a close-up of Ella and Anita's heads on the pillow, facing each other. As they smile at each other, Anita strokes Ella's hair (figure 3.4). Ralf enters the frame again from above the pillow and the two kiss his cheeks. The camera then cuts to a close-up of Ella drinking from the glass, then a medium shot of Kerstin sitting off to the side. Ralf enters the frame and whispers something in her ear, hugging her head. The camera then cuts to a close-up of the upper thighs and pantied bottoms of two women lying face down on the bed. One bottom turns over on its side toward the other bottom, and the woman's hand caresses the other woman's leg, moving up the leg to just below her bottom, followed by a dissolve to Gertrud's smiling face (figure 3.6). The camera then cuts to a woman's hand pulling a long, sheer scarf off of the dresser, over Gertrud's face. Ralf reaches for it and puts it over his head. Gertrud giggles as he continues performing. The camera then cuts one last time to a close-up of Anita

Figure 3.4. Orgy. *All My Girls.* ©DEFA-Stiftung/Wolfgang Ebert.

Figure 3.5. Ella and Anita during the orgy. *All My Girls.* ©DEFA-Stiftung/Wolfgang Ebert.

with the scarf tied around her head, as the extra-diegetic music changes to a faster, disco funk beat. Anita gets up from the bed and begins dancing around the room in her bra and panties, waving the long arms of the scarf around, as if performing a dance of the veils. She turns on the lights and spins them around, creating a disco effect. She then approaches the camera in extreme close-up, and as she moves away, the mise-en-scène changes from the hotel room to a black screen with painted flowers. Anita dances backwards into a medium long shot, as she and the flowers are superimposed onto one another. The sequence ends with the music being replaced by the sound of a rooster crowing and a medium close-up of Ralf and Kerstin as the only two bodies left in the bed.

This sequence is one of the few moments in DEFA history wherein a homoerotic relationship between women is directly suggested. The cinematography, in particular, foregrounds the erotic nature of the women's bodies. The fragmentation of their bodies into distinct parts—hands, legs, breasts, bottoms, faces, mouths—emphasizes the diffuse nature of women's eroticism, reflecting not only Rich's notion of the lesbian continuum, but also the feminist imperative to "question the standardization of sexuality according to masculine parameters."[45] The "problem" of Ralf can thus be read as a formal safeguard. Ralf enables and validates

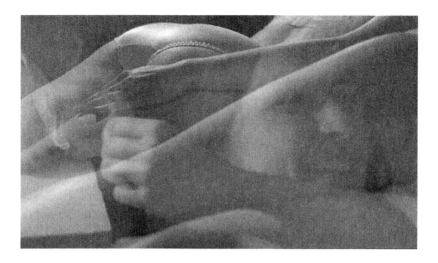

Figure 3.6. Female pleasure. *All My Girls.* ©DEFA-Stiftung/Wolfgang Ebert.

the women's mutual kisses and caresses because his presence "guaran-
tees" the heteronormativity of the nearly all-female mise-en-scène. Ralf
necessarily acts as a catalyst within that mise-en-scène for an already existing homoerotic potential that becomes the film's most intense climax:
the women's physical enjoyment of each other. Further, given that Ralf's
perspective is only one of six perspectives within the frame (the other
five being female) and that the final point-of-view shot of Anita dancing
follows a shot of Gertrud and Ralf on the bed next to her with the scarf,
it is impossible to ascribe a definite gender to the gaze through which we
watch Anita dance. Given the nearly all-female space, however, the scene
clearly privileges a female viewing perspective, that is, a viewer position
that identifies with a woman's gaze directed toward another woman.
These images—close-ups of female hands on female arms and legs, of a
naked female torso toasting another woman's near nakedness—explode
official prohibitions against same-sex desire in the GDR and invite the
spectator, regardless of gender, to indulge in this female fantasy. Privileging the female point of view and female desire for the female body,
the camera constructs the spectator's voyeuristic look within a lesbian
continuum by positioning the women simultaneously as subjects and objects of desire.[46] The camera emphasizes, through close-ups, the women's

delight in each other's bodies and alludes to other moments in DEFA cinema that emphasize women's homosocial/homoerotic pleasure: for instance, between Margit and Lucie in Günther's *Her Third* and between Sonja and Tilly in Carow's *Until Death Do Us Part*.[47]

Yet, in all three of these films, the same-sex pleasure is presented as a brief, utopian moment, impossible to sustain. In each film, social constraints loom in the background and eventually break through to thwart women's same-sex pleasure. The extinguishing of this lesbian impulse has to do with the contradictions between individual desire and socialist ideology. In the case of *Her Third*, it is the contradictory nature of Margit's emancipation that disrupts, if incompletely, the film's lesbian continuum. Partially embodied in her emotional and physical enjoyment of Lucie, her emancipation is undercut by her more traditional desire for a third husband.[48] In *Until Death Do Us Part*, it is the failure of the collective to accept labor's limited emancipatory potential and Sonja's feelings of abandonment within marriage that construct the lesbian continuum as an incomplete (if critically important) alternative to heterosexual love: Tilly and Sonja celebrate Sonja's new job by dressing up as a married couple, drinking and dancing, and forgetting for a moment the domestic abuse Sonja has endured as a result of her husband's patriarchal demands.[49] In each film, the homoerotic taboo eventually reasserts itself, leaving women's "sharing of joy, whether physical, emotional, [or] psychic" as a repressed fragment in the text that cannot be ignored but is itself refused by the text's hegemonic discourse of socialist subjectivity as necessarily heterosexual.

In the final scene of *All My Girls*, the film returns to the issues of spectatorship presented at the beginning of the film: that of "seeing oneself." The screening sequence depicts the documentary film-within-the-film as Marie, the other women, Ralf, and his professor attend the film's first private screening, followed by Ralf's departure from the factory and the final credits. The mise-en-scène is the private screening room, in which the above-mentioned characters are seated as viewing audience. The sequence begins with a long shot of the onscreen spectators and then cuts to the first clip of the documentary, a "clip" that we as spectators have already seen earlier during the filmmaking process at NARVA. In it, the women welcome a group of Party officials to the factory but miss their chance to present the Party leader with the obligatory

Figure 3.7. Pleasure in seeing ourselves. *All My Girls.* ©DEFA-Stiftung/Wolfgang Ebert.

bouquet of flowers. Initially frustrated, the women realize they are still being filmed and choose to recreate the scene with Anita as Party official and Susi as bearer of the bouquet. The women gesture and congratulate one another in exaggerated fashion, patting each other on the back and hugging, while the diegetic sound is replaced with a comic soundtrack reminiscent of the silent era. The extra-diegetic camera then cuts back to the women in the screening-room audience, laughing at their own images on screen.

Here the mise-en-scène constructs the conditions of Ralf's initial concern regarding spectatorship: "The people don't want to see themselves." However, the result is quite different from what he expected. Ralf's homage to Chaplin—the women's parody of the workers' obligatory performance of gratitude for the Party—fulfills what Bisky and Wiedemann have determined are the "basic viewer expectations": entertainment and social critique. In the footage, the Party officials are all men, dressed in suits, while the workers are all women, dressed in work clothes and aprons and bearing flowers. The women's exaggerated enactment of the Party congratulating one of its most productive brigades is therefore doubly critical: the Party is portrayed as twice removed from those it represents—it is representative neither of the class (marked by dress) nor of the gender (the Party is all male) of its workers.[50] Further, the officials' brief presence on the factory floor, which takes up a total of approximately thirty seconds of footage, points to both their mislocation and their relative absence in the sphere of *work*. The women's lack of disappointment and comic performance suggests that East German workers had little other than empty formalities to seek from the "workers' and peasants' state."[51] The emphasis in this sequence on female spectatorship further encourages same- and trans-gender identification in *All My Girls*'s viewing audience by aligning the women in the brigade with "workers," the characters with whom the audience is most likely to identify, rather than with the Party.

The screening sequence ends with a cut to the final documentary clip, in which Anita is filmed in a medium close-up, speaking directly into the camera.

> I once had a friend, who had come up with a theory of not wanting anything from the world so that he could be completely himself... [jump cut] Bored? Nope—you can see for yourself that it's really hard work; it tires the eyes and really wears out your body. [jump cut] "You're all always so rational," he always said, "you plan everything so that you don't ever have to be afraid, that something won't work. Always keep with the program!" Yeah, yeah... [jump cut] We've put together a committee... and have been thinking about how we can improve the working conditions for the women here, for example switching jobs on the line each hour... [jump cut] No, I don't know where he is now. He didn't really take the work here seriously. Just disappeared.

In this penultimate scene, it is once again overtly suggested that women, rather than men, are the true laborers in the East German economy. The male co-worker who has left the factory is mediated through Anita's onscreen presence. As she voices his critique for him, her own answers function as an indirect support of this critique. His argument that overplanning is a manifestation of the fear that things might otherwise not work or go wrong finds its expression in Anita's assertions. Her mention of the commission to improve women's working conditions comes across as pointless and futile—clearly, the planning continues even without much change for the workers. After her male co-worker has "simply disappeared," she and the other members of the brigade are left to continue the monotonous work.

While Anita describes the male co-worker as not taking the work at NARVA seriously and leaving without a trace, the spectator is presented with the opposite in Ralf, who has come to take the women's work seriously and refuses to abandon their story until they resolve it. However, while Ralf can be considered "on their side," he still remains at a distance from the women in terms of class and in terms of narrative function. As the mediator of their narratives, he stands between them and the final narrative product, between the "real" women of NARVA and the spectators.

DESIRE, NARRATIVITY, AND THE ARTIST

The film's final sequence also raises questions regarding the documentary filmmaking process and the relationship between the documentary filmmaker and his object. The framing narrative presented in the opening and closing sequences deals directly with Ralf's desires as a filmmaker, while the story of the brigade itself complicates Ralf's narrative. When considered together, the sequences analyzed—the factory sequence, the splintering of the brigade in Marie's office, and the orgy sequence—call into question what might be considered a male narrative of desire (to master his female objects who are, at the same time, the objects of his documentary study). In the factory sequence, the women's mastery of their space (exhibited through their physical intimacy on the assembly line, the ease with which they accomplish their labor, and their verbal "mastery" of Ralf upon his arrival) establishes their narrative presence. Their recalibration of the "us"/"them" in Marie's office asserts their desire to speak and their unwillingness to be spoken for. In the orgy sequence, the camera's negotiation of the women's pleasure in one another asserts their positions as subjects (not just as objects) of desire. As a result, the question of who is the subject and who is the object in the documentary process becomes contested.[52]

This is most evident in the meaning of the film's title, *All My Girls*. To whom does the *my* refer? The opening sequence of the film suggests that this is Ralf's story; thus, the viewer is likely to assume that the *my* in the title refers to him and that the women, whom he will represent on film, are *his*. This would also give strong support to a reading of the title as a

revision of the children's song "Alle meine Entchen." The song allegorizes
the private/political dichotomy that the SED would like to assert. In
teaching children that all ducks, geese, chicks, and doves act happily as
a group, it encourages collective participation in an authoritarian power
structure.[53] The obvious comparison of these women to a gaggle of geese,
"*immer bereit!*" ["always prepared!"] to parrot the acts of others around
them is easy to make, especially given the obvious allusion to slang terms
for *girl*: "chick," "silly goose," etc.

Yet the women's resistance to "orders from above" and the shift from
an emphasis on the documentary filmmaker's perspective to that of the
brigade's perspective in each of the sequences I have analyzed suggests
that *my* be read differently. Particularly in the factory sequence, Marie's
highlighted concern that the brigade will be split up and individually assigned to other lines while their new line is being installed suggests that
we ascribe the *my* to Marie, asserting that this is, in fact, a story about
Marie and *her* "girls." Further, the structure of looks between the women
in this sequence reinforces their belonging to the collective. Their collective identity as a brigade would necessarily lead each of the women
to see the others as part of *her* group, shifting the *my* to each of them.
Similarly, the extra-diegetic camera's exclusion of Ralf from the frame
during Marie's breakdown in her office and Kerstin's obstruction of the
diegetic camera at the end of that sequence resist Ralf's ownership of
the story. Instead, the *my* again refers to the women and Marie, who are
personally involved in the story of their struggle and the splintering of
their small collective, and who refuse the diegetic filmmaker access to
certain moments of their collective experience. Further, the camera's
privileging of a female perspective during the orgy sequence reiterates
the *my* as belonging to the individual women. That is, by simultaneously
emphasizing various female looks within the frame and as the assumed
camera perspective, the camera adopts a (predominantly) female gaze,
anchoring the meaning of *my* with the women (i.e., the women are *hers*—
the objects of the camera's gaze). Finally, the positioning of the brigade
in the screening room as the "mass spectator" mirrors their position
within the film narrative as "mass subject." As each woman in the audience identifies with the diverse positions of the other women on screen,

the *my* reflects back onto each of them as they come to identify the group portrait as their own.

The film's overt problematization of the male filmmaker's gaze relates directly to Ralf's frustration in the opening sequence. At the beginning of the film, Ralf complains that he has not been allowed to make *his own* film based on *his own* ideas, which suggests that the *my* in the title refers to the artist as sole owner of his work. Yet, as I have demonstrated, the brigade is a resistant object of his desire: in terms of gaze, voice, and agency, Ralf exists primarily on the margins of the film's narrative. Instead of being a film about a filmmaker and his film, *All My Girls* is a film about a filmic object that resists its own objectification while asserting its subjectivity both outside the moments of diegetic filmmaking (i.e., in scenes not actively filmed by Ralf) and inside the filmmaking process (e.g., by being filmed and by asserting what should be included and excluded from the final cut). Although Ralf makes artistic decisions regarding representation, it is not just his film, but also the women's film. Ralf cannot own the brigade's story; he is not the speaking subject of that story at the same time that he is not the singular desiring subject of the orgy sequence, nor of the screening sequence. Similar to his function as a catalyst for the women's desire for each other, Ralf also functions as the medium through which they tell their story. Ralf cannot determine the story without the voice of his object, which is at one and the same time a group of active subjects who assert their own voices throughout the documentary process.[54] I am therefore suggesting that Ralf functions in the text not as author but rather as editor of or mediator between the women's stories and the viewers' expectations, and also as a medium through which the women negotiate their mutual stories, i.e., their personal narration of their relationships with and desires for one another. This function is most clearly illustrated in Ralf's choice to leave the footage of the argument and breakdown of collectivity in Marie's office out of the film's final cut: Kerstin has argued against its inclusion because it is too personal and painful to be shared with a wider public. Ralf's acquiescence serves as a conscious acknowledgment of his "object's" voice, and of his role as negotiator between his and his objects' competing narrative desires.[55]

As a result, the film complicates the traditional alignment of subject/object with male/female at the same time that it resists a singular subject position through a group portrait of the female brigade. In her book entitled *Alice Doesn't*, Teresa de Lauretis problematizes this configuration of male : subject :: female : object by returning to Freud's questions "what does a woman want?" and "what is femininity?" De Lauretis argues that Freud's question is an articulation of (male) desire that generates a narrative of femininity *for men*. She makes a correlation between Freud's notions of masculinity : subjectivity and femininity : objectivity and Jurij Lotman's notion of the mobile character and the immobile character/plot space. Lotman, whose focus is on the cyclical nature of mythical texts, suggests that characters can be divided into those who are mobile and free to move about the plot space (e.g., the male heroes Oedipus and Perseus), and those who are immobile, who are functions of the plot space and are essentially "personified obstacles" (female "topoi" such the Sphinx and Medusa).[56] De Lauretis focuses on Lotman's overtly gendered reduction of possible plot functions to two: "entry into a closed space, and emergence from it. Inasmuch as closed space *can be interpreted* as 'a cave,' 'the grave,' 'a house,' 'a woman,' . . . entry into it *is interpreted* on various levels as 'death,' 'conception,' 'return home,' and so on."[57] De Lauretis argues that if myth works to establish this distinction, then:

> The primary distinction on which all others depend is not, say, life and death, but rather sexual difference. In other words, the picture of the world produced in mythical thought since the very beginning of culture would rest, first and foremost, on what we call biology. Opposite pairs are merely derivatives of the fundamental opposition between boundary and passage; and if passage may be in either direction, from inside to outside or vice versa, from life to death or vice versa, nonetheless all these terms are predicated on the *single* figure of the hero who crosses the boundary and penetrates the other space. In so doing, the hero, the mythical subject, is constructed as human being and as male; he is the active principle of culture, the establisher of distinction, the creator of differences. Female is what is not susceptible to transformation, to life or death; she (it) is an element of plot-space, a topos, a resistance, matrix and matter.[58]

De Lauretis gives us an opportunity to consider how the narrative space of *All My Girls* complicates the roles of male : subject :: female : object in the narrative, revealing the film's attempt to engage the question of desire in narrative, specifically the desire of the artist both within (diegetic) and outside (extra-diegetic) the space of the narrative.[59] Diegetically, one can read Ralf as a reformulation of the heroic male who "crosses the boundary and penetrates the other space" in order to become the hero and author of his story, as the one who narrates history. Clearly, Ralf imagines himself to be a "revolutionary" who passes into the space of labor in order to emerge with an artistic product that reveals the "true" labor relations within that space. Given that the object of Ralf's study is an all-female brigade, one might be tempted to read "woman" as the space/topos of his revolutionary artistic act. However, as I have shown, the singularity of the male hero is contested in the film by establishing the brigade, not the filmmaker, as the narrative hero and the subject of the film. Further, that subject, the *Mensch* at the center of the text, is "woman," not "man." It is less likely to be the filmmaker, and more likely to be the brigade, with whom the viewer identifies, the "girls just like us," who are "not heroes," but who are "sympathetic" and "honest" characters. In addition, the overt tension between Ralf's and the women's desire to narrate the brigade's story asserts that the documentary belongs just as much to the women as it does to Ralf.

Yet we cannot dismiss the role of the framing narrative as a story of the male artist (hero) struggling to assert his vision of history in a cinematic landscape overdetermined by state control and official ideology. Ralf's desire to model himself on a "revolutionary" artist, along with the "great directors" Chaplin, Fellini, and Romm, reveals the conundrum of the socialist filmmaker: how to marry entertainment with a critical eye, how to make films that will bring people into the theater and also raise their consciousness, how to prevent "the people" from turning the channel while also presenting the "truth" of life without taboos? De Lauretis' discussion of myth and historiography is helpful in understanding Ralf as the mythic socialist hero. De Lauretis connects the myth-making function of narrative with that of history:

> History . . . in the modern definition, achieves both narrativity and historical-ity by filling in the gaps left in the annals and by endowing events with a plot structure and an order of meaning. What is involved in the discovery of "the true story" within or behind the events that come to us in the chaotic form of "historical records"? What wish is enacted, what desire gratified, by the fantasy that real events are properly represented when they can be shown to display the

formal coherency of a story? In the enigma of this wish, this desire, we catch a
glimpse of the cultural function of narrativizing discourse.[60]

This question of discovering the "true story" of history, of desire as the
mediating agent in the equation of narrativity with meaning, is thematized through the character of Ralf, the diegetic filmmaker. Ralf's desire
to get at the true story of the brigade, to bring the viewers truth with "no
taboos," reveals his desire to arrange real events in the formal coherency
of a story to narrate the history of the everyday in an East German factory. Ralf explicitly reiterates Honecker's own official declaration of "no
taboos" and in doing so, overtly problematizes the role of the artist in
the GDR. But what are we to make of Ralf as the diegetic representative
of the artist, particularly in relation to the *Gruppe Berlin*? Why would
the *Gruppe Berlin* choose to portray the filmmaker as a man, given that,
with the exception of the cameraman, the artistic circle was all female
(the artistic adviser, Tamara Trampe; the screenwriter, Gabrielle Kotte;
and the director, Iris Gusner)? This question points to the larger enigma
of artistic desire in this group of East German women artists. If an all-
female group of artists has come together to create a film about filming
a documentary about an all-female brigade, what desires and anxieties
are revealed through the choice of a man to represent the artist, and
how does that play out in the construction of subjects and objects in the
documentary process?

First, given East European women's complicated rejection of Western feminism, it is unlikely that the *Gruppe Berlin* was trying to create a simplistic division between men and women in the film. And, as I
have shown, any strict division along gender lines in the film is resisted
through mode of class in the film. One might argue that a desire to balance possible gender tensions with gender solidarity is visible in the varied representation of the few men represented in the film.[61] The men in
the factory who are representative of a kind of socialist paternalism are
only rarely represented (Marie's boss, Lauterbach; the Party officials),
whereas Ralf, the only male represented regularly, stands in as the figure
of the artist, who is a sympathetic mediator of the women's story, and
whose position is complicated through his location outside the everyday.
Although Ralf's status is questioned throughout the film, he also represents a position of social privilege in the GDR that was unique in many

respects.[62] Further, because women's emancipation in the GDR never involved gender isolationism, it was more common to see solidarity being built along the lines of class, rather than gender. And yet, while Ralf does identify with the group of women in the end, he is still not marked as a "worker," and so remains an outsider in terms of class. Finally, given the high percentage of male directors at DEFA, choosing a male film student might simply reflect a more "realistic" artistic choice at the same time that it might be considered a subtle critique of the gendered division of labor at the studio.[63]

I suggest instead that Ralf can best be read as representative of the divide that exists between the women working on the film (Trampe, Kotte, and Gusner) and the actual women working at the NARVA plant in Berlin. Ralf functions as a diegetic surrogate for the extra-diegetic filmmakers' location outside the everyday of the GDR, and the *Gruppe Berlin*'s desire to represent that everyday of which they are always only marginally a part. If we consider the personal history of just one of the women making the film, the artistic director Trampe, and her desire to create a realistic *Alltagsfilm*, the choice of a male film student might make even more sense. Trampe's first job during her teenage years was at the actual NARVA plant in Berlin, an experience she describes as both positive and formative, mainly because it was a factory populated predominantly by female laborers. After working there for three years, Trampe went on to work at another factory, and then, after studying at the university, went to work for the journal *Forum*. She was fired from *Forum* after refusing to write for the paper during her visit to Prague, which coincided with the Prague Spring uprisings, and ended up at DEFA after two women writers from DEFA discovered her in Eisenhüttenstadt, producing theater pieces written by local workers. She describes her resulting choice to develop a feature film about her first place of "real" work as an exciting opportunity to portray those aspects of working women's lives that were rarely addressed in other aspects of East German culture. Trampe and Kotte, both having experienced work on the assembly line, devoted over four months to researching women's experiences at the NARVA plant, hoping to get closer to the "reality" of the women working there, many of whom Trampe had worked with as a teenager.[64] Trampe's personal history suggests yet another layer of the meaning in the film's title. If we consider Trampe's desire to return to this very formative space, where she became a woman *and* a worker, then the *my* in *All My Girls* could reflect this desire to see herself among these "real" women. Her more complicated position as an artist, on the margins of these women's everyday experiences, could therefore be mediated through a male protagonist as she reconnects with her origins, "her girls."

Thus, the choice to portray a male directorial student in place of the women in the *Gruppe Berlin* might have something to do with an awareness of and desire to represent their own distance from the "real" women of the actual NARVA factory. Clearly, Trampe and Kotte wanted to do justice to a reality of which they were no longer a part. Their choice of a male director could therefore be read as a manifestation of the desire to represent this divide through gender, to express their distance as artists from their object of study. If "woman" comes to represent the new socialist subject in the *Alltagsfilm*, the new *Mensch* with whom the masses are to identify, then "male" becomes a marker—even if an unconscious one—of the outside. Whether conscious or not, this choice can thus be read as a way of working through the distance in East German society between the artist/intellectual and the "real" workers; between Trampe, Kotte, and Gusner as female artists, and their laboring counterparts at the NARVA factory. Given the disproportionately few number of women in leading artistic positions at DEFA, Trampe and Kotte cannot be seen as representative of the "artist" per se. Yet, given their roles as artists, they cannot be read as representative of the "worker," in the way that the NARVA women are. While Kerstin might represent this distance on a certain level, her character is not placed in any position of authority, either as worker or as artist. The character of Ralf, on the other hand, exhibits myriad aspects of the intellectual as artist, making him an overt metaphor for the "non-working" women working on *All My Girls*.

This (un)conscious recognition and portrayal of artistic difference thematizes and attempts to reconcile not only the class differences inherent in the artist/worker division, but also the power differences in the subject/object relationship, between the filmmaking subject(s) and his/their object(s), the women at the NARVA. Ralf's eventual identification with and investment in the brigade's situation is reciprocated by the women's acceptance of him. His choice to ignore deadlines in favor of standing by the brigade until their struggle to remain together is won can be read as a commentary on the role of filmmaking as a social practice. Trampe and Kotte's devotion to researching the "real" experiences of the women at NARVA, to putting art in the service of life, is reflected in Ralf's persistence to get it right, to show the "truth" of that experience. Further, it reflects a particularly Marxist understanding of personal freedom and fulfillment. Marx suggests that the division of labor "only becomes truly such from the moment when a division of material and mental labor appears. From this moment onwards consciousness *can* really flatter itself that it is something other than consciousness of existing practice, that it *really* represents something without representing something real; from now on consciousness is in a position to emancipate itself from the world."[65] *All My Girls* attempts to represent something "real" by bringing to light aspects of women's everyday lives in the GDR. But it also develops a metacritique of the division of mental and physical labor, and its gender specificity in the GDR, emphasizing the role of the artist in negotiating that division. By manipulating art in the service of "lived experience," by negotiating between the voice of the filmmaker and the voice of the documentary "object," the diegetic and extra-diegetic filmmakers reveal a desire to move toward an emancipatory notion of personal freedom possible only through the abolition of the division of labor.[66]

SPACE, REALISM, AND VIEWER PLEASURE

Some contemporary critics of *All My Girls* questioned its supposed idealization of the factory space, suggesting that the social milieu of the female laborers and factory life was portrayed in too bright a light, resulting in a lighthearted film that avoided the darker side of labor in the GDR. Trampe herself stated that the film she had envisioned would have been sadder, grayer, more bitter, and uncomfortable. In an interview with *Sonntag,* Gusner talks about this critique of the film:

> Younger filmmakers have accused us of seeing the factory milieu as too beautiful, they found our representation duplicitous. But, if we brought in more light than is normally present, it is because we wanted to visually express the human warmth of the relationships between the female workers. It was more important

to me to show internal, rather than external, truth. Sure, the work of our girls
is monotonous and it takes place in an ugly factory atmosphere. But it's also
true that our society can't do without their work. This contradiction is what we
wanted to show, in terms of making sense of social necessity. It's for that reason
that we emphasized that interpersonal relationships are often more important
than individual accomplishments.[67]

In this interview, Gusner uses the term *believable* to describe the film's
artistic reflection on the interpersonal relationships between the women
and their environment, asserting that "human warmth" is the "internal
truth" that proves more important and holds greater meaning for the
collective than solitary achievements do. Gusner thus constructs a film
that resists a definition of realism based solely in representation (e.g.,
the factory is portrayed in "too bright a light") instead focusing on a
narrative atmosphere that is "believable." Gusner's assertion that the
film's believability is located in the "human warmth of the relationships
between the female laborers" and not in the physical representation of
the factory locates the film's believability in the group inhabiting the
space, in their relationships, rather than in the space itself.

However, neither does the film construct an unrealistic factory
space. The film clearly represents the monotony of the women's work,
and the film's portrayal of the contradictions between the collective on
the small scale (the group of women) and the collective on the large
scale (the state represented by "orders from above") reveals the film's
realism. In representing the group's struggle to assert its desires in the
space of the factory—staying together as a brigade rather than being split
up and temporarily assigned to other brigades while a new line is being
installed—the film resists a complete "brightening up" [*Verschönerung*]
of the relationship between the state and the collective on the small scale.
Further, the film foregrounds, as part of this conflict, the women's fears
that splitting up the brigade even briefly would mean the end of the brigade altogether, since it is their camaraderie and conflict, not the work,
that actually keeps them going. In fact, it is the overt monotony of their
labor to which their group solidarity stands as opposite, as meaningful
existence, that results in a critique of labor per se. The result is a film
whose "believability" or "realism" lies in its narrative of camaraderie
and conflict, a realism that stands in opposition, however, to less critical

socialist realist texts, which attempted to "see the world of today with the eyes of tomorrow."[68]

I would like to suggest further that we consider how the notion of "believability" problematizes cinematic, specifically feminist, debates about the ideological control of "classic cinematic realism" and how other forms of realism in East German texts, such as that produced in *All My Girls*, can create a critical viewing perspective. To suggest that a film is believable usually means that some form of realism holds sway over the text. The most common critique leveled at cinematic realism is that it tends toward transparency in representation—i.e., the film seems to reflect the "real world" and/or does not make the spectator aware of his or her role in the process of making meaning—and that it offers the viewer uncontested closure, most often in the form of the happy ending.[69] However, *All My Girls* does deconstruct the transparency of representation through the character of Ralf. As the representation of the East German artist, Ralf questions the ethics of the subject/object divide in narrative and in documentary filmmaking, making the power hierarchies involved in filmmaking one of the film's central questions. The viewer thus becomes aware of the role of the artist in the often conflict-laden decision-making process of filmmaking. Film as such is therefore constructed within the film as a medium in which narrative is constructed and power is negotiated, not as a transparent medium. Further, the film's incomplete closure with regards to Kerstin challenges the viewer to reflect on her absence as an instance of collective, rather than personal, loss.[70]

What are the possible critical uses of realist techniques that suture the spectator and enable identification with the characters on the screen, especially in the East German artistic context, which often exploited "realist" methods in order to ideally represent a non-ideal social context? The film's engagement with the East German everyday was, as Feinstein has argued, an attempt to deal with those aspects of East German experience that were neglected by dominant East German discourses. *All My Girls* combines aspects of documentary realism, which some have termed "kitchen-sink" realism, as in the works of Ken Loach, as well as comic strategies that work together to produce a text that is neither properly "socialist realist" nor representative of escapist or fantastical "cinematic realism." In its foregrounding of the documentary process, *All My Girls* reveals both the "real" and the "fantastical" nature of the filmmaking process as it produces meaning. Further, the location of the film in Berlin's NARVA plant as an overt homage to Böttcher's *Stars* asserts the filmmakers' desire to draw on DEFA's documentary tradition, a tradition that, while more often subjected to censorship than the feature film industry, managed to produce a variety of critical films.

Gusner emphasizes the contradictory space of the factory, a dialectical space of monotony and social necessity, precisely because it enables believability and thus, spectator identification. That is, it creates positions on screen with which the spectator can identify, either as a result of suture and narrative, or as a result of personal experience, or as a result of both. These identificatory positions are both enjoyable—the spectator is easily sutured into the narrative through the compelling construction of subject positions on screen—and critical—the positions within the narrative do not offer simplistic or didactic solutions to the complex and contradictory relationships constructed on screen but, rather, encourage viewers' critical engagement, most likely as a result of personal experience.

In foregrounding the contradictions of this space, within which interpersonal relationships take shape and are represented by women workers, *All My Girls* offers Western viewers in particular a representation of femininity that is almost completely absent in Hollywood film. Because of the difference in cinematic contexts—that of DEFA and of Hollywood—*All My Girls*'s critical potential and possibilities for viewer pleasure also differ. For the Western viewer, the film represents women's work, women's bodies, and women's agency in a way that is practically absent in dominant cinematic discourse. The film's critical potential for a Western audience lies partially in representations of women's labor that were made possible by the different socioeconomic and ideological context of socialism and the necessity of women's labor. Women's everyday presence "at work" in the GDR altered the scope of possibilities for embodying women on the screen in ways that were not possible or believable—on a mainstream level—in Hollywood. Because 90 percent of East German women were in the workforce, with a large percentage of those in unskilled and semiskilled jobs, certain (though not all) traditional expectations regarding representing women's bodies were overcome and new traditions were established. The extensive focus on women as manual laborers in the film, combined with an absence of the obligatory romantic or sacrificial/maternal narrative that makes the female protagonists in Hollywood cinema "complete" women, constructs for the viewer an alternative community of women—a lesbian continuum—outside of domestic and romantic interests, a representation very uncommon in mainstream Western film. It therefore goes beyond Western feminist attempts to create an "in the kitchen atmosphere" by almost completely restricting its representation of the women to their work spaces.[71]

In the 1970s, however, Hollywood produced numerous films that portrayed women working outside the home, including films as diverse as *Alice Doesn't Live Here Anymore*, *An Officer and a Gentleman*, *An Unmarried Woman*, *Working Girl*, *9 to 5*, and overtly feminist films like *The 24 Hour Woman*. Yet we can see the radicalism of *All My Girls* in its immediate cinematic context and its importance for the history of women's cinema by asking certain questions: What is the focus of these Hollywood films, and do they differ significantly from *All My Girls*? Do these films attempt to deal with gender roles and social tensions produced as a result of changes in those roles? Or are the melodramatic romance and domestic sacrifice that were present in early Hollywood women's films simply shifted to the office space, where the "frigid bitch boss" is contrasted with the seductive secretary?[72]

One notable difference is that all of these Hollywood films focus on pink-collar work or on feminized labor, and not on representations of working-class women or collective consciousness in the way that DEFA does. Robin Wood put it quite succinctly when he said that "in Hollywood films—even in the most determinedly progressive—there is no 'Women's Movement'; there are only individual women who feel personally constrained."[73] Wood deals specifically with the films *Alice Doesn't Live Here Anymore* and *An Unmarried Woman*. However, his argument regarding the restriction of progressive films to non-working class heroines and to the recuperation of women into either maternal or romantic positions in the end holds for all of the films mentioned above. The women in these Hollywood films are individuals (not members of a collective) who, in the end, are saved from their dangerous independence by strong, protective males who will look after them.[74]

In both East European and Hollywood contexts, *All My Girls* achieves two very important narrative reconstructions. First, the female brigade at the center of the film sets up the possibility not only for female identification, but for a differentiated, multiple, and constantly shifting identification as a result of the film's focus on a group of women, rather than on a single female protagonist. The camaraderie and tensions between the women, which are established and developed throughout the film, splinter the individuality of identification into a collective identity. At the same time, and even more interesting within both the Eastern and Western cinematic contexts, it transforms the space of manual labor— traditionally labeled masculine—into a feminine space. That is, based on the little representation men enjoy in the film, manual labor becomes a space within which women not only feel "at home," but within which they argue, make decisions, and exercise relative authority.[75] As a result, the gendered specificity of public/private spaces is complicated.

For an East German audience, *All My Girls*'s focus on unskilled female laborers creates slightly different possibilities for viewer pleasure. One argument against the critical potential of the film might be that the factory is not a new space of representation (though the focus on unskilled women workers *is* new) and that the film's closure rests on a partial, superficially happy ending: the agency that the women in the film enjoy is miniscule (fighting to keep the brigade together) compared to a lack of agency, which "real women" in the GDR were complaining about.[76] However, the brigade's achievement at the end comes also with loss: Anita accuses Kerstin of stealing money collected for the "solidarity kitty," when, in fact, Anita has simply misplaced the money. As a result of the accusations, Kerstin does not return to work and all attempts to locate her are unsuccessful. This loss is a direct result of the brigade's brief yet significant failure to trust her, which underscores the primacy of the women's interpersonal relationships. While Ralf is also complicit in the circle of mistrust, Kerstin's absence is felt primarily in the work space. Anita's lonely mourning scene in the factory bathroom at the end of the film, together with the arrival of a new girl, again lays bare the unresolved tensions between Anita, the exemplary brigade leader, and Kerstin, the intellectual outsider. This complication of the group dynamic asserts the partiality of the happy ending and emphasizes the tensions of class and power within the collective. In not assigning blame or simplifying these tensions through didacticism, the film problematizes the seeming cohesiveness of collectivity and engages the viewer in an ethical re-vision of equality and egalitarianism under socialism.

One could certainly make the opposing argument that representing women "at work" reflects a Party ideology that unquestioningly attempted to harmonize women's "natural" roles as mothers with their necessary participation in the socialist economy. However, the film clearly participates in the turn in DEFA filmmaking toward portraying the less glorious aspects of working life and the everyday of socialism, which involves a shift from portraying female protagonists as educated engineers, heart surgeons, veterinarians, and lawyers (*Her Third, The Seventh Year, Because I Love You, Destinies of Women* to name a few), to portraying unskilled women working on the line. Further, like the other films discussed in this book, *All My Girls* reflects a shift in the East German cinematic images of women, by resisting aspects of the gender ideology at the heart of the SED's so-called women's policies. The women in *All My Girls* are not mothers; they are single, promiscuous, "other women," and they are assertive in their presence and speech. Further, this uncommon representation of women in the space of the factory is used simultaneously to critique the essence of that space—labor—as the central signifier of the "all-round developed socialist personality." Although the film is set in the space of the factory, the film is not a glorification of labor. Rather, the *space* of labor—both empowering and alienating—is what enables the women to build a camaraderie not based on labor, which consequently leads to forms of agency different from those structured by the domestic space. While emphasizing the problem of alienated labor under socialism—labor must sell itself even in the worker's and peasants' state—the film also privileges moments in which the women realize their individual worth and power within a lesbian continuum. As a result, the contradiction between the social necessity of industrial labor and the alienation of the individual workers becomes a critical tool for illustrating "that interpersonal contacts are often more important than individual accomplishments."[77]

4

Real Women: *Goodbye to Winter* and the Documentary Women's Film

We shouldn't be surprised that in a socialist society conflicts come to the fore that have, for years, been left in the dark to stew and to poison people's lives. We first become conscious of conflicts once we can afford to overcome them. We have come to see our position as women in a more differentiated way since the moment we were faced with the opportunity to change it.
—Maxie Wander. *Guten Morgen, du Schöne.*

DOCUMENTARY FORM AND FEMINIST FILM THEORY

How do we see and understand documentary? If we cannot rely on the images and the narrative to provide us with "authentic" and "truthful" representations of "real" history, then what do we make of documentary? This has been the question at the center of most international debates on documentary since the 1970s. Since that time, questions have been raised about the documentarian's disruption of the "reality" that she or he is filming, about the camera's mediation of its object, and about the dramatization of material "reality."[1] Brian Winston suggests that the issue of "truth" as a marker of the documentary film (in supposed opposition to the feature film) is a contradiction that has been ignored and sustained since the beginning of the documentary tradition: "[T]he need for [cinematic] structure implicitly contradicts the notion of unstructured actuality. The idea of documentary, then and now, is sustained by simply ignoring this contradiction."[2]

For many contemporary filmmakers and film theorists, this contra-dictory "truth" is best countered with a style of filmmaking that is overtly political and self-reflexive, a cinematic form that draws attention to docu-mentary's participation in the narrative process of meaning-making. The work of Trinh T. Minh-ha and Claire Johnston is representative of this trend. In contrast, when looking at the East German documentary tra-dition, it is almost impossible to find this type of formal self-reflexivity. While DEFA experienced moments of artistic independence throughout the history of the GDR, DEFA's documentary studio remained closely watched by the party. The close relationship between the documentary film and television studios was strictly enforced, which meant that a great majority of documentary films were commissioned by the state for televi-sion. Thus, while there always remained a relative amount of artistic free-dom at the studio, documentarians, in contrast to their colleagues in the feature film studios, were especially put upon to produce ideologically correct films that would support the party's political and cultural goals.[3]

The preferred style at DEFA was "socialist realism," which demanded "*Lebensnähe*" ["being near to life"] and "*Widerspiegelung des 'Typischen'*" [reflection of the typical].[4] Yet the question of how typical or near to life this form could actually be is easily disputed when one considers the ideal form that documentary socialist realism was expected to take: "Our mission consists of seeing the world of today with the eyes of to-morrow."[5] Filmmakers were faced with official resistance to any kind of aesthetic avant-gardism and were discouraged from reacting formally to most international movements in documentary filmmaking.[6] Thus, for a cinema that was closely bound to the state, the definition of "politics" was often equated with party slogans, not, as has been the case in inter-national debates, with an activist cinema that perpetually questioned its political foundations.

Yet many documentarians were able to produce films that interro-gated East Germany's historical imaginary, thus creating a public space for critical reflection on official ideologies. Helke Misselwitz' film *Winter adé* [*Goodbye to Winter*] (1988), a film that reflects on women's experi-ences of gender difference in the GDR, achieves just this. Like other documentarians who came before her, Misselwitz focuses in particular on aspects of everyday socialist life. Similar to the work of her colleagues,

Misselwitz' social critique lay almost exclusively in the particular images and in the montage, rather than in the verbal aspects of the film. While scripts for feature films and the audio of documentary footage were screened for possibly inflammatory language, the images remained relatively uncensored. Like her predecessors Jürgen Böttcher, Winfried Junge, and Volker Koepp, Misselwitz juxtaposes seemingly benign images, dialogue, and voice-over commentary to avoid overtly critical meaning and instead uses them to construct various levels of ambiguity when commenting on the contradictions of and alienation experienced in East German society.

As other scholars have suggested, filming the everyday of socialism thus carries with it seemingly contradictory meanings.[7] On the one hand, these films provide an escape from larger, overtly political topics. On the other hand, this shift from the "public" to the "private" is a shifting of critique from not from one "sphere" to another, but rather, from official to less directly political issues.[8] Attempts to document and probe the lives of the everyday, for example in Junge's Golzow documentaries and Koepp's Wittstock films, illustrate this tension between the personal and the political. As Barton Byg has suggested, the sometimes politically motivated narrative choices made by filmmakers were often complicated by the contradictions in participants' personal responses, and the visual reality of domestic duties and personal space. While the "larger" problems of socialism (issues of official politics) were not dealt with at length, a more critical engagement with the everyday was achieved that engaged viewers' desires to encounter socialism as it was lived, not in the form of socialist realist idealism. That critical engagement is discussed by Elke Schieber as a particular cinematic tradition at DEFA documentary studio, in which the films construct a kind of "critical truth":

> A style was developed that was characterized by long, observational takes with few cuts, creating a quiet flow of images. Viewers accepted these films because they didn't interrupt or condense the words spoken by their subjects, and because they freely offered up the opinions of their subjects, who were allowed to move about in spaces that were familiar [to them and to the viewers]. . . . The camera stressed nothing, discredited no one, idealized nothing.[9]

Goodbye to Winter successfully constructs such critical truths by conforming to a trend within DEFA documentary filmmaking, in which "woman" comes to represent the "truth" of everyday life. Misselwitz' film is representative of a movement, also visible in DEFA feature films and in GDR women's literature, in which the contradictions of real, existing socialism are dealt with through a gendered lens. Whether or not one can speak distinctly about a genre of "documentary women's film," it is clear that documentary films about women, especially in the 1970s and 80s, differed greatly from those about men. The most significant and renowned among them are Böttcher's *Stars* (1963), about a female brigade in the Berlin-based light bulb factory NARVA, as well as his film *Wäscherinnen* [*Washer Women*] (1972), about a group of women working at an industrial laundromat in Berlin; Gitta Nickel's *Sie* [*She*] (1970), about female workers in a Berlin confectionary factory; and *Wir von ESDA* [*We Women of ESDA*] (1976), about women working in a hosiery factory in the Ore Mountains; and finally Koepp's Wittstock films *Mädchen in Wittstock* [*Girls in Wittstock*] (1975), *Wieder in Wittstock* [*Back in Wittstock*] (1976), *Wittstock III* (1977), and *Leben und Weben* [*Living and Weaving*] (1981), a longitudinal study in cinematic form about a small group of women living and working in the town of Wittstock in Brandenburg, that includes a post-*Wende* return, *Wittstock, Wittstock* (1997). Like so many other social theorists, Eduard Schreiber sees this focus on women and the everyday of socialism as an awareness on the part of artists that women functioned as a site of crystallization for social contradiction and rupture:

> [Women] carry the weight of social developments and their deformations into the most private spheres.... In film, they are the ones most able to inform us about the fragility of our social circumstances, to allow us to sense these circumstances and to make them sensually discernable/perceptible.... Women prove to be more radical and are more convincingly able to express, reflect and question East German reality.[10]

Goodbye to Winter constructs this critical truth by creating a sense of authenticity through a documentation of women's experience of these social contradictions and ruptures. "Authenticity," however, is a problematic notion for documentary, since it supports a notion of documentary truth as a way of describing the genuine, the real, and the factual. Yet *Goodbye to Winter*'s construction of authenticity serves a critical function in subverting official gender ideology by legitimizing various aspects of women's lived experiences in the GDR that are refused or ignored by that ideology. Therefore, both notions—truth and authenticity—are not absolutes but, rather, textual constructs that have critical value.

Additionally, *Goodbye to Winter* uses different cinematic techniques to create a sense of authenticity of experience in the GDR, which specifically lies in the interrogation of official ideologies of gender in the GDR. In particular, Misselwitz's use of the talking-heads technique, a traditionally realist structure, engages directly with feminist film debates regarding the social and political role of documentary film practices. Both Sonja Michel and Julia Lesage have argued for the importance of certain realist structures for achieving feminist goals in filmmaking. Lesage asserts that many feminist filmmakers deliberately use traditional realist structures like the talking-heads technique—"a simple format to present to audiences . . . a picture of the ordinary details of women's lives, their thoughts—told directly by the protagonists to the camera—and their frustrated but sometimes successful attempts to enter and deal with the public world of work and power."[11] These forms of realism can be understood as "an urgent public act" aimed at making these biographies and experiences simple, accessible, and trustworthy. Lesage questions the notion of "truth" or "transparency" by suggesting that conventional textual techniques create a structure for the viewer that is recognizable and enjoyable, not transparently or factually true. At the same time, this structure demands the viewers' critical engagement with established social narratives.[12] Thus, in using this technique, Misselwitz participates in the demystification of the past by providing women a public forum in which they can speak about their lives and articulate new knowledges—new truths—of socialist experience.[13]

Interestingly, the film does not limit itself to one space and time, as is often the case in previous East German documentaries that focus on a single woman, on women working in a particular brigade, or on women working in one factory or living in one town. The women who speak in *Goodbye to Winter* are located around the country, are in various stages of life, and lead a variety of lifestyles. In a sense, the film attempts to create something that other East German documentaries had yet to accomplish—a collage of East German women's experiences. This use of various positions, of an assortment of women in differing social positions and family roles speaking into the camera, makes it more difficult to generalize about the particular women interviewed and creates a differentiated, less stereotypical and therefore more authentic picture of GDR womanhood. It thereby complicates and even contradicts official media images of women.[14]

This technique of various voices challenging the "truth" of official narratives is strongly rooted in the oral tradition of women's history. Reconstructing a social history from the bottom up has been the focus of many feminist historians and cultural critics who attempt to question monolithic historical narratives.[15] However, as Joan Scott argues, the use of women's personal narratives—both the autobiographical and the interview / life-story forms—threatens to become its own form of foundational knowledge standing opposite to official ideology.[16] Yet *Goodbye to Winter* does not suggest a single truth or reality. In its emphasis on autobiography and life story, on the individual telling and interpreting of experience, the film creates a kind of *metissage*, a "braided text of many voices that speak their cultural locations dialogically."[17] In narrating their experiences, the women interviewed participate in their composure and discomposure as historical subjects. *To compose* here means to participate in the cultural activity of constructing a narrative about the self, a narrative that is then constantly reinterpreted and revised at different historical moments.[18] The dis/composure of the subject of life-story telling occurs when the narrator must engage with the competing and contradictory public discourses surrounding those personal experiences.[19] Thus, the authenticity of *Goodbye to Winter* is located both in the plurality of the experiences narrated and in the composure and dis/composure through narration, in the act of narrating experience that contradicts both official representations of women's experiences and women's own representations of experience voiced in the film itself.

The collaborative process of *Goodbye to Winter* creates a dialogue of voices that control the text: "the autobiographical 'I,' with its authority, is replaced by a less stable 'we.'"[20] In this sense, the *author(s)* and the *editor/writer* of the text are not one and the same.[21] This self-reflexive technique suggests that Misselwitz is aware of the fact that, while enabling an alternative narrative of women's experience in the GDR, the text remains constructed by an author who does not stand outside history.[22]

GOODBYE TO WINTER

The film's autobiographical frame is established by the opening sequence, in which Misselwitz narrates her own personal history in voice-over monologue. Beginning with a shot from inside a car, waiting at a railroad crossing, she says: "In front of this closed railroad gate my mother gives birth to me. In the ambulance. Grandmother helps her. . . . She writes in her diary: 'What a glorious birthday gift you are. Daddy is very happy, even if you, too, aren't the son he so desired.'" The camera cuts to the still image of a family photo: a grandmother holds one small girl and one baby girl; a younger couple, presumably Misselwitz's parents, stands behind them. The image is replaced with a second still of two girls receiving diplomas, while the sound of the opening sequence (a passing train) is replaced by the sound of creaking. The still image is replaced by a medium shot of a man cranking the railroad gate open. Misselwitz asks to see the tattoos decorating his chest and back, wondering aloud what kind of women he has inscribed there. His answer: *"scheene* Frauen" ["purty" women].

The film's establishing shot, waiting for the train to pass over the tracks, becomes a visual metaphor for Misselwitz's entrance into and experience of the world. Having been born a daughter, rather than the son for whom her father had longed, Misselwitz was a mixed blessing. Her metaphorical standstill supports the two privileged sentences from her mother's diary. While she is born into a state of supposed gender equality, her sex is clearly presented as a barrier. She must wait for it to pass, or for a man to open the gate to her emancipation. The contradictions of Misselwitz's personal experience are then grotesquely multiplied in the figure of the railroad worker. Not only is he represented as an agent of (women's) release, but the visual representations of women on his body are static and one-dimensional: his only definition of them is *"scheen"* [pretty]. This secondary screen of the tattoo reflects on the visual medium with which Misselwitz must struggle in order to represent "women and girls in this country." It is a medium that traditionally binds woman to her to-be-looked-at-ness.[23]

Importantly, this sequence illustrates that alternative forms of history writing, like the diary or autobiographical forms, give voice

Figure 4.1. "Scheene Frauen." *Goodbye to Winter*. Dir. Helke Misselwitz, DEFA, 1988.
©DEFA-Stiftung/Thomas Plehnert.

to experiences that are often silenced in official narratives—here, the
supposed gender equality in the GDR. The mother's diary and the still
photos of Misselwitz become tools of a public discourse, participating
in the production of knowledge and historical narrative. Misselwitz's
use of still photos, rather than her own talking head, illustrates that she
remains at a kind of standstill: while she is shown receiving her diploma,
this moment is frozen, thus raising the question of women's progress in
the GDR by alluding to the reifying tendency of official socialist discourse. By contrasting the still images with the moving images of her
documentary footage, she intervenes in public discourse and gives the
women's experiences catalogued there a previously unattained historical agency.

The second third of the opening sequence takes place in the main
hall of the Planitz train station, beginning with a close-up of a pair of
woman's legs in nylons with a pinstriped seam, then moving into a medium long shot of the entire station hall. As the camera tracks slowly

forward through the hall, Misselwitz recounts the first time she left her small town:

> At the age of nineteen I leave this city in order to go my own way. Vocational training, marriage, divorce. Furnished room; varied, yet intensive employment. Career, birth of my daughter, second marriage. Pursuit of a degree while childrearing, second divorce. Insistence on meaningful work. I know many women whose worries and desires I share. The self-assuredness of my nearly grown daughter makes me simultaneously unsure and hopeful.

This section of the monologue functions like an abbreviated resumé, noting major life changes. It also functions as a commentary on the previous third of the opening sequence, in which Misselwitz obliquely suggests that all official attempts to enact emancipation from above through social policy—marriage and divorce rights, inexpensive housing for married couples, access to higher education and job training—have only partially alleviated the problems women face in society. The challenges of single motherhood (and its naturalized meanings) and finding meaningful work are exacerbated by residual sexism women experience at various levels of society, reflected in Misselwitz's father's expectations, in the railway worker's tattoos, and in the pinstriped nylons. She uses the words *worries* and *desires* to bridge her personal experience (work, marriage, divorce, childrearing) with that of the women she will interview throughout the film. This second section of the opening sequence makes obvious her own investment in the film project, therefore avoiding an omniscient perspective that will present "facts," at the same time that she uses voice-over monologue to remind the viewer that she maintains a certain level of textual authority.[24]

At this point, the camera cuts to the film's title and a woman's voice announces that passengers should now board the train. This narrative device invites the viewer to join Misselwitz in a personal journey that is also a public attempt to rewrite history through dialogue. From inside the train car, the camera looks out the window as the train passes through the countryside. Misselwitz tells the viewer that she is departing, "in order to experience how others have lived, how others would like to live. On this trip we will talk to each other . . . sometimes we will only look at them—women and girls in this country." Yet Misselwitz also depicts this attempt at dialogue with her documentary object as problematic. The numerous secondary screens in the film—like the photos and the tattoos—reflect on the visual medium and its tendency toward objectification. Thus, in looking out the window of the train, the camera suggests the problems with the documentary gaze. Misselwitz's voice-over, "sometimes we will only look at them," is doubled by the camera's look, thus equating the viewer's gaze with the gaze invited by the tattoos. In reminding us of our participation in this objectification, Misselwitz admits her own textual authority, while also expressing her desire to get closer to these "real women," a rapprochement that the photos and the tattoos cannot enact.

Misselwitz's first attempt to approach these women is with Hillu, an advertising economist, aged forty-two, living in Berlin. Although the camera does not include Misselwitz in the frame, her presence is made clear through her voice in dialogue with Hillu. Hillu's description of her life, as with most of the women in the film, centers around family and work. She begins by talking about her marriages, the first having oc-curred after becoming pregnant at age nineteen. She credits her father's authoritarianism with her early conservatism and her hesitance to escape this first marriage:

> It was a stupid marriage because my upbringing hindered me from freeing myself from it at the appropriate time. . . . There were six of us children growing up, and we had an incredibly authoritarian father . . . and this authoritarianism in my childhood home always placed the father figure in the best light, and perhaps I just carried that over into my own marriage. . . . It took me a long, long time to free myself of that, to rid myself somehow of this superiority of "Father/ Husband."

Hillu's own interpretation of her experience suggests that she underwent a form of feminist coming to consciousness. An awareness of the male's special role in the home (as husband and father) that thwarted her own escape from a dead-end marriage was eventually worked through and led to her emancipation from that first relationship.

Hillu's familial experiences, especially those of overt gender inequal-ity, are closely related to her professional experiences. While working at the HO-Berlin, she was awarded the Banner of Labor. The way in which she narrates her memory illustrates the contradictions between her ex-pectations and her experience:

And then came my initial thoughts, and I was really shocked, and until the end I just couldn't shake it: Why are there so few women? The whole hall was full, and there were only men.....There were about 300 award winners . . . and only about five percent of them were women. And I thought, *why* are there so many men? So many people from all areas of the economy and the sciences and so few women. . . . Where are the women?! And I, too, was the only woman present from my entire collective.

In this single monologue, Hillu very clearly and concisely expresses both the gender inequality in the GDR and astonishment at how that inequality has been maintained. As Christine Schenk so aptly describes it, the "paternal" and "protective" SED state both constructed an official narrative of gender equality necessary to engage over 90 percent of the female population in the production process, while maintaining the primacy of men in positions of authority, thus not engendering an overtly political feminist movement in the GDR.[25] Hillu's surprise at the lack of women at the award ceremony should actually have been expressed as expectation, given her own situation as the only woman from her brigade in attendance that night. However, she expresses disbelief, which is most likely a result of expectations, developed within a dominant social discourse that constantly reiterates women's equality and emancipation, having been frustrated or disproved through experience. The state continues to represent gender relations in a way that mirrors Hillu's own early familial experiences: the male figures are "put in the best light" while the women are left to follow their lead. And, although her expectations, informed by official discourse, are contradicted by her personal experiences, Hillu continues to express some surprise. In this way, Hillu exhibits what Summerfield has called "dis/composure"—Hillu's own feelings of personal emancipation, supported by official discourse, are contradicted by her direct experience with the state and by her experiences at work.

These contradictions are also formally highlighted in the following sequence by Misselwitz's use of montage. The contradictory meanings of *woman* in the public/private distinction, and the role of the visual media in perpetuating these contradictions are emphasized through a variety of secondary screens within the film. These secondary frames or screens—television monitors, posters, storefronts, and domestic windows—emphasize the myriad ways in which woman's identity is visually constructed and call attention to the viewer's participation in that construction. In the reception of images, and of this film in particular, viewers participate in women's objectification, in their to-be-looked-at-ness, and in either the questioning or perpetuation of ideological distinctions that determine gendered identity (male/female, public/private, etc.). The role of visual images in questioning or maintaining these ideological distinctions is made most obvious in the montage sequence following Hillu's interview. It begins with an image of a storefront where numerous televisions report on the festivities for International Women's Day. From the multiple screens emanates a voice from *Aktuelle Kamera*, covering the ceremony of the Clara Zetkin Medal, a national honor awarded annually to one woman for outstanding achievements in developing and advancing socialist society.[26] Given in honor of Clara Zetkin, the award recognized a "model socialist woman," whose life and work reflected the fulfillment of her dual duties as laborer and mother. The camera cuts from the multiple tiny screens of the *Aktuelle Kamera* coverage to another storefront in which female mannequins dressed in various "gender appropriate" wardrobes (negligees, aprons, dresses) sell the newest models of lingerie and double beds, kitchen towels and tableware, living room furniture and appliances. The disjuncture created by the soundtrack and the visual frame, the voice announcing woman's emancipation, and the images trumpeting her domestic retreat, create a very real and alienating sense of the contradictions East German women faced. This sequence visually and aurally emphasizes the contradictions expressed in Hillu's interview. Is the socialist woman's fulfillment to be found at work or at home? Are the two positions reconcilable? Does her fulfillment lie in state policies that enable her to efficiently manage her career and motherhood? The sequence also asserts the visual ideology Misselwitz is critically engaging by asking the viewer how one visually and aurally represents "women and girls in this country" without perpetuating the ideological distinctions represented by the frozen mannequins and the award ceremony.

One of the most poignant encounters Misselwitz includes in the film, and one that deals specifically with woman's role as working

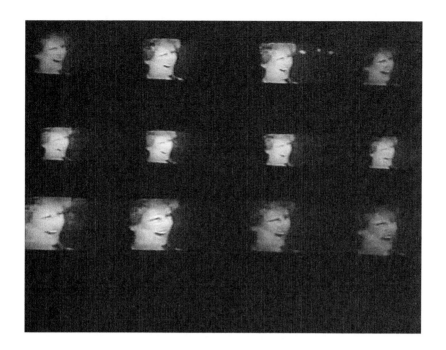

Figure 4.2. Clara Zetkin Medals awarded on International Women's Day. *Goodbye to Winter*. ©DEFA-Stiftung/Thomas Plehnert.

Figure 4.3. Store window—kitchen. *Goodbye to Winter*. ©DEFA-Stiftung/Thomas Plehnert.

mother, is the encounter she has with Christine Schiele, a thirty-seven-year-old single mother living with her two teenage children in Meuselwitz, near Altenburg. This sequence begins with a view from the train window of the factory in Meuselwitz, an iron giant releasing thick columns of smoke into the sky. The camera cuts to a medium shot of a dark room in which a worker is banging on pipes. As the worker appears, back first with coveralls and hardhat on, it is not clear that this is a woman. However, after emerging from the second dark room, Christine turns briefly to face the camera. The camera follows her in a medium shot as she walks along seemingly endless corridors in the dark factory, banging pipes along the way, the noise of the machines often drowning out the sounds of the pipes. The camera cuts to a medium close-up of Christine as she sits writing in the work log. Here, the viewer discovers that she makes this trip eight times per hour, banging the pipes to keep the soot from settling, ensuring its release into the air above the factory town.

Although the sequence begins in the factory space, most of Misselwitz' encounter with Christine is spent in her kitchen, conversing at the kitchen table. Their conversation begins over a long shot of a small cluster of houses framed by the factory smokestacks in the distance. The image creates a sense of isolation that was not felt during the previous encounter with Hillu. The viewer suddenly becomes acutely aware of the geographic and class differences between the women being interviewed. The image of the tiny, isolated town directly contrasts with the hustle and bustle of the Berlin train station. Also, Christine's thick accent is a marker of her rural surroundings, and she is considerably less articulate than Hillu. The sequence in Christine's kitchen is dominated by her narration of her marriage, begun at the age of nineteen, and her troubles as a single mother. Her interpretation of this long chapter in her life reveals little more than disappointment. Christine's recounting of her early pregnancy and marriage reveals her conflicted feelings about her "natural" role as a mother. She interprets her disappointment through the lens of youth—"me' war'n zu jung" ["we were too young"]. Yet she also exhibits a form of dis/composure while narrating. In telling her story—"Me' wollte jetzt sein Leben genießen, me' wollte noch die

Freiheit genießen, me' wollte noch für sich"—Christine shifts from the subject *we* to *one*.[27] The *me'* functions both as a dialect form of *wir* and of *man*. What is most telling is that she never once says "I." In shifting from an interpretation that would likely be supported by official discourse—"we were too young"—to an interpretation that reveals personal disappointment and that would likely go unrecognized by that discourse—"one wanted to enjoy one's life, one wanted to enjoy [one's] freedom, one wanted [to live/exist] for oneself"—Christine uses a third- rather than a first-person pronoun. Using *one* rather than *I* universalizes rather than particularizes the disappointment she feels. In doing so, Christine constructs an alternative interpretation, composing a "factual" discourse that interprets her personal feelings as a form of public knowledge.

Christine's disappointment with early motherhood is only compounded by her daughter's mental illness. Her fears and isolation stem from the troubles she has with Ramona. At one point while describing her experience of motherhood, Christine's face dominates the frame in close-up. She is on the verge of tears. Her mouth is turned down and she trembles as she talks. She looks down at the table and her eyes are glassy as she speaks:

> CHRISTINE. [*I* have] fears about *my* daughter, that she doesn't return the love that *I* try to give her. And then there is *our* uncertain future, what *I* can hope for in the context of *my* life, given *my* daughter's situation.
>
> [Christine looks directly at Misselwitz and pauses, then looks back down at the table.]
>
> That's an idea that *one* can't shake, because *one* has given birth to a child that belongs to *one*, but from which *one* has to separate *oneself* to a certain degree, something that *one* has to consider over the course of *one's* entire life . . .
>
> MISSELWITZ. Do you have anyone who is tender toward you?
>
> CHRISTINE. No, no one at all. No one at all. Because of *my* daughter it's assumed that *one* is also ridiculed and pitied, or that *one* is also a sick person. (my emphasis)

There is an interruption from outside of the frame. Christine's daughter, Ramona, enters the room and is belligerent toward her mother. Christine looks briefly into the camera, then uneasily in Ramona's direction, then again into the camera, and back again toward Ramona at the sound of a door slamming shut. She seems afraid of Ramona's aggressiveness. She continues:

> People in these situations show no understanding, they have no understand-
> ing and that *one* is treated *like someone* used to be treated, who had aborted a
> child . . . where *one* is in a situation, where that person is good for nothing, is
> worthless, where he's so down-and-out according to other people, that it doesn't
> matter what's inside of him.
> MISSELWITZ. But *you* didn't give *your* child up, *you* raised her despite her
> illness.
> CHRISTINE. But that's not really accepted in our society. That's not at all
> noticed or respected. For other people, it means that *you're* good for nothing,
> that *you* aren't fit to raise *your* children and can't give them the things that others
> have or help them feel the way others feel, and for that reason *you're* outcast,
> *you're* rejected, because *you* have a child that is a burden. . . . (my emphasis)
> [The camera cuts to the window, which frames the neighbors in the garden as
> they walk away.]

The story Christine tells is fraught with contradictions between expectations and experience, between a social discourse of motherhood and
Christine's personal tragedy. The most painful experiences, also the
most unbelievable and difficult for Christine to accept, are constructed
in the third person (*one*) rather than the first person. In order to assert
the need to separate from her daughter, from this person to whom she
gave birth, she uses the general pronoun *one*. Then, a couple of sentences
later, Christine shifts in mid-sentence: "Because of *my* daughter it's assumed that *one* is also ridiculed and pitied, or that *one* is also a sick person" (my emphasis). Christine continues to use *one* when describing
how people treat her: the way in which they used to treat women who
had had abortions, or those members of society who had been deemed
generally worthless.

When Misselwitz counters with "but *you* did not give your child
up, *you* raised her, regardless of her sickness," Christine shifts from the
third person *one* to the second person *you*, following Misselwitz's lead.
In doing so, she also shifts from a generalized discourse to an extremely
personalized discourse. The *you* that Misselwitz speaks is reflected by
Christine back onto Misselwitz and the viewers: "But that's not really
accepted in our society. That's not at all noticed or respected. For other
people, it means that *you're* good for nothing, that *you* aren't fit to raise

your children and can't give them the things that others have or help
them feel the way others feel, and for that reason *you're* outcast, *you're*
rejected, because *you* have a child that is a burden" (my emphasis). In
German, *you* is never replaced with *one* as it is in English. The *you* functions therefore as a particularly personalizing word. This *you* acts as what
Lesage has called a "deep structure," an organization of language that
psychologically incorporates both Misselwitz and the viewer into the
conversation with Christine. The details of Christine's life are thrust
onto the viewer through the form of the *you*, binding the details of her
life to those of the viewers' lives.

Further, the shift of the camera from a close-up on Christine's face
to the image of the neighbors as they walk away visually completes this
bond between the viewer and Christine. It incites critical reflection on
the part of the viewer: should the viewer identify with Christine or with
"people," "others," these neighbors who possibly have participated in
ostracizing Christine? The tension created between Christine's painful
narrative and facial expressions and the seemingly harmless behavior of
the neighbors as presented in the film is a moment in which the viewer,
as both Lesage and Michel argue, may develop a critical consciousness
regarding official ideologies of motherhood in the GDR. The film com-
pels the viewer to ask how "common sense" notions of motherhood are
undergirded by an ideology of motherhood that serves to exclude women
like Christine, and whether equality and humane treatment should be
reserved for those who fit the mold of the "normal" socialist individual.[28]
Misselwitz restructures the truth of social and gender equality in the
GDR by confronting the viewer with the marginalization of women like
Christine and her daughter and compelling the viewer to contemplate
his or her own participation in that marginalization.

Misselwitz compounds this critique in the next brief sequence.
The sequences are bridged once more with a shot of tracks moving and
diverging, indicating that Misselwitz is back on the road. The many
divergent tracks allude to the potentially infinite number of women to
be sought out, an endless number of women whose stories might re-
semble those of the women Misselwitz has already encountered. It also
asserts a recalibration of the identity "mother," as we shall see in the next
sequence. From the moving tracks, the camera cuts to a medium shot of

a storefront, Helene Wall's *Puppenklinik* [Doll Clinic] in Delitsch. Inside, we see a medium shot of Helene wrapping a recently repaired doll; a slow pan of a wall of baby-doll heads and several headless, naked baby-doll bodies; and still close-ups of smiling, angelic doll faces leaning tenderly against one another. From outside of the frame, the viewer hears Misselwitz ask, "What are those?" Helene turns over a small tin box in her hand and answers, "These are mama voices," to which Misselwitz replies, "Are there also papa voices?" Helene: "No, but we have bear voices." Helene illustrates this by turning over a canned bear growl. The camera cuts again to a close-up of several baby-doll faces and then pans slowly to the left as the viewer repeatedly hears the canned cry of "Mama!"

This sequence, placed immediately after the sequence of Christine Schiele, reinforces the film's ideological critique of motherhood in the previous sequence. The absence of any canned voices crying "Papa!" naturalizes women's roles as mothers, suggesting that regardless of the discourse of gender equality and women's emancipation in the GDR, it is little girls and not little boys who are trained from their earliest years to be primary caregivers for their children. Further, the mass-produced baby-doll heads lining the wall, with their shining eyes and happy mouths, contrast starkly with the expressions of pain and disappointment on Christine Schiele's face and suggest a mother-child bliss that is far from the realities of motherhood experienced by women like her. The sweet sound of "Mama!", contrasted with the abrasive and aggressive tone of Christine's daughter from the previous sequence, results in an eerie feeling of disjuncture, hinting that the young girls awaiting their newly repaired baby dolls might be in for a rude awakening as real mothers.

Misselwitz constructs a slightly similar critique in a later sequence about Margarete Busse, 85, who lives with her husband in Großfriedenwalde in the Uckermark. Misselwitz interviews her at the celebration of her diamond wedding anniversary. However, in this sequence, it is the discourse of marriage, not motherhood, that forms the basis of Misslewitz's critique. The sequence begins with a long shot of a house in a small village as Misselwitz tells us in a voice-over that this is the home of Margarete Busse. The camera then cuts to a medium close-up of Margarete and Hermann, sitting at the dinner table while an accordion plays

Figure 4.4. Mama voices. *Goodbye to Winter*. ©DEFA-Stiftung/Thomas Plehnert.

outside the frame. They are surrounded by children, grandchildren, and great-grandchildren as everyone congratulates them. The scene is one of longstanding familial warmth and happiness. The camera then cuts to a medium shot in the kitchen, in which Misselwitz interviews two granddaughters and one great-granddaughter about the family's history of marriage. When asked if any of their family members have gotten divorced, the oldest granddaughter answers, "No, right? Not in our family.... Wait! Yes! Marianne, one of the grandchildren . . . but she lives in the West." The other granddaughter and the great-granddaughter then confirm the success of each other's marriage, noting that one of them has already celebrated her silver wedding anniversary while the other is "approaching her silver anniversary with giant steps!" The sequence ends with their expressions of happiness that they have been able to celebrate their grandparents' diamond wedding anniversary.

It is clear from this short interview that these three women value the fact that none of their family members—except that one granddaughter in the West—have ever gone through a divorce. The diamond wedding anniversary of Margarete and Hermann, the silver wedding anniversaries of the two granddaughters, and the pending silver wedding anniversary of the great-granddaughter become proof of a solid and happy family, a family that is bound for better or worse, for richer or poorer, until death do them part. This solidity and happiness is supported visually by the images of Margarete and Hermann sitting together at the table, by images of Margarete dancing with her great-grandson, by images of Margarete surrounded by great-granddaughters and great-grandsons who snuggle up close to her and wrap her in their arms, and by the last image of the entire family—children, grandchildren and great-grandchildren—gathered for a family portrait.

However, this image of familial bliss is deconstructed by Margarete's own telling of her life story. The granddaughters' conflation of public propriety with private happiness reminds us of the critique in *Lot's Wife*,

Figure 4.5. Margarete Busse, family portrait. *Goodbye to Winter*. ©DEFA-Stiftung/Thomas Plehnert.

in which Richard equates divorce with a lack of political commitment, a lack of devotion to the Party. As with Katrin in *Lot's Wife*, Margarete's private critique is relocated to the space of the bedroom. There the viewer finds flowers on the nightstand, a painting on the wall, and a made bed, all indications of a happy home. The camera then cuts to a medium shot of Margarete sitting next to a table, holding a black-and-white, portrait-sized photo of herself at age twenty-two. Margarete says that the photo was taken at a mansion where she worked and learned certain housekeeping skills as a maidservant. The camera then cuts to the open window and back to a medium shot of Margarete, now without the photo.

> MISSELWITZ. You *had* to marry?
> MARGARETE. Yes, I was pregnant.
> MISSELWITZ. What did your father say?
> MARGARETE. He said he would kick me out if that happens again and I'm not married. So I got married right away.
> MISSELWITZ. Otherwise you wouldn't have married Hermann?
> MARGARETE. No. [Shakes her head and purses her eyebrows together.]
> MISSELWITZ. And how has it been with Hermann? Did you ever regret marrying him?
> MARGARETE. [Looks down at her lap.] Yes, if I were to tell you everything, I had a difficult time, yes, especially at first. He was unfaithful, even though I already had three kids. [In a whisper:] He just passed by the door.... He drives me crazy. He's no good, really. I should have married a better man. I had one, too... . He was a forest ranger. [She sighs:] I can't let myself think about it. [She purses her eyebrows together, shakes her head, and looks away.]

The scene ends with a cut to a long shot of the house with Margarete and Hermann standing in the doorway. The contrast between the meaning of the diamond wedding anniversary for the granddaughters and great-granddaughter and Margarete's own experience of marriage is as startling as the contrast between the discourse of motherhood as represented by the baby dolls in Helene Wall's Doll Clinic and Christine Schiele's experience of motherhood with a mentally ill daughter. Margarete's diamond anniversary is, from her perspective, no reason to celebrate. Not only did she not want to marry Hermann in the first place—she is forced into the marriage through the threat of being disowned and barred from her family home—but her unhappiness is

Figure 4.6. Margarete Busse. *Goodbye to Winter*. ©DEFA-Stiftung/Thomas Plehnert.

compounded by Hermann's infidelity after she had already borne three children. Further, the location of the interview—a seemingly cozy marital bedroom—asserts an unambiguous critique of Hermann's infidelity and Margarete's feelings of betrayal and isolation in her marriage. Margarete's narration of her marriage—"He's not a very good man. I should have married a better one. I could have, too. . . . I just shouldn't think about it"—undermines the discourse of marriage that her granddaughters and great-granddaughter perpetuate in their idealization of the diamond wedding anniversary. Further, their insistence on wanting to make it to their own diamond anniversaries also attests to the fact that Margarete has not told any of them the secret truth of her personal history. Margarete's narration of her personal experience is silenced by their expectations and is shared instead with Misselwitz and with viewers.

　　The final image of Margarete and Hermann standing in the doorway of their family home alters the previous family portraits in this sequence and functions as yet another revealing secondary screen. The initial family images of celebration and togetherness have been uncovered and produce a sense of isolation and emptiness. This seemingly happy image becomes a visual frame of Margarete's disappointment, sadness, and anger. The family portrait at the beginning of the sequence is reframed, and the darkness from the open door behind the couple symbolizes the hopelessness and isolation that emanates from her domestic space, serving as a visual metaphor for her secret sadness: her family remains "in the dark" about her marriage. The "truth" of this solid marriage has been restructured through Margarete's voice. Maxie Wander's quote from the beginning of the chapter is especially interesting here:

> We shouldn't be surprised that in a socialist society conflicts come to the fore that have, for years, been left in the dark to stew and to poison people's lives. We first become conscious of conflicts once we can afford to overcome them. We have come to see our position as women in a more differentiated way since the moment we were faced with the opportunity to change it.[29]

While Margarete might have chosen to divorce her husband once divorce became inexpensive, available, and commonplace in the GDR, her own familial discourse of marriage most likely would have prevented her escape. Like Richard's perspective in *Lot's Wife*, the family's obvious disdain for divorce is expressed as a national, systemic difference that separates East and West—an ideological distinction of public/private that serves to keep Margarete tied to a loveless, disappointing marriage.

Misselwitz turns her attention at the end of the film to the problem of girlhood in a sequence that focuses on two runaways. Here, questions of equality and emancipation are constructed from the perspective of marginalization, for which the two young punks, Kerstin and Anja, become markers. Misselwitz focuses particularly on the gendered image as a way of creating a bridge for identification between the mainstream viewer and the marginalized girls. Throughout the scene, the girls look almost directly into the camera, toward Misselwitz, whose presence is marked through her voice, and the sound of passing trains can be heard sporadically above them. The girls wear their dyed hair—Kerstin's black, Anja's white—teased and spiked. Their pose against the trestle is nonchalant and lazy, suggesting boredom and disaffection. The placement of the girls below the tracks, rather than inside a train car as in other interviews, is crucial. They are runaways and punks and as such are positioned outside the "normal" social fabric. Further, their position below the tracks in this opening scene symbolizes their having "fallen through the cracks," their having been "lost." Misselwitz begins by asking how and why it is that they have run away.

> KERSTIN. It all just made us sick, was just too much.
> MISSELWITZ. What made you sick?
> ANJA. The rules and everything.
> KERSTIN. We were always getting into trouble at home.
> ANJA. Wanted to really assert the things *we* wanted to do . . . .
> MISSELWITZ. Did you ever think about the fact that your parents might be sad or that they might worry about you?
> KERSTIN. Of course, I think that's also what I wanted to achieve. I mean, *I* can consider all the things I did wrong, and my mother. . . . Well, I also wanted *her* to consider what *she* had done wrong. (emphasis in original)

Although Kerstin and Anja will later be labeled as asocials by government youth agencies, their explanation for their dissatisfaction with their home life is hardly asocial. Rather, their hatred of rules and of parental and communal expectations is a typical marker of youthful rebellion and of DEFA feature films centered around youth culture.[30] Kerstin and Anja's simple explanation for having run away offsets their seemingly abnormal status as punks and runaways, making it easier for the viewer to identify with their disappointment and more difficult for the viewer to marginalize them.

The larger social critique of this sequence becomes clear in the following scene, in which we discover that, after the period of filming, Kerstin and Anja are punished by the state for not following social rules. The viewer watches Kerstin and Anja depart the scene, walking the tracks hand in hand, laughing. This image conjures up that of the Western hero walking off into the sunset, and the feeling is made slightly triumphant by the girls' laughter. However, Misselwitz's voice-over monologue, which can be heard just over the laughter of the girls in the frame, introduces a feeling of foreboding:

> Anja and Kerstin regularly stay away from home for days at a time and don't go to school. Kerstin is admitted to a youth work camp for *Schwererziehbare* [troubled youth or "youth who are difficult to raise"] four weeks after shooting on location. Half a year later Anja, accompanied by her mother and sister, is sent

to a youth work camp in the district of Karl-Marx-Stadt [Chemnitz]. Her father
arrives from his night shift in order to say goodbye to her.

The camera cuts to a medium close-up of Anja standing on the train platform, whose worried look is directed again just to the left of the camera at
Misselwitz. The change in Anja's image from a self-confident and happy
girl is altered not just by her worried look but also by her appearance. Her
hair is no longer spiked and dyed white, and it is pulled back into a pony-
tail. She is no longer wearing her punk clothes but, rather, a pair of jeans
and a button-down shirt with matching earrings. This imposition of nor-
mativity—the change from punk to "normal" clothing—is symbolic for
the arbitrary definition of *Schwererziehbare*. While Kerstin and Anja's
disappointment and resistance to rules might be considered a typical
aspect of teenage existence, the ways in which it manifests itself is considered dangerous enough that they are removed from their homes and
placed in "youth work camps."[31] While this was not uncommon, the way
in which Misselwitz encourages the viewers' identification with the two
girls is. In this final scene, after Anja has boarded the train and is about
to depart, she meets Misselwitz at the open window of her train car. No
longer outside or underneath the tracks, Anja has assumed her "normal"
place in the socialist everyday. Her position inside the car, however, does
not suggest travel or movement in the way it does for the other women
Misselwitz meets on her train travels. Rather, Anja is being shipped off,
most likely to be forgotten by the very normal, everyday that the train
represents. At the window, Misselwitz places both of her hands on the
sides of Anja's face, calling her "meine Kleine" [my little dear]. Anja answers with a half-hearted smile. As the train pulls away, Misselwitz waves
goodbye. The camera then cuts to a deserted platform with the sound of
the train still pulling away. In a medium shot, we see Misselwitz's hand
raised, holding against the backdrop of the station a picture of Anja as a
small girl. Misselwitz's connection to Anja and her sadness at her departure mirrors the feelings she expresses for her own daughter in the train
station of the opening sequence. Her daughter's self-confidence, which
makes Misselwitz both unsure and hopeful, has found its reflection in
Anja's self-confidence, which has consequently resulted in marginalization and internment. Misselwitz's choice to include this scene revealing

her attachment to Anja completes the bridge of viewer identification by emphasizing the cross-generational bond between them and by putting the girl's seemingly asocial posturing into the understandable terms of familial conflict, teenage rebellion, and individual freedom. Finally, the camera cuts to a perspective from inside a train car, looking out onto the passing winter landscape, as the sound of the train continues from the previous scene. The overlapping sound and the shift of viewer perspective from the platform to inside the train car further encourage spectatorial identification with Anja's position. As we watch her depart, we are forced also to imagine and identify with her perspective as she sets out on her journey to the youth camp.

The film's closing sequence places the viewer in a similar perspective. From within a train's caboose, we depart from the final station on the journey. Snow covers the tracks and the sound of moving over the tracks can be heard slightly under a woman's voice-over: "And I think that I will have to fight very hard indeed for the things I want. For in the end, one has but one life to live. Yes . . . that's what I'll have to do." These final words compose a story of struggle defined by personal desire. The woman's voice-over, rather than tying each woman's story into one neat narrative, asserts the particularity of each woman's experience—each of them has "but one life." The course of that life, represented in the image of the tracks, involves perseverance and struggle, coping with change, and moving on.

Suddenly the tracks disappear and the vessel of travel is now a ferry. The viewer is left to stare at the open waters below as Janis Joplin's voice is heard singing the lyrics to "Summertime." The camera remains in this perspective, looking down onto the water for another few seconds, and then there is a cut to a long shot of the ocean from the deck. The camera pans the ocean, with the horizon falling into the center of the frame. The perspective from the ship reflects a previous sequence in which one of the interviewees asks a group of children gathered on the beach if they have seen any ships today, and they all answer no. The woman responds with "Doch!" [yes, you have!]. Pointing toward the horizon, she says she sees a ship. It is faint, but it is there. In taking the perspective from the ship toward the horizon, this final sequence hints at an optimistic sense of movement and accomplishment in the final voice-over.

Yet this sequence is ambiguous. One could argue that it serves to provide the viewer with a somewhat optimistic, forward-looking culmination to the collage of faces and voices to which the film gives space. As I asserted at the beginning of this chapter, while the film presents a variety of perspectives and voices, Misselwitz maintains a certain level of artistic control over the text. While creating a collage of women's voices that resists any singular narrative of gender in the GDR, Misselwitz also acknowledges her directorial construction of a narrative frame—autobiography and personal interest in oral history— that contextualizes these voices. The final sequence, therefore, functions as a partial conclusion to the preceding narratives and suggests a particular reading of the title, *Winter adé,* that reflects the artistic and critical goals of the film. Meaning "goodbye winter" or "adieu winter," the title suggests a movement away from a season of cold, death, emptiness, and silence. The "winter" in the title alludes to the state in which Misselwitz finds women's voices and narratives in the GDR of the late 1980s. The marginalization of such stories from the dominant socialist discourse of women's experience is the winter from which women must depart.

Yet it is questionable if the lyrics to "Summertime" point to the season of women's true emancipation in the GDR, in which their voices will be heard, their personal narratives acknowledged, and a new journey toward freedom will begin. While the ending of the tracks and the introduction of water, of uncharted seas, suggest that this journey exists beyond the frame of East German women's current narratives, the image is not one of summer. Instead, the black and white of the film blurs the sky into a monotone gray, leaving the viewer to seek the warmth of summer elsewhere. While the film does not overtly suggest that a journey toward freedom for these women exists outside the frame of socialism, the ambiguity of the ship's course and its destination is juxtaposed to the "easy livin'" and "jumpin' fish" of the song. As a result, the song's ironic tone underscores the gray ambiguity of the image. It becomes difficult to believe that any of these women will "spread their wings and take to the sky." In fact, the viewer is compelled to ask, "Where to? To the expansive nothingness of the sea?"

Misselwitz concludes the film in a way that maintains the diversity of the voices within, constructing her own biography as one narrative perspective among others. Just as her daughter's self-assurance causes her to feel both apprehension and hope, her desire to imagine these women taking their leave of winter and embracing the summer is contrasted with the gray tones and the open expanse of an uninviting sea. The film's continued emphasis on personal experience and life story highlights the uncomfortable and seemingly irreconcilable narratives of Hillu, Christine, Margarete, Kersten, and Anja, while the final sequence refuses closure in the direction of an optimistic, foundational narrative of a new beginning. Thus, the film does not assert any concrete truths of East German women's experience. Rather, in emphasizing the diversity of voices that compete to construct a braided text, a *metissage,* the film intervenes in official, political discourses of East German women's history and becomes a site of critical truth that lays bare the inconsistencies and contradictions of real existing socialism.

Conclusion: After the Fall

I have my problems with the word *Wende*. What does it mean? What changed
and what did it change into? . . . It is called a "start" or a "new beginning," the
"upheaval," the "collapse"; and the totally unaware call it the "revolution."
  —Tamara Trampe, "Filmmaking after the Wende"

This project began with the question of absence—why has so little research been done on DEFA *Frauenfilme*, given the explosion of research
on DEFA in the past twenty-five years? While there are myriad possible
reasons, I have attempted to frame an answer by suggesting that the
politics of gender are both at the center of the films' social critique and
their exclusion from contemporary research.

As I have discussed throughout this project, the East German
women's films are representative of a particular shift in East German
filmmaking toward representations of the *Alltag*, a shift that has often
been equated with a retreat from overtly political critiques of socialism
to critiques centered around the personal and private issues of everyday life. This equation is most often made due to an emphasis on the
Kahlschlag and banning of East Germany's "rabbit films." Yet as I have
shown throughout this book, these notions of "political" and "critical"
are limited to a view of East Germany as a totalitarian state with complete control over artistic production and of everyday issues as secondary and unimportant in comparison to the larger issues of state politics.

Such positions do not take into account several things. First, they reject or ignore that artists and intellectuals, as well as ordinary citizens, actively participated in the construction and contestation of East German culture. Second, they assume a division between public and private that has been refuted as an ideological falsehood in fields as diverse as sociology, history, women's studies, and Marxist studies, a division that was—not without contradiction—both enforced and disavowed by the social policies of the East German state itself. These supposedly private issues became, through the East German women's film, the site of social critique and debate between the artist, the viewing public, and the state. Further, as I have shown, the importance of viewer expectations must be reevaluated as both an artistic and political tool. Because both the state and artists were dependent on viewers' desires to receive this "most important art," both the state and the artist had to take into account viewer expectations of more enjoyable, believable, and critical films, expectations that most often led to changes in cultural policy and enabled more diverse artistic expression.

The focus of this book has been on the function of "woman" as a narrative tool of identification and social critique in the shift toward the *Alltagsfilm* and issues of the everyday. The emphasis on female protagonists in the *Alltagsfilm* reveals both a residue of gendered stereotypes—woman is equated with the private—as well as an awareness that the contradictions of East German socialism were best revealed through women's everyday struggles. As I have argued throughout, in DEFA women's films, these struggles often become the springboard for engaging with a broad spectrum of needs and desires that were silenced and left unfulfilled in East German society, and it was "woman," as the locus of these contradictions, who could function best as the site for spectatorial identification that would offer realistic, rather than socialist realist/idealist, representations of the *Alltag*.

But the question remains why these films in particular evoke only marginal critical interest and why they have not been taken up more often by feminist film theorists and feminist Germanists in particular. Given the importance of academic debates regarding divisions between public and private critique, as well as regarding viewer identification and pleasure, these films present the feminist film theorist, the feminist

Germanist, and the scholar of socialist studies with a plethora of material for fruitful analysis. This book begins to fill a gap in each of these fields of inquiry by bringing questions of cinema, feminism, and socialist studies to bear on the individual films.

In chapter one, "Happily Ever After," I consider Günther's *Lot's Wife* as a contemporary of the rabbit films that escaped the wrath of the *Kahlschlag* and that illustrates the overt political critique of the *Alltagsfilm* genre. At the same time, the film serves as the basis for a reconsideration of questions of gaze and voice as potentially emancipatory tools for the female protagonist. I consider how Katrin's voice resists received romantic narratives and confronts the residue of bourgeois ideology in socialist marriage. Katrin's rejection of the reification of socialist ideals as manifested in the institutions of marriage and divorce constructs for the viewer an alternative narrative of self-realization that stands outside the socialist discourse of labor. Katrin's personal definition of happiness is not contained in the system that will ultimately hold her captive. Yet her refusal to participate in her own show trial undermines the validity of that system and encourages the viewer to identify with a troublemaker as the new socialist heroine.

In chapter two, "The Lonely Woman?" I consider two films that respond, one hopefully, one despairingly, to the GDR's discourse of motherhood. In *The Bicycle*, motherhood functions as an alternative discourse of subjectivity that resists the socialist discourse of labor and historical progress. Motherhood offers the protagonist both an escape from her otherwise alienated existence as an unskilled worker and an affective pleasure that cannot be experienced in the public sphere. In *On Probation* single motherhood is much bleaker. For the protagonist of Zschoche's film, motherhood is overdetermined by socialist norms and expectations that are as alienating as the unskilled labor she performs. In *On Probation*, woman is bound to her biology through a social discourse that simultaneously assumes her "natural" inclination to reproduce while also punishing her failure to successfully perform her biological responsibilities in socially acceptable ways.

In chapter three, "Pleasure in Seeing Ourselves?" I analyze the ways in which the *Gruppe Berlin* constructs a film about the filmmaking process in which the central problem is representing an object on screen that is seemingly unknowable and unpalatable. This object, a female brigade, raises specific questions about representing women on screen and constructing viewer pleasure. *All My Girls* reconstructs labor as particularly female, and "woman" becomes the marker for *Mensch* as the film illustrates the primacy of interpersonal relationships rather than work in the process of socialist emancipation. This results in an alternative viewing pleasure that is not simply constructed through voyeuristic or masochistic identification but, rather, through both the enjoyment of and identification with the female collective on screen, within a lesbian continuum. The desire to "see oneself" in the narrative overrides divisions of gender and class, thus enabling the construction of the brigade as the new "mass subject."

In the final chapter, "Real Women," I consider one of DEFA's most important documentary films, *Goodbye to Winter*, in constructing an alternative history of women in the GDR. I consider how the film engages with questions of realism, documentary, and authenticity in the context of documentary filmmaking internationally and at DEFA. While acknowledging the problem of truth in documentary forms, I consider how the film constructs a kind of "critical truth" that retains a subjective rather than objective position. The film does not attempt to reflect or document reality. Rather, it constructs a feeling of authenticity of experience through an emphasis on narrativity, autobiography, and life story that is recognizable, enjoyable, and also critical. Through the collage of interviews and the autobiographical frame, the film becomes not a foundational narrative, but rather a plural, sometimes unstable text that emphasizes the telling and interpreting of experience, rather than "objective truth."

By framing DEFA women's films in the context of international cinematic trends of their respective historical moments, I have attempted to accomplish several things. First, contextualizing these films within an East and West European cinematic landscape enables us to reconsider monolithic definitions of *communism* and *liberal democracy* at a historical moment in which the latter seems to be our only political possibility. Recovering and reconsidering East European women's films enables us to engage the complexity of socialist ideologies in our "post-historical" moment and reveals the crucial role that gender plays in understanding the possibilities for social critique and imagining a radical politics of representation. In critiquing labor and progress as the fundamental values of the individual and society, these films participate in a longstanding tradition of questioning an Enlightenment discourse that stands at the heart of both Western liberal democracy and Eastern socialism. As a lost moment of critical reflection on the failures of and possibilities for social utopianism, these films use women to speak against technical rationality and instrumental reason, offering alternative modes of being in the world that are more *"menschlich"* [human(e)] because they are based in love, intimacy, and radical collectivity. Further, this is particularly pertinent at a historical moment in which most subjects, especially women, live precariously under late capitalism. The critique that DEFA women's films offer depends on the stability of labor—the right, even the imperative, to work. Recovering a canon of films in which women are primarily defined as workers, yet call into question labor as the foundation of subjectivity, destabilizes the conviction that socialism was totalitarian at a historical moment in which different forms of *affective labor*—child and elder care, housekeeping, and sex work being the most common—have become the most dependable sources of income for many women of the former Eastern bloc.

Second, by contextualizing DEFA women's films within the cinematic landscape of Eastern and Western Europe, we begin to understand the diversity of local histories and political ideologies, and the ways in which "woman" can function as a narrative trope of political resistance. This enables us to revise the history of women's films, recovering a lost canon of texts that supplement and alter our understanding of the genre's importance for both women's studies and cinema studies. Analyzing these films from the perspective of Western feminist film theory emergent at the time gives us the opportunity to revisit foundational concepts in feminist theory and to consider their potential resonance and limitations for understanding those films that have been historically absent from the cinematic canon.

EAST GERMAN WOMEN'S FILMS AND BEYOND

In opening up the canon to include these texts within a theoretical context that is seemingly dated, we are also given the opportunity to consider the theories' relevance for contemporary scholarship. Recent developments in German cinema reveal a continued interest in femininity as a site of political critique, and continuities with the DEFA tradition of the *Alltagsfilm* are notable. Several of these recent films rework the cinematic conventions that have been the focus in this book and address issues of women's work, motherhood, and female subjectivity under a new regime of precarious labor under late capitalism. Andreas Dresen's *Die Polizistin* [*Policewoman*] (Germany, 2000) and *Sommer vorm Balkon* [*Summer in Berlin*] (Germany, 2005); Maria Speth's *In den Tag hinein* [*The Days Between*] (Germany, 2001), *Madonnen* [*Madonnas*] (Germany, 2007), *9 Leben* [*9 Lives*] (Germany, 2011), and *Töchter* [*Daughters*] (Germany, 2014); Christian Petzold's *Yella* (Germany, 2007) and *Barbara* (Germany, 2012); as well as Valeska Grisebach's *Sehnsucht* [*Longing*] (Germany, 2006) represent a handful of recent German films that explore the politics of the personal through female protagonists.

Interestingly, works by Berlin School filmmakers, especially those of Christian Petzold and Maria Speth, exhibit thematic and occasional aesthetic similarities to DEFA women's films. The Berlin School has primarily been read in relation to the French New Wave and the New German Cinema, as part of a longer tradition of German avant-garde filmmaking. Scholars cite a diverse range of influences on these directors, including the Munich journal *Filmkritik* and its privileging of observation and description; the German legacy of realist filmmaking and particularly Kracauer's *Theory of Film: The Redemption of Physical Reality* (1960); and directorial predecessors as varied as Michelangelo Antonioni, Hartmut Bitomsky, Jürgen Böttcher, Robert Bresson, John Cassavetes, Harun Farocki, Jean-Luc Godard, Michael Haneke, and Jean-Marie Straub.[1] While the individual works of the Berlin School are as diverse as their purported influences, Eric Rentschler has suggested that they share certain predilections including "an aesthetics of reduction and restraint, a penchant for image-focused rather than plot-driven constructions, a veristic resolve marked by an investment in the here and now, and a desire to negotiate the quotidian spaces as well as the less charted places of contemporary Germany and Europe."[2] Roger Cook, Lutz Koepnick, and Brad Prager describe protagonists as "unattached, undistinguished, and wayward persons in the process of confronting that dearth of sense and meaning associated with everyday life in the Western world," whose character development is deemphasized and whose milieu is foregrounded primarily through an emphasis on "environs and habits, atmospheres and objects."[3]

While DEFA women's films do not reveal affinities with the Berlin School's deemphasis on plot—what Cook, Koepnick, and Prager refer to as "dysnarration," a formal strategy in which the very concept of narrative is disrupted through disorganization and irony—they do reveal commonalities in their exploration of everyday life, their emphasis on protagonists who live on the edge of precarity, and their opposition to Hollywood's illusory forms of reality that reign as a "tyranny of fantasy."[4] DEFA women's films construct a realism of resistance to social issues— the inevitable march of "progress," the alienation of the laboring subject, the possibilities of self-realization within a social collective—that continue to resurface in Berlin School films, most often through a female protagonist. DEFA women's films' emphasis on life as halted and static under real existing socialism is eerily similar to Berlin School films' view of contemporary, capitalist neoliberalism in which "fulfilling, purposeful action" is a political impossibility.[5]

One could argue further that this rejection in Berlin School films of the possibility of progress offers the viewer a glimpse of post-unification Germany as a dystopia of neoliberal, global capitalism. This happens particularly through the use of mise-en-scène and the (mostly) female protagonists' precarious relationship to both space and labor. The films persistently emphasize what Marc Augé has called the "non-places" of supermodernity, spaces of transience—airports, supermarkets, hotels, highways—that refuse the individual identification with a collective history, creating

> neither singular identity nor relations; only solitude, and similitude. There is no room there for history unless it has been transformed into an element of spectacle. . . . What reigns there is actuality, the urgency of the present moment. . . . Everything proceeds as if space had been trapped by time, as if there were no history other than the last forty-eight hours of news, as if each individual history were drawing its motives, its words and images, from the inexhaustible stock of an unending history in the present.[6]

The malaise and absence of progress in DEFA women's films is rebooted in Berlin School films as the global experience of neoliberal supermodernity. Whereas the DEFA films considered here privilege the private sphere as a space of political resistance to productivity, Berlin School films place their protagonists in non-spaces to emphasize the "end of history" and the eradication of "spheres" under supermodernity. Refusing to embed themselves in history and participate in ideologies of progress, Berlin School films present the viewer with primarily female protagonists, who "live in/for the moment" because that is the state of the precarious laboring subject under global capitalism.

"Living for the moment" is the literal translation of Maria Speth's second feature, *In den Tag hinein* [*The Days Between*]. The film reveals a lack of forward historical movement in the cyclicality of its protagonist's ennui and precarity. Lynn, a twenty-something living with her brother and his family in a nondescript *Plattenbau* apartment on the edges of a Berlin recognizable only through the color of its subway cars, has no "future" in the film. She spends her days working a menial job in a university cafeteria and her nights dancing at clubs, drinking to excess and riding her bike from (non)place to (non)place. Her romantic encounters are emptied of intimacy. Sex with her longtime boyfriend, Daniel, a swimmer whose rational, apathetic relationship to his profession— represented through scientific apparatuses and a cold color palette—is unfulfilling and occasionally unfinished. Her romance with the Japanese student Koji is hindered by a linguistic barrier that reduces their halted conversations to banalities and is set against the nondescript expanse of parking lots, the airport, the mall, and the arcade. Lynn's meaningless death mirrors the meaninglessness of her material circumstances: walking inebriated down the middle of the street in the wee hours of the night, she is hit by a car and presumably suffers from a concussion. The morning after sex with Koji, shot in a red light that does nothing to rectify the absence of intimacy between them, Lynn lies on the bed face down, motionless, while Koji weeps. Yet the viewer can feel little loss, as Lynn's inability to meaningfully relate to others results in the viewer's inability to relate significantly to her. Instead, the alienation she experiences and exudes is transferred to the viewer, and we can react to her passing only in the way we would react to a headline.

Similarly, Speth's first feature, *Madonnas*, emphasizes a lack of forward historical movement through the female protagonist's precarious material circumstances. The film opens with a medium shot of Rita, a young mother with an infant in arms, in a telephone booth begging the person on the other end for an address. The first three minutes of the film emphasize the precarity and hopelessness of her transitory existence: she washes baby clothes in a public restroom, is unable to scrounge up two Euros to pay for her coffee and danish at a roadside café, and directs an empty gaze out the window as her baby cries in the carrier. A delinquent mother who moves in and out of jail, detention centers, and halfway houses, Rita has abandoned her other four children to her own mother's care. Allowing an American soldier stationed in her town to acquire and furnish an apartment for her, she maintains a border of inaccessibility through banal conversation and vacant presence. Rita spends her days sleeping late, chain smoking, and drinking with her youngest on her hip. Using her children as momentary objects of attachment, Rita's experience of motherhood mirrors Nina's in *On Probation* as simultaneously fulfilling and constraining. Having abandoned her children one final time to her own mother, Rita is absent for the final sequence. Her eldest daughter, Fanny, appears as a post-*Wende* reincarnation of Jacqueline in *On Probation*: "she's not coming back," Fanny explains to Rita's American boyfriend in the empty domestic space. Shot primarily in medium long and long shots against a backdrop of *Plattenbau* apartment buildings, bars, and the monotonous void of suburbia, Rita never aspires to anything, and her urban landscape reinforces that there is nothing to aspire to. Motherhood, in the end, is just another institution of containment and stasis.

In these films we can see if not a continuation then at least a continuity of narrative interest in femininity as representative of marginalized social consciousness and the material circumscription of self-realization. Recent developments in the American mediascape seem also particularly ripe for analysis in the context of revived feminist theories. While aesthetically and narratively very different both from DEFA women's films and the films of the Berlin School, serial shows like Lena Dunham's *Girls* and Jenji Kohan's *Orange is the New Black*, as well as Abbi Jacobsen and Ilana Glazer's *Broad City*, rely on an engaged, feminist awareness of the male gaze, voice, narrativity, and collectivity that affect their subsequent representations of female bodies and female desire on screen.

My research has clearly raised questions that were unresolvable in the limited space of a single book project, one of which is regarding former Eastern and Western tensions in remembering the culture of the former East Germany. With the rise of *Ostalgie* [Eastern nostalgia] studies, there is a growing debate as to how, why, and whether we should engage with former East European culture and the role of memory and desire in that process.[7] The question of *Ostalgie* often invites a discursive return to Cold War ideas of totalitarianism and liberal democracy, of dictatorship and personal freedom. I have attempted to uncover some of the ways in which East German women's films reveal the problems of this discourse, specifically through the lens of public/private political engagement. However, one might also reframe the persistence of these films' popularity on German TV and in second-run movie theaters in terms of recent German cinematic developments—the Berlin School, for example—and "post-historical" cinematic attempts to come to terms with the "failures" of neoliberal democracy in the *Alltag* of the masses.

Notes

PREFACE

1. The film-within-the-film is *Ivan's Childhood* (dir. Andrei Tarkovsky, USSR, 1962).

2. Brecht, "Theater for Pleasure or Theater for Instruction?" 73.

3. Throughout the film, this pose is repeated, along with the sound of church bells, to remind us of Margit's youth spent in a convent as a result of her mother's sudden death. In chapter two I discuss how repetition is used to mark cyclical time, as theorized by Julia Kristeva. Here, it emphasizes the cyclicality of Margit's romantic endeavors as the story ends with "her third."

INTRODUCTION: RESCUING HISTORY FROM THE RUINS

1. Since first viewing these films at the archives, I subsequently discovered that many continue to run on MDR (*Mitteldeutscher Rundfunk*—Middle German Television) and RBB (*Rundfunk Berlin Brandenburg*—Berlin Brandenburg Television).

2. This has been accomplished only insofar as films about women have functioned in the framework of larger arguments. For example, while Anke Pinkert uncovers the critical potential of mother and daughter figures in the years leading up to 1965, these characters serve to illustrate her larger argument about historical trauma and melancholy. Daniela Berghahn's extensive history of DEFA devotes one chapter to women on film. Leonie Naughton discusses women's films only to the extent that they serve as an important historical and cultural backdrop to her work on post-unification film culture. John Urang's book, *Legal Tender*, provides an examination of gender in East German commodity culture, literature, and film but does so in a broad manner that mirrors trends in Cultural Studies rather than Cinema Studies. This tension between Cultural Studies and Cinema Studies is one that continues to inform work on DEFA and, barring the works of a few scholars, results in little engagement with established cinematic theories.

3. On the issue of Western ignorance and continued marginalization of DEFA in the construction of the German film canon, see Barton Byg "Reassessing DEFA Today," Naughton, and Pinkert; on the hegemony of Western intellectual trends and the marginalization of a critical discourse regarding Eastern bloc culture, see Susan Buck-Morss, Byg, Paul Cooke, Anikó Imre,

Naughton, Renata Salecl, Tamara Trampe, and Slavoj Žižek, *Did Somebody Say Totalitarianism?*; on the importance of gender for these issues, see Buck-Morss, Susan Gal and Gail Kligman, Imre, and Pinkert.

4. Byg, "Reassessing" 3.

5. The term *Wende* means "turn" and is used to denote the shift or turn from socialism to liberal democracy after German unification.

6. Naughton, *That Was the Wild East* 14–21.

7. Pinkert, *Film and Memory in East Germany* 3.

8. Žižek, *Did Someone Say Totalitarianism?* 168.

9. Buck-Morss, *Dreamworld and Catastrophe* 4–7.

10. Ibid., 68.

11. Ibid., ix–x.

12. Raymond Williams defines "structure of feeling" as a manifestation of practical consciousness—that which is different from official consciousness, "what is actually being lived . . . a kind of feeling and thinking which is indeed social and material" (130–131). He also uses the term "structures of experience" to emphasize "not feeling against thought, but thought as felt and feeling as thought: practical consciousness of a present kind, in a living and interrelating continuity," and he insists we consider them "as a 'structure': as a set, with specific internal relations, at once interlocking and in tension . . . still *in process*, often indeed not yet recognized as social but taken to be private, idiosyncratic" (132). He asserts that its shift from emergent (culture) to dominant (culture) is most often revealed in certain forms and conventions (art and literature), but that these remain only one articulation of those structures of feelings (133–134).

13. See http://www.umass.edu/defa /biblio.shtml. For recent research that gives significant priority to DEFA in the context of German film history, see Allan and

Heiduschke, Hake, Heiduschke, Kapczynski and Richardson, Silberman and Wrage, and Wagner.

14. See Gisela Bahr, Bundeszentrale für politische Bildung, Irene Dölling, Margrit Fröhlich, Christel Gräf ("Waren Ostfrauen wirklich anders?"), Susan Linville, Ute Lischke McNab, Ingeborg Majer-O'Sickey and Ingeborg von Zadow, Andrea Rinke, Karen Rosenberg, and Helke Sander.

15. Although the women's film as a genre was given a certain amount of attention in the GDR and some critics attempted to sketch a working definition of the term, the ways in which woman was constructed as a narrative and cinematic tool was somewhat under-theorized. The near omission of gender from DEFA film criticism and the practical absence of DEFA from feminist interventions in German cinema is curious, given the importance of women protagonists in DEFA films and given East German critics' obvious interest in asking the question "The 'women's film,' what is it?" Examples include Rudolph Jürschik, Horst Knietzsch, Hans-Rainer Mihan, Heinz Müller, Maya Turovskaya, and Margit Voss.

16. The list of potential works is overwhelming. In addition to the collection by Majer-O'Sickey and von Zadow, see Sandra Frieden, Julia Knight, Susan Linville, and Richard McCormick, as well as Eric Rentschler's edited volume *West German Filmmakers on Film*.

17. By taking this approach, this book contributes to the growing body of work on East European cinema that is inflected by gender critique. See especially Imre and Iordanova.

18. Marciniak, "Second World-ness and Transnational Feminist Practices" 5.

19. Most East European women filmmakers vehemently rejected any feminist positioning. This was certainly the case for Věra Chytilová and Ester Krumbachová

(Czechoslovakia), Márta Mészáros (Hungary), and Agnieska Holland (Poland). West German filmmaker Helke Sander makes a distinction between "feminine" and "feminist" imagery in her essay, "Feminism and Film," arguing that, while feminism has been defined "in the most contradictory and utterly irreconcilable" ways, it is very much the case that "certain as yet unrealized feminine qualities—that is, characteristics which have been socially smothered in men, such as sensitivity, fantasy—can be expressed with confidence first in art works by women" (76). Helma Sanders-Brahms and Margarethe von Trotta have similarly resisted the label *feminist*, a label that can be "the kiss of death for a film that seeks to be commercially viable" (Linville 145).

20. Imre, *East European Cinemas* xviii.

21. Anton Kaes uses the term *counter-cinema* to describe the avant-garde sentiment shared by directors of both the Young German Film and the New German Cinema. This, he argues, was made possible by new economic, social, and political constellations in West Germany in the 1960s, including the establishment of the West German film schools; new state and local funding of small film projects through subsidies, loans, advances, prizes, and awards; the promotion of West German culture abroad via film festivals, Goethe Institute retrospectives, and university use; as well as television as a new landscape for filmmaking. The substitution of subsidies for a studio system, he argues, thus enabled filmmakers a certain amount of economic and aesthetic independence from the mainstream film market (20–24).

22. For a cursory overview, see Berghahn 178–180. For an extensive analysis of the relationships between the developing West German women's movement of the late 1960s and early 70s, West German institutional changes like those Kaes discusses, and West German

women filmmakers' attempts to construct a "feminine aesthetic," see Knight 73–149 and Sander.

23. Berghahn, *Hollywood Behind the Wall* 182.

24. Kuhn, "Women's Genres: Melodrama, Soap Opera and Theory" 129.

25. See especially the works of Márta Mészarós (Hungary); Agnieszka Holland, Andrzej Wajda, and Krzysztof Zanussi (Poland); Vera Chytilová and Ester Krumbachová (Czechoslovakia); and the various West German filmmakers already mentioned.

26. Merkel, . . . *und Du, Frau* 34.

27. Ibid., 38.

28. Ibid., 44.

29. Ibid., 54.

30. Hake, *German National Cinema* 91, 92.

31. Chapters one and two in Hell's *Post-Fascist Fantasies* are especially enlightening here: "Specters of Stalin: Constructing Stalinist Fathers" (25–63) and "Stalinist Motherhood" (65–88). Pinkert analyzes the maternal function specifically as a public site for working through the trauma of the air raids and for displacing the trauma of the Holocaust, for expressing the "universal experience of loss, pain, and death caused by war" (103). See especially her brilliant analysis of the postwar films *The Murderers Are Among Us, Rotation, Destinies of Women, Story of a Young Marriage,* and *Sun Seekers* (83–141).

32. Pinkert, *Film and Memory in East Germany* 88.

33. Berghahn, *Hollywood Behind the Wall* 177.

34. Pinkert, *Film and Memory in East Germany* 117.

35. Hake, *German National Cinema* 100.

36. Berghahn, *Hollywood Behind the Wall* 187.

37. Marx, *Economic and Philosophic Manuscripts of 1844* 83.

38. The literature on this topic is vast. See in particular the work of Hanna Behrend, Donna Harsch, Daphne Hornig and Christine Steiner, Eva Kolinsky, and Hildegard Maria Nickel.

39. Verfassung 1949, Article 18.

40. For an excellent overview of reproductive services, see Harsch, chapter four, "Restoring Fertility." On access to the pill, see also Kolano 34. On maternity and montly child support, see also Kolinsky 105.

41. Kolinsky, "Gender and the Limits of Equality in East Germany" 102. See also Behrend 34, 38–40; and Harsch 246–261.

42. The *Haushaltstag* [housework day] is an excellent example of the persistence of an official gendered division of labor in the domestic sphere. Introduced in 1961, it guaranteed all single, full-time working mothers one day off per month to catch up on housework. Later, the *Haushaltstag* was expanded to include women without children, as well as women working part-time. However, the law never applied to men (*Lexikon des DDR-Alltags* 145). Kolinsky includes an informative table comparing the differences between these types of provisions in the GDR and the FRG (106).

43. Kolano, *Kollektiv d'amour* 40–41.

44. Kurt Starke, qtd. in Kolano, *Kollektiv d'amour* 46.

45. Wander, *Guten Morgen, du Schöne* 9.

46. Emmerich, *Kleine Literaturgeschichte der DDR* 289–291. Other collections include Christiana Barckhausen, *Schwestern* (1985); Meta Borst, ed., *Partnerschaft: Geschichten vom Zusammenleben* (1987); Gabriele Eckart, *So sehe ick die Sache* (1984); Christine Lambrecht, *Männerbekanntschaften: Freimütige Protokolle* (1986); Irina Liebmann, *Berliner Mietshaus* (1982); Christine Müller, *Männerprotokolle* (1986); Erika Rüdenauer, ed., *Dünne Haut: Tagebücher von Frauen* (1987).

47. Nagelschmidt, "Frauenliteratur der siebziger Jahre . . ." 68.

48. Emmerich, *Kleine Literaturgeschichte der DDR* 286–287.

49. Ibid., 287.

50. Ibid.

51. Ibid., 346.

52. Von der Emde, "Irmtraud Morgner's Postmodern Feminism" 118.

53. See especially Morgner's *Hochzeit in Konstantinopel* (1968), *Leben und Abenteuer der Trobadora Beatriz nach Zeugnissen ihrer Spielfrau Laura* (1974), *Amanda. Ein Hexenroman* (1983), and *Rumba auf einen Herbst* (1992). For a more thorough analysis of Morgner's use of fantasy, see Alison Lewis.

54. Von der Emde, "Irmtraud Morgner's Postmodern Feminism" 119–121.

55. Hell, *Post-Fascist Fantasies* 217.

56. Ibid.

57. Ibid., 219.

58. Wolf, *Kassandra* 296.

59. Hell, *Post-Fascist Fantasies* 219.

60. Wolf, *Kassandra* 262.

61. Hell, *Post-Fascist Fantasies* 220.

62. See Dorothea Becker, Günther Holzweißig, Karen Ruoff Kramer, Hans Joachim Meurer, Joyce Marie Mushaben, Dagmar Schittly, Regine Sylvester, and Klaus Wischnewski. While Meurer and Schittly have provided two of the most comprehensive sociopolitical histories of DEFA since Ralf Schenk's seminal *Das zweite Leben der Filmstadt Babelsberg*, they overwhelmingly emphasize a totalitarian reading of DEFA's institutional culture. Meurer even goes so far as to define DEFA's cultural policies as "Stalinist" (97–107). In contrast to these approaches, Allan and Sandford's *DEFA: East German Cinema 1946–1990*, Allan and Heiduschke's *Re-Imagining DEFA*, Berghahn's *Hollywood Behind the Wall*, Heiduschke's *DEFA and Film History*, Naughton's *That Was the Wild East*, and Pinkert's *Film and Memory*

in East Germany provide readers with a more balanced approach to understanding the creative and political possibilities and obstacles experienced by former East German filmmakers.

63. Ralf Schenk, "Mitten im Kalten Krieg" 55.

64. Ibid., 10–11, 14, 24.

65. Ibid., 51, 55. For an exhaustive overview of the GDR's foundational notion of socialist culture, and of the cultural goals and implementation of a particularly "socialist" cinema within that context, see Meurer 59–70.

66. This is a forestry term, which describes the systematic felling of trees. Differing slightly from the use of terms such as "freeze" and "thaw," the image of whole forests being felled creates a sense of complete and utter destruction, suggesting the obliteration of potential future growth. This adds to the sense of finality that is often attributed to this moment in DEFA history, in which all cinema worthy of examination seems to have been struck down with one fell swoop.

67. See especially Schittly, Holzweißig, and Wischnewski.

68. Feinstein, *The Triumph of the Ordinary* 196. On the private as a "political retreat," see Schittly 163 and Meurer 94. Schittly frames her analysis in terms of political retreat and withdrawal; Meurer argues that social issues are "concealed" by the private.

69. See Allan and Heiduschke, Berghahn, Feinstein, Heiduschke, Pinkert, Rinke, Silberman and Wrage, Urang, and Wagner. Berghahn provides a brief, chapter-long comparison of West German, East German, and Russian women's films, roughly outlining the differences between "feminist" consciousness in East and West and the subsequent differences in films developing out of inherently dissimilar social contexts (175–183). Pinkert's approach to

early DEFA films about women reveals the ways in which female characters functioned to work through the trauma of the immediate postwar period. Rinke's much more extensive study of women's films from 1972–1982 provides an in-depth analysis of one decade of women's films. While her book offers insightful sociohistorical readings of eight women's films of the period, it does not engage at great length with cinematic theory and international cinematic trends, something this book sets out to do.

70. I will address the ideological conflation of the public/private and political/personal dichotomies in greater detail below.

71. See espeically Stefan Bollinger and Fritz Vilmar, Dölling, Wolfgang Engler, Petra Junghans, Thomas Lindenberger, Merkel, and Michael Rauhut.

72. Jungnickel, "Produktionsbedingungen bei der Herstellung von Kinospielfilmen und Fernsehfilmen" 47.

73. Ibid., 47–48.

74. Ibid., 48; Meurer, *Cinema and National Identity in a Divided Germany 1979–1989* 66. For a brief overview of film production at DEFA, see Naughton 23–44; for an extensive history of production, distribution and exhibition see Meurer 88–107, 123–138, 154–169. Naughton includes an interesting and informative consideration of the downsizing and dismantling of the studios, including the political and cultural implications for postunification German identity.

75. Meurer, *Cinema and National Identity in a Divided Germany 1979–1989* 66. For an exhaustive overview of the arduous process of developing subject matter, see Schönemann 73–80.

76. This acceptance procedure was often the first time that the studio board had seen any part of the film, and involved an initial screening and in-depth discussion with the filmmaking collective regarding

the film's artistic and political merits and failures. As a result, the film would be *abgenommen* [accepted] or changes would be required. After the studio acceptance procedure, the film would then be submitted to the state for its *staatliche Abnahme* [state acceptance procedure]. The film would then be *zugelassen* [let through or "permitted"] or *nicht zugelassen* [not let through, not "permitted"] by the Minister of Film, Director of the *Hauptverwaltung Film* [Central Film Administration—HV Film], and a representative of the Minstry of Culture (Jungnickel 56). For an overview of DEFA's centralized structure, see Berghahn 23–35, Meurer 90–94, and Naughton 36–42.

77. Schönemann, "Stoffentwicklung im DEFA-Studio für Spielfilme" 75.

78. Naughton also mentions the "indirect criticisms [that were] clearly discernable to local audiences" and the intimation of social themes that were otherwise taboo (26), noting that these "begrudgingly tolerated" criticisms were brought into public discourse by DEFA films in the 1980s in particular (32).

79. Schönemann, "Stoffentwicklung im DEFA-Studio für Spielfilme" 78.

80. Wischnewski, "Die zornigen jungen Männer von Babelsberg" 364.

81. Ibid., 355–356. Regarding socialism as the only viable option for most East German artists, see Dalichow, "Die jüngste Regiegeneration der DEFA—Aufbruch oder Abgesang?" 73.

82. Wischnewski, "Die zornigen jungen Männer von Babelsberg" 358.

83. Schönemann argues that only a select few "were allowed to cast a critical perspective on reality [in the GDR] . . . because their political integrity had been proven after many years of membership—at DEFA and in the Party—and thus, could no longer be questioned, because they were predictable assets." She considers the "individual arts" (painting, writing) as "freer," arguing that these "critical spirits" could

find their venues—abroad, if necessary—whereas "for filmmakers, their dependence is total . . . they cannot work without state support, namely because they have access neither to the finances, nor to the technical materials necessary, because there is only the one studio" (Schöneman, "Stoffentwicklung im DEFA-Studio für Spielfilme" 76–77).

84. Naughton, *That Was the Wild East* 35–36, 38–41.

85. Schönemann, "Stoffentwicklung im DEFA-Studio für Spielfilme" 76.

86. Buck-Morss details how the private space of the apartment functioned as an alternative public sphere in the former Soviet Union, particularly in the 1960s (*Dreamworld and Catastrophe* 199).

87. While this does not hold true for East German experimental art, produced primarily underground, it does pertain to the feature film landscape. On East German avant-garde and experimental work, see Randall Halle and Reinhild Steingröver.

88. Naughton, *That Was the Wild East* 36.

89. Lothar Bisky and Dieter Wiedemann's important work, *Der Spielfilm. Rezeption und Wirkung,* includes research on film reception in the GDR, which suggests that film was one of the most popular artistic media in the GDR. They note 75–80 million viewers annually and project that a 25-year-old viewer in the mid-1980s had already seen an average of 2,000 films either in the theater or on television, an overwhelming number in comparison to the possible number of novels read, paintings viewed or theater performances attended. Naughton emphasizes the fluctuation in the viewing public's interest in DEFA: in the early 1970s, DEFA was poorly received and the phrase "I'd even go see a DEFA film with you!" became a well-used ironism; by the mid-1970s, that phrase actually expressed genuine interest, as DEFA increased in popularity with

spectators; by the late 1970s, its meaning had shifted again; and by the early 1980s there was, once more, a "rise in the pictures that found favor with audiences and critics alike" (34–39).

90. Feinstein, *The Triumph of the Ordinary* 8.

91. Bisky and Wiedemann, *Der Spielfilm* 7.

92. See Bisky and Wiedemann, *Der Spielfilm*, table 5, "Beliebtheit ausgewählter Freizeittätigkeiten," and table 3, "Vergleich der Altersstruktur der DDR-Bevölkerung über 14 Jahre mit der Altersstruktur der Kinobesucher über 14 Jahre," respectively (23, 13).

93. Bisky and Wiedemann, *Der Spielfilm* 8.

94. Emmerich, *Kleine Literaturgeschichte der DDR* 120, my emphasis.

95. Byg, "Two Approaches" 87.

96. See Wischnewski 361, Feinstein 221, and Meurer 67–69.

97. Bisky and Wiedemann's research asserts the overwhelming regularity with which East Germans could view Western films: "In 1977, 332 films broadcast by the West German television stations ARD and ZDF were also shown in East Germany. Only 5% of those films were produced in socialist countries, and almost half of them were produced in American film studios!" (40). Meurer asserts that 80% of the East German population had access to West German broadcasts (68).

98. Wischnewski, "Die zornigen jungen Männer von Babelsberg" 362.

99. Ibid.

100. Bisky and Wiedemann, *Der Spielfilm* 28–30, emphasis in original. The figures are based on surveys done in the 1970s, in which viewers finished the statement, "I expect a feature film to . . . " with varying degrees of agreement (disagree, somewhat disagree, agree, strongly agree, definitely agree). 84 percent answered "entertainment" with either *strongly agree* or

definitely agree, 94 percent answered "good artistic realization" with either *strongly agree* or *definitely agree*, and 65 percent answered "realistic portrayal of reality" with either *strongly agree* or *definitely agree*.

101. Feinstein, *The Triumph of the Ordinary* 6–7.

102. Ibid., 194.

103. Ibid., 195.

104. Ibid., 199.

105. Qtd. in Engler, *Die Ostdeutschen* 174.

106. Bisky and Wiedemann, *Der Spielfilm* 30.

107. Mihan, "Die ganze Wahrheit" 12.

108. Bisky and Wiedemann, *Der Spielfilm* 19–20.

109. See Joan B. Landes. Landes is specifically referring to Simone de Beauvoir's *The Second Sex*; Sherry Ortner's "Is Female to Male as Nature is to Culture?"; Friedrich Engels' *The Origin of the Family, Private Property and the State*; and Gayle Rubin's "The Traffic in Women: Notes on the Political Economy of Sex."

110. Gal, "A Semiotics of the Public/Private Distinction" 86.

111. See Gal and Kligman, *The Politics of Gender after Socialism*, and Katherine Verdery, *What Was Socialism and What Comes Next?*.

112. Gal, "A Semiotics of the Public/Private Distinction" 80–81.

113. Ibid., 87.

114. Feinstein, *The Triumph of the Ordinary* 196.

115. Engler admits that there were significant economic differences based on education and training, and that this often resulted in a gendered division of labor in which women disproportionately ended up in professions that earned less money. Nickel provides a more specific analysis of the division of labor in the workforce and in the home in "Geschlechtertrennung durch Arbeitsteilung: Berufs- und Familienarbeit in der DDR." See also the

collection of essays in Gislinde Schwarz and Christine Zenner's *Wir wollen mehr als ein "Vaterland": DDR-Frauen im Aufbruch.* What is most important about Engler's argument is his emphasis on gender parity in economic independence and security, i.e., neither women nor men had to marry for financial reasons. Engler uses the term *soziale Gleichheit* [social equality] to express this systemic containment and limitation of achievements and success. That is, in terms of financial gains, professional titles, goods and services, etc., one could only accumulate or aspire to a particular limit, and most could achieve this limit in one form or another (*Die Ostdeutschen* 175–197).

116. Engler, *Die Ostdeutschen* 217. Engler argues that new socialist economic and social policies relieved men and women of their previously definitive social roles, making gendered roles less stable and resulting in conflicting desires that were based on both the redefined gender order and inherited gender divisions (*Die Ostdeutschen* 220–222). What Engler fails to deal with, however, are residual bourgeois gender norms that led to the uneven development of women's (and men's) emancipation, specifically in relation to the SED's *Muttipolitik.*

117. Mihan "Sabine, Sunny, Nina" 12.

118. The title of Helke Sander's seminal West German materialist-feminist film, *Die allseitig reduzierte Persönlichkeit* [*The All-Round Reduced Personality—ReDuPers*], is a direct allusion to and precise cinematic critique of this failure, and will be discussed at greater length in chapter 2.

119. Schieber "Anfang vom Ende" 267–270.

120. For more on the problematic concept of an East German *Ersatzöffentlichkeit*, see especially the work of Feinstein and Engler.

121. Voss specifically addresses Martin Ritt's *Norma Rae* (1979) and Fred Zinnemann's *Julia* (1976/1977).

122. Voss, "Frauenprofile gefragt" 167.

123. Turovskaya, "Der 'Frauenfilm'" 22–23.

124. Ibid.

125. The films I have chosen to work on are a good example of this: Helga Schütz worked with her then husband, Günther, to write the screenplay for *Lot's Wife,* and Christel Gräf worked as the film's dramatic adviser; *All My Girls* was practically an all-female production, with Iris Gusner directing, Gabriele Kotte producing the scenario, and Tamara Trampe acting as dramatic adviser; *Goodbye to Winter* was written and directed by Helke Misselwitz. Women, although rarely directors, could often be found in the role of scenarist and dramatic advisor, as was the case in *Apprehension* (scenario by Helga Schubert, dramatic advising by Erika Richter); *Until Death Do Us Part* (dramatic advising by Barbara Rogall); *The Legend of Paul and Paula* (dramatic advising by Anne Pfeuffer); and *The Bicycle* (directed by Evelyn Schmidt, dramatic advising by Erika Richter).

126. Bisky and Wiedemann give identificatory structures and viewer pleasure a great deal of attention: "The effectiveness of a literary or cinematic story depends very strongly on whether it presents sympathetic protagonists, and the extent to which it enables identificatory and distanciation processes" (*Der Spielfilm* 58). The result of such identificatory possibilities is the ability of film to construct the individual, but only if film texts speak to individual needs and desires: "The result expresses itself in [the bodies and psyches] of the individuals in this communication process—through validation or changes in the personal dispositions and types of behavior.... The effects of films are always bound to concrete social and individual situations. They presuppose individual needs and a larger social desire or interest to satisfy those needs" (94–95).

127. Lim, "Summoning Halcyon Days of Failed Ideals."

128. Kristeva, "Women's Time" 449.

1. HAPPILY EVER AFTER? THE
EMANCIPATORY POLITICS OF
FEMALE DESIRE IN *LOT'S WIFE*

1. Films that exhibit stylistic influences from Italy, France, and West Germany include Martin Hellberg's adaptation of *Emilia Galotti* (1958); Frank Beyer's *Königskinder* [*Star Crossed Lovers*] (1962); Konrad Wolf's *Sonnensucher* [*Sun Seekers*] (1959), *Divided Heaven* (1964), and *Ich war neunzehn* [*I Was Nineteen*] (1968); and nearly all of the films produced and then banned in 1965/1966, most notably Frank Beyer's *Spur der Steine* [*Trace of Stones*] (1965/1990), which visually alludes to both Akira Kurosawa's *Seven Samurai* (1954) and John Sturges' *The Magnificent Seven* (1960); Jürgen Böttcher's *Born in '45* (1966/1990); Kurt Maetzig's *The Rabbit Is Me* (1965/1990); and Herrmann Zschoche's *Karla* (1966/1990). See also Berghahn and Feinstein.

2. Egon Günther's *Wenn du groß bist, lieber Adam* [*When You Are Grown Up, Dear Adam*] (1966/1990) is clearly influenced by Vojtech Jasny's *Az prijde kocour* [*Cassandra Cat*] (Czechoslovakia, 1963).

3. Richard Neupert makes a sound argument for reading the French New Wave in the larger context of other artistic movements, such as the New Novel and the Theater of the Absurd, as well as within the context of structuralism and semiotics, arguing that the New Wave was participating in larger cultural debates about significa-tion, generic tradition, and textual structure (12–25). Günther's use of oblique and sideways camera angles, jump cuts, and his experimental use of the close-up, along with intertextual references to French phi-losophy—Diderot figures prominently in one of the film's dialogues—suggests that his film is more than marginally influenced by the French New Wave's transformation of postwar cinema. Other films of this generation—*Divided Heaven, The Rabbit is Me, Born in '45*—clearly exhibit similar

cinematic influences. For more on the French New Wave influences on these three films, see Feinstein 110–131, 151–175 and 194–200, respectively.

4. Sellier, *Masculine Singular* 4. The French New Wave is periodized by contem-porary scholars as beginning in 1956, with the release of Roger Vadim's *Et Dieu . . . créa la femme* [*And God Created Woman*], and ending in 1962. However, the "official" birth of the French New Wave is considered to coincide with the 1959 Cannes Film Festival, with the release of *Les quatre cents coups* [*The 400 Blows*] (dir. François Truf-faut) and *Hiroshima mon amour* (dir. Alain Resnais). While it is clear that Resnais's films were overtly political from the begin-ning and Godard's filmmaking has, since the mid-1960s, become increasingly more political, the early films of the French New Wave are decidedly less so. See Monaco, Neupert, and Sellier.

5. In the West German context, this is most clearly the case with Rainer Werner Fassbinder's work. Fassbinder's interest in traditional cinematic genres—film noir, science fiction and melodrama, espe-cially—and his particular love for Douglas Sirk is well documented. See Fassbinder's *Anarchy of the Imagination* and his essays in Rentschler's *West German Filmmakers on Film*. In the East German context, the influence of traditional cinematic genres is primarily visible in the so-called *Indianer-filme* [Indian Films], which attempted to rewrite the genre of the Western from the proto-communist perspective of the Native Americans, and in the East German musicals.

6. On the West German model, see Alexander Kluge, "On Film and the Public Sphere." Sellier argues that the emphasis on "individual genius" in *Cahiers du cinéma* is indicative of the French directors' socio-political myopia, which she sees as further problematized by their contradictory emphasis on Hollywood filmmakers

Hitchcock and Hawks, incarnations of "the Hollywood dream factory," whose "films [were] produced more or less on the assembly line" (25–28).

7. Sellier, *Masculine Singular* 95–97.

8. For the French context, see Sellier and Neupert. For the West German context, see Rentschler's *West German Filmmakers on Film*, and Knight.

9. Monaco, *The New Wave* 70.

10. Sellier, *Masculine Singular* 149.

11. Ibid.

12. Neupert, *A History of the French New Wave Cinema* 80.

13. In the final scene of *Lot's Wife*, Katrin Lot is driven off to her site of incarceration accompanied by the sole colleague who supported her during her trial. His line delivers the film's final scathing critique of the East German justice system: "Go ahead and look back, Katrin. Don't worry; you won't turn into a pillar of salt."

14. In *A Married Woman*, Macha Méril's character, Charlotte, speaks in voice-over throughout the film, adding minimalist, stream-of-consciousness commentary to the images. In the second instance of this sound/image combination, Charlotte's lover brings the car around after their morning tryst while she comments in voice-over: "Who am I? I've never really known for sure. The verb 'to follow.' Other reasons. I used to be. Not here, a year ago. Just once, right? . . . It's difficult. I'm on vacation. As the days pass . . . Happiness. I don't know." This use of female voice-over commentary is also present in Günther's film, yet Katrin's voice serves to emphasize the correlations between female desire and political resistance, as I will argue throughout the chapter.

15. Sellier, *Masculine Singular* 149.

16. Ibid., 115.

17. The previously referenced voice-over also emphasizes this: Charlotte repeatedly states, "I don't know." On the alignment of femininity with consumption

as a recurring trope in the French New Wave, see Sellier, *Masculine Singular* 14–16, 18–21, 67–69, and 180–183.

18. Kluge, "What Do the 'Oberhauseners' Want?" 10.

19. Hake, *German National Cinema* 151.

20. Ibid.

21. The prevalence of childlike female protagonists is very common in the French New Wave, being most obviously represented in the figure of Anna Karina but also in Brigitte Bardot's early performances. See Sellier, *Masculine Singular* 145–146 and 153–164.

22. Silberman, "Beyond Spectacle" 186–187.

23. Heide Schlüpman provides an interesting critique of Kluge's notion of "femininity as productive force" and its relationship to fantasy, arguing that, while Kluge uses women protagonists to provoke fantasy, "what matters for Kluge in women's films is not women's cinema in general, but what the vision of femininity can contribute to his own work . . . he separates the theme of femininity as a productive force from that of the relationship between the sexes, and that of sexuality within society, and never reunites them" ("Femininity as Productive Force" 77).

24. The result was unsuccessful, however, in that artists, in particular, believed in and strove for a more intellectually rigorous engagement with "socialist modernity" and "socialist morality" than the SED could stomach. Ulbricht denounced these "counterrevolutionaries," whose "immorality" and "skepticism" were "objectively in line with those of our enemy," and who were, in fact, "softening the GDR from within with their so-called liberalization" while using state funding to do so (Engler, "Strafgericht über die Moderne" 20).

25. Ibid., 24.

26. Ibid., 17.

27. Reimann, *Alles schmeckt nach Abschied* 170.

28. Hake, *German National Cinema* 151.

29. Feinstein offers an excellent reading of the ways in which gender is structured along a binary of science/rationality and emotion/intuition in the film, arguing that Rita's decision to remain in the East "is grounded in a way more fundamental than reason," and ultimately provides the means "for legitimizing the new society, for grounding the truth of socialism" (*The Triumph of the Ordinary* 117, 119). For a more in-depth analysis of the influence of the French New Wave on Wolf's film, in particular that of Resnais's *Hiroshima mon amour*, see Feinstein 118–121 and 131–132.

30. The film is based on the "novel of arrival" of the same name, written by Christa Wolf. Wolf helped write the screenplay for the film as well.

31. Urang, *Legal Tender* 65, my emphasis.

32. Ibid., 76.

33. Feinstein argues that Maria's sexuality places her in a liminal position and gives her a strength of character that, like her insistence on truth at all costs, sets her apart from other characters in the text, who are complacent. However, his focus emphasizes her self-reliance without engaging the ways in which her sexuality represents a form of agency contained by masculine power structures.

34. *Frauenschicksale* [*Destinies of Women*], directed by Slatan Dudow in 1952, would probably be considered the first DEFA *Frauenfilm*. The propagandistic tenor of the film, however, makes it an unlikely candidate for arguments wishing to tease out the critical aspects of DEFA films. The programmatically biased portrayal of the "capitalist-imperialist" West as "evil" and the simplistic, melodramatic depiction of the young female protagonists' emancipation through work and collectivity hampers the film's critical potential, even

if its aesthetic value perseveres. For an interesting, in-depth analysis, see Berghahn, "East German Cinema after Unification" 183–189.

35. Gräf, Letter to Strafvollzugsanstalt Görlitz.

36. Loth, Letter to Arbeitsgruppe "Roter Kreis."

37. See Jackie Byars, Molly Haskell, and Annette Kuhn.

38. As such, it functions in much the same way as in Malle's *The Lovers* and Godard's *A Married Woman*.

39. Silverman, "Lost Objects and Mistaken Subjects" 104.

40. Silverman, "Dis-Embodying the Female Voice" 309.

41. See Byars, Haskell, and Kuhn.

42. This narrative function of female desire as a tool for resisting the institution of marriage is what aligns Günther's film most with those of the French New Wave. See especially Varda's *La Pointe Courte* (1954), Malle's *The Lovers* (1958), Truffaut's *Jules & Jim* (1962), Godard's *A Married Woman* (1963), and Rohmer's *Suzanne's Career* (1963). What sets Günther's film apart from those of his French contemporaries is his overt alignment of the personal with the political through an overt critique of the law.

43. The tension constructed here between these three notions of romantic narrative reflects Engler's argument in *Die Ostdeutschen* regarding inherited notions of romance and gendered expectations developed under the new East German social order. As I will argue later in the chapter, Katrin's ideal of love can be connected to the film's utopian impulse for social change.

44. Engler provides an interesting reading of the contradictory nature of the SED as an "Arbeiter- und Bauernpartei" ["workers' and peasants' Party"]. His research reveals that, while 70–99 percent of East Germans in all career groups felt they belonged to the "working class," membership in the Party

was actually much higher in professions not typically considered "working class." For instance, while 91–95 percent of "production workers" identified as members of the working class, only 17–24 percent were members of the SED, while 94–95 percent of them were members of the union (FDGB—*Freier Deutscher Gewerkschaftsbund*). In contrast, 78–85 percent of "management and intelligentsia" identified as members of the working class, while 45–93 percent of them were members of the SED. Engler reads this in two ways: first, in order to assert their integral role in socialist society, middle- and upper-management and those in highly skilled careers joined the SED; second, the "workers' Party" was never representative of the workers because "intelligentsia and management often set the tone" (*Die Ostdeutschen* 191). Engler concludes that the discourse of work, rather than the nature of work, determined membership in the Party, and that blue-collar workers actually sought out other avenues for leadership and representation (*Die Ostdeutschen* 190).

45. Gal 87.

46. Günther's use of nonsynchronous sound to comment on the image here is reminiscent of Godard's use of the same in *A Married Woman*.

47. Mulvey, "Visual Pleasure and Narrative Cinema" 27–28.

48. This use of claustrophobic close-ups of Richard is what makes Günther's film distinct from *A Married Woman*. Whereas Godard presents Charlotte in pieces—belly button, legs, knees, arm, face—via close-ups, in Günther's film it is Richard who is broken up into abstract pieces. Godard's viewers are invited, along with Charlotte's diegetic lover, to focus on the beauty of her body parts, even as they are simultaneously made aware of the structures of masculine power in this method of representing the female body (we often see the hands of Charlotte's lover placed on her body in such a way as to denote control and

possession). In Günther's use of the close-up, however, the traditional fetishization of the female body is replaced with a critical gaze directed at the *oppressor's* body, broken into its abstract, offensive pieces.

49. Here, I am referring to Hell's analysis of the Communist hero. Hell relies on Žižek's notion of the sublime body when describing the foundational narrative of antifascism, an ideological formation, she argues, that is based on the family: "these unconscious fantasies revolve around an identification with the father's body. Or, to recall Lefort's analysis of the totalitarian project, it is around the leader's body that the social is made to cohere. . . . The identification with the father's body results in the fantasy of the *post-fascist body*: in these novels [of arrival], sexuality is defined as that part of subjectivity which links the subject to its fascist past, and the new subject comes about as a result of the erasure of its material body, its sexual body" (*Post-Fascist Fantasies* 19).

50. Kluge and Negt, *Öffentlichkeit und Erfahrung* 404.

51. See Engels, *The Origin of the Family, Private Property and the State* 742.

52. Engler provides an interesting reading of work as a kind of East German *Vergangenheitsbewältigung* [coming to terms with the (fascist) past] in *Die Ostdeutschen* 11–31.

53. This semantic and ideological issue of domestic labor was taken up by East German authors, as well as sociologists and historians of East Germany already mentioned. This problem is considered only secondarily in the film, in Katrin's attempt to expose Richard's bourgeois expectations of marriage.

54. Obviously, issues of economic stability and self-sufficiency are necessary prerequisites for domestic tranquility, a concern that stands at the center of two other films discussed in this book, *The Bicycle* and *On Probation*. I only wish to em-

phasize that the film problematizes "work" (here, paid labor) as the most important factor in creating the conditions for the "all-round development of the socialist personality."

55. This is the second reference in the film to Katrin's "poetic" reasons for escaping her marriage. The first occurs when Katrin first demands a divorce for lack of love—she reads to Richard aloud from the French author Diderot: "I once saw a respectable woman shudder with horror as soon as her husband came near her. I saw her throw herself into the bath and wash herself, over and over, because she didn't believe she could clean herself enough after performing her wifely duties." This allusion to French culture reiterates the film's international influences; Godard and Truffaut include multiple, recurring references to French literature and philosophy as well. The lawyer's assertion, "this isn't a case for the courts, it's a case for poets" can also be read as a self-reflexive gesture on the part of Günther, revealing skepticism about socialism's ability to meet the needs and desires of its citizens, and ironizing art's ability to change that system in accordance with those needs.

56. There is a rather strong similarity between this scene and the opening sequence of Zschoche's On Probation, which I discuss in the next chapter.

57. Schittly, Zwischen Regie und Regime 163.

58. Ibid., 124.

59. Gal, "A Semiotics of the Public/Private Distinction" 90.

60. Ibid., 89.

61. Günther, "Die verzauberte Welt" 57.

62. Schittly, Zwischen Regie und Regime 9.

63. Günther, "Die verzauberte Welt" 64.

64. The new divorce law is found in §24: "(1) A marriage can only be dissolved when the court has determined that certain serious grounds have been met: that the marriage has lost its significance for the spouses, the children, and therefore also for society." The Zerrüttungsprinizip [principle of breakdown] removes all questions of guilt from the divorce process: "A marriage can be considered "failed" and thus, can be dissolved, when the spouses no longer cohabit and it cannot be expected that they will do so in the future." http://www.ilexikon.com/Scheidung.html.

2. THE LONELY WOMAN? (RE)-PRODUCTION AND FEMININE DESIRE IN *THE BICYCLE* AND *ON PROBATION*

1. Kaplan, *Motherhood and Representation* 26.

2. Brückner, Interview 254.

3. Ibid., 256.

4. Linville, *Feminism, Film, Fascism* 3.

5. Susan Linville analyzes several West German films within the context of the postwar discourse of melancholy and mourning developed by the husband and wife team, Alexander and Margarete Mitscherlich. The Mitscherlichs argued that German authoritarianism and avoidance of mourning and *Vergangenheitsbewältigung* were rooted in the son's failure to accept or fully identify with the patriarchal authority (*Feminism, Film, Fascism* 3). Linville suggests that the "bad mother" fantasy is bound up with the melancholic tradition, which serves as the discursive basis for sustaining the sufficiency and integrity of the male subject (6). Sanders-Brahms' film opens with a direct allusion to this myth, wherein the daughter of Bertolt Brecht reads aloud from his poem "Germany" (1933).

6. In chapter four I discuss the aesthetics and politics of autobiography and biography in much greater detail in relation to Misselwitz's *Goodbye to Winter* (1988). Interestingly, Misselwitz's

opening sequence is also accompanied by a voice-over, in which she foregrounds the intergenerational experience of women, beginning with a reference to her mother's diary—the entry narrating the day of Misselwitz's birth—and ending with Misselwitz's hopes for and fears about her own daughter's future.

7. Linville, *Feminism, Film, Fascism* 14.

8. In Schmidt's film, the mother-daughter dyad travel via bicycle into the green of a nearby park. Although it is dissimilar to Sanders-Brahms' liberation of the female protagonists via wartime bombing—the private sphere is actually destroyed—the shift from Susanne's small, cramped apartment into the lush, expansive green of the park (constructed via framing and camera work, color, and light) reveals a similar emotional experience of liberation for Schmidt's protagonist.

9. Linville, *Feminism, Film, Fascism* 68.

10. Ibid., 69, 71.

11. Knight, *Women and the New German Cinema* 77.

12. Rich, B. Ruby, "She Says, He Says" 44.

13. See especially Iordanova (*Cinema of the Other Europe* 126–30). Examples include *Zerkalo* [*The Mirror*], dir. Andrei Tarkovsky (USSR, 1975); *Szerelem* [*Love*], dir. Karoly Makk (Hungary, 1977); *Matka Królow* [*Mother of Kings*], dir. Janusz Zaorski (Poland, 1983); *Przesluchanie* [*The Interrogation*], dir. Ryszard Bugajski (Poland, 1989); *Angi Vera*, dir. Pál Gabor (Hungary, 1978); and Márta Mészáros' autobiographical trilogy, in which the loss of the mother is closely bound up with Stalinism: *Napló gyermekeimnek* [*Diary for My Children*], (Hungary, 1982); *Napló szerelmeimnek* [*Diary for My Loved Ones*], (Hungary, 1987); and *Napló apámnak, anyámnak* [*Diary for My Father and Mother*], (Hungary, 1990).

14. Szaloky, "Somewhere in Europe" 93.

15. Ibid., 94. Szaloky provides an enlightening analysis of the relationship between the public/private dichotomy in Hungary, the absence of race and gender from the "unified exilic Hungarian self-image," and the mother figure as "inconsequential, incapacitated, or—worse—self-serving and altogether unmotherly" in the Hungarian orphanage cinema (85–95).

16. Iordanova, *Cinema of the Other Europe* 134.

17. The title and focus of Mészáros' film alludes directly to what Szaloky calls the "Hungarian cinema of orphanage," one particular manifestation of the "internal exilic" cinema of communist Hungary. Connecting the Hungarian experience of Soviet occupation and control between 1956 and 1989 with residual feelings of colonization (under the Ottoman and Austro-Hungarian empires), Szaloky argues that Hungarians have a long history of not identifying with the ruling system, and of "seeing themselves, not without a melancholy satisfaction, as blameless 'historical victims' and hapless 'historical losers,'" who exist in a state of simultaneous entrapment and deterritorialization ("Somewhere in Europe" 84, 92). This manifests, she argues, in a particular national exilic consciousness she calls the "orpha-nation." Each of Mészáros' films discussed here could fall into this category.

18. During the second half of the film, Kata and Anna are filmed in a restaurant, being watched by a group of men at the bar. In an intimate medium shot, their absorption with each other is contrasted with long shots of the men watching them. Kata and Anna never look outside of their own immediate space. The framing becomes tighter, eventually replacing the medium shot with a medium close-up of the pair and close-ups of each emphasizing both their physical and emotional closeness.

Their mother-daughter intimacy thus becomes impenetrable.

19. Marciniak, "Second World-ness and Transnational Feminist Practices" 7–10.

20. Ibid., 18.

21. Kristeva, "Women's Time" 446.

22. Ibid., 447.

23. Ibid., 445–46, my emphasis.

24. Ibid., 446, my emphasis.

25. Ibid., 448.

26. See Nagelschmidt, "Frauenliteratur der siebziger Jahre. . . ."

27. See especially Nagelschmidt, Hornig and Steiner, and Behrend. Behrend's interview in 1987 with an editor for *Junge Welt* is especially telling in this respect. In answer to her question, why there were no female "heroines of work" in the publication's recent issues, his answer is that, after school and the university "comes love, marriage, children and all of the other responsibilities related to family life" ("Frauenemanzipation made in GDR" 43). Behrend sees this as a typically pragmatic way of dealing with discrimination against women in the GDR by failing to question woman's naturalized role as mother.

28. Hornig and Steiner emphasize the naturalization of motherhood as the key to understanding the GDR's paternalism: "But: she should be a *happy* mother, which is why she received all possible forms of state help in the raising of *her children*. And various sociopolitical and family-oriented measures were taken in the 1970s to encourage women's willingness to give birth . . . these official considerations did not envisage social change that would call for men's equal participation in the reproductive and socialization process," (Hornig and Steiner, "Der alltägliche Frauenk(r)ampf zwischen Küche. . ." 58–59, emphasis in original).

29. O'Brien, *Reproducing the World* 10. See also Urang. Michéle Barrett's introduction to Friedrich Engels' *The Origin of the*

Family, Private Property and the State provides an analysis of Engels' naturalization of woman's reproductive role and feminist anthropological critiques of thereof. Barrett argues that the definition of the family is of primary concern. For Marx and Engels, it is defined in terms of property and class society, i.e., "the family" as a unit remains unquestioned, analyzed as "a consequence of the amassing of private property." Hence, the family is understood as a superstructural phenomenon, an expression of the economic base. The analytic priority of the nuclear family thus subsumes any separate consideration of the division of the sexes as an antagonistic one. What remains is the need to specify more precisely what is at issue, namely sexual relations and the economic organization of households/domestic ideology.

30. *Kleines politisches Wörterbuch* 762–763, my emphasis.

31. Kristeva, "Women's Time" 448–449.

32. Hans Dieter Mäde, "Stellungnahme zum Film *Das Fahrrad*" (Nov. 11, 1981): 2.

33. Ibid.

34. Müller's anxiety about the film's, and Susanne's, "failure to progress" reveals once more the official resistance to dealing with the public/private distinction. A generational and gendered problem cannot, by definition, be understood in terms of the private, but rather invokes the need to reconcile individual experience with its larger (collective) sociohistorical reality, which is exactly what *The Bicycle* achieves. Müller's critique of the film reads as follows: "The film convincingly illustrates a phenomenon that has become obvious in the life of our younger generation: an unwillingness and inability to surrender themselves to the responsibilities of partnership and the conflicts that arise therein; an unwillingness to overcome difficulties, adverse

situations and psychological barriers. This unwillingness leads to the renunciation of important social experiences . . . unfortunately, [the film] deals with this problem solely from the perspective of *individual frustration*." Müller, "Einschätzung des DEFA-Spielfilms *Das Fahrrad* zum staatlichen Zulassungsverfahren" (25. September 1981): 2 (emphasis in original).

35. Marx describes the function of living labor as a (barely) living cog in the production process as follows: "In no way does the machine appear as the individual worker's means of labour. Its distinguishing characteristic is not in the least . . . to transmit the worker's activity to the object. . . . Not as with the instrument, which the worker animates and makes into his organ with his skill and strength . . . rather it is the machine which possesses skill and strength in place of the worker, it itself is the virtuoso, with a soul of its own. . . . The worker's activity, reduced to a mere abstraction of activity, is determined and regulated on all sides by the movement of machinery. . . . Labour appears, rather, merely as a conscious organ, scattered among the individual living workers at numerous points of the mechanical system; subsumed under the total process of the machinery itself, as itself only a link of the system, whose unity exists not in the living workers, but rather in the living (active) machinery, which confronts his individual, insignificant doings as a mighty organism. In machinery, objectified labour confronts living labour within the labour process itself as the power which rules it . . . [it is] the transformation of . . . living labour into a mere living accessory of this machinery" (*The Grundrisse* 279).

36. Later in the film, it is also suggested that she is raped after leaving a bar. Aside from Thomas, the only other man she interacts with in the film is the police officer who files her claim for the bicycle. He is also the same officer who discovers,

on her way home from the picnic with Jenny, that she fraudulently reported her bicycle missing.

37. Kristeva, "Women's Time" 456.

38. The fairy tale in *The Bicycle* functions differently than Sanders-Brahms' use of the fairy tale "The Robber Bridegroom" in *Germany, Pale Mother*. While Schmidt's editing contrasts the "real" happy ending of the mother-daughter dyad with that of the fairy tale Susanne narrates, "The Robber Bridegroom" reflects the real experiences of the mother-daughter dyad as it is being narrated and as a trope of the possibilities of agency through female solidarity in the face of male violence.

39. Kristeva, "Women's Time" 445.

40. Ibid.

41. This is most obvious during Susanne's exploration of the apartment while Thomas sleeps: the camera follows her in a medium shot as she discovers a cabinet with glasses and china in the living room; a study with a desk, bookshelf, and extra bed (where Jenny now sleeps); a bright, modern kitchen with well-stocked cabinets; and lastly a pristine, private bathroom with a built-in bathtub. Smiling and closing the door, Susanne partakes in the timeless feminine ritual of the solitary bath. When Thomas enters, she places her hand on his, and says, "Now push a button so that everything stays just the way it is." Here, the film implies through the visual emphasis on the middle-class domestic comforts that she's "marrying up" with (or without) "true love."

42. During the move in, the chasm of class difference between them is emphasized again when Thomas asks, "Hast du schon daran mal gedacht, dich zu verändern?" [Have you ever thought about changing yourself?] In asking this question, he asserts a class-based assumption about improvement: not only should Susanne attempt to climb the production ladder, but she should drink and smoke less, go out less often, etc. Susanne's face and eyes suggest

that she immediately assumes he means this as a class-based inquiry.

43. Families with four or more children and single mothers with three or more children received numerous financial benefits from the state, including things as diverse as free laundry service and reduced prices at cultural events (Sommer, *Lexikon des DDR-Alltags* 182).

44. "Gleichberechtigung der Frau," *Kleines Politisches Wörterbuch* 328 (my emphasis).

45. "Persönlichkeit," *Kleines Politische Wörterbuch* 686.

46. Wolf, Foreword 20–21, my emphasis.

47. Kaplan, *Motherhood and Representation* 64.

48. Ibid., 66.

49. Ibid., 69, 70–71.

50. Ibid., 151.

51. Wolf, Foreword 20.

52. Urang, *Legal Tender* 65–68.

53. Ibid., 68.

54. Silberman, "Discipline and Gender" 168–169.

55. Ibid., 169–170.

56. Ibid., 172.

57. Ibid., 174–175.

58. In his "Stellungnahme zur Staatlichen Abnahme des Films," DEFA General Director Hans Dieter Mäde both draws a connection between Nina and other DEFA heroines, at the same time that he articulates how these particularly feminine characteristics serve to uncover larger questions about the individual and the collective: "Nina, like Paula, Sabine Wulff, and Sunny, to mention only a few of our recent female protagonists . . . is searching for warmth, love, fulfilling partnership. Yet, Nina is unable to take things in her own hands and organize her life accordingly. . . . Here, the film makes clear how responsibility for oneself and for society can only articulate itself in the many individual deeds of individuals, and it also shows

that this process does not unfold without contradictions" (2).

59. "Kurzprotokoll über das Auswertungsgespräch zum DEFA-Film *Bürgschaft für ein Jahr*" 2–3, my emphasis.

60. "Einschätzung des Spielfilms *Bürgschaft für ein Jahr* zur staatlichen Zulassung" 1–2.

61. Ibid.

62. Silberman, "Discipline and Gender" 165.

63. Ibid., 166–167.

64. Ibid., 168–169.

65. Ibid., 167.

66. Ibid., 176.

67. Ibid., 167–168.

68. Kristeva, "Women's Time" 456.

69. Butler, *Gender Trouble* 90.

70. In this respect, *On Probation* reminds the viewer of the use of repetition in representing Paula's alienated experience of domesticity in *The Legend of Paul and Paula* (dir. Heiner Carow, 1973). Yet *On Probation* critically surpasses that film's engagement with woman's double burden. While it has been argued that *The Legend of Paul and Paula* is the most popularly received explicit articulation of private desire as overt resistance to socialist bureaucracy and collectivity, the film's use of femininity (and motherhood in particular) is rather conservative and falls more in line with the politics of the maternal melodrama than the maternal women's film Kaplan describes. See especially Sander and Schlesier, and Dölling, "We all Love Paula but Paul Is More Important to Us: Constructing a 'Socialist Person' Using the 'Femininity' of a Working Woman."

71. Silberman, "Discipline and Gender" 168.

72. Ibid., 169.

73. The kindergarten teacher shows no sympathy for Mireille's needs, and after Mireille's absence, she resists Mireille's return, stating that she already has "two problem children" to deal with. In the end,

Mireille is accepted back into the kindergarten, but unwillingly. Halfway through the film, Mrs. Behrend offers to take care of Mireille for the afternoon so that Nina can attend a parent-teacher meeting. We see Mrs. Behrend and Mireille missing their stop because the tram is crammed with people, walking home while the milk in the grocery bag leaks out, and Mrs. Behrend struggling to get Mireille to walk the rest of the way home; no amount of reasoning or threats can convince Mireille to keep up. This sequence in particular also underscores the ways in which the work of mothering is *laborious* in ways that are unaccounted for in the socialist discourse of labor.

74. The "problem" of masculinity in the film was also overtly addressed by DEFA's Chief Director, Hans Dieter Mäde, in the protocol of the *Studioabnahme*, wherein he describes their "failures" as a potential liability for the film's social critique.

75. Silberman, "Discipline and Gender" 174.

76. Ibid.

77. Wolf, Foreword 21.

78. Kristeva, "Women's Time" 445.

3. PLEASURE IN SEEING OURSELVES? *ALL MY GIRLS*

1. Knight, *Women and the New German Cinema* 73–79.

2. Ibid., 117–118.

3. Brückner, "Searches for Traces" 86–87.

4. See Helke Sander, "Feminism and Film."

5. Knight, *Women and the New German Cinema* 89–90.

6. See Knight, *Women and the New German Cinema* 76–78. Examples of films primarily focused on the problem of female labor include Claudia von Alemann's *Es kommt darauf an, sie zu verändern* [*The Point Is to Change It*] (1972–1973); Barbara Kasper's *Gleicher Lohn für Mann und Frau*

[*Equal Wages for Men and Women*] (1971); Ingrid Oppermann's *Frauen—Schlußlichter der Gewerkschaft?* [*Women—At the Tail End of Trade Unions?*] (1975); Helke Sander's *Eine Prämie für Irene* [*A Bonus for Irene*] (1971); and Valeska Schöttle's *Wer braucht wen?* [*Who Needs Whom?*] (1972).

7. In East Germany, the best example of this trend is the construction of the *VEB Gaskombinat Schwarze Pumpe*, which would become the primary facility for producing coal in the former GDR. The foundations for the town of Hoyerswerda, which would become the new home for the laborers at Schwarze Pumpe, were laid on the same day as the groundbreaking for the factory in 1955.

8. See Iordanova, *Cinema of the Other Europe* 130–133.

9. Hames, *The Czechoslovak New Wave* 194.

10. The class differences between the Party and the people is, I would suggest, part of the sequence's covert critique: the opulence of the banquet—the posh hall and chandelier, the excessive amount of food and alcohol, etc.—allude to the Party's access to a higher standard of living which, in East Germany, was reflected in the Party's use of imported automobiles (Citroën, Volvo) and access to imported Western goods in the *Exquisit-Läden* [luxury shops].

11. Hames, *The Czechoslovak New Wave* 195.

12. Knight, *Women and the New German Cinema* 89–90.

13. For a discussion of the *Kinosterben* see Bisky and Wiedemann 10–11.

14. Bisky and Wiedemann devote considerable attention to the influence of television on film reception in the GDR. According to studies performed by the *Hauptverwaltung Film*, more East Germans watched television than went to the movies in the 1970s and 80s, and between one and four million East Germans saw films

through the medium of television (34–35). As I discussed in the introduction, competition from Western films being shown on West German television stations and broadcast in the GDR was tight, and resulted in the need to produce popular television programs and films that could draw a larger East German audience.

15. Bisky and Wiedemann discuss how each genre (Western, romance, police procedural/detective story, drama, musical) meets differing viewer desires based on questions of age, gender, and class. Their research is, in part, an appeal to official institutions like the Central Committee and the *Hauptverwaltung Film* to support rather than limit the variety of generic texts available to the East German public. Their approach emphasizes the role of film and television as part of an East German culture of leisure, wherein the East German subject participates in the formation of the social fabric but during which she or he also must recuperate from a day's work. According to Bisky and Wiedemann, therefore, art (here, film) must be inherently entertaining for spectators to choose it as one leisure activity among many.

16. Contemporary reviews and viewers' responses were overwhelmingly positive. All viewer responses quoted in this paragraph were taken from the following newspaper reviews: "Fünf Mädchen, die auch zu uns gehören könnten: Werktätige im Gespräch über den Film *Alle meine Mädchen*"; "Mit Vergnügnen gesehen: *Tribüne*-Leser diskutieren *Alle meine Mädchen*"; "Sympathische Frauen und Mädchen aus unserer Mitte: Zuschauer diskutieren *Alle meine Mädchen*"; Heinz Kerstin, "Ein nichtfeministischer Frauenfilm"; and Margit Voss, "Vertrauen—Prüfstein für alle." This positive reception is also thematized in the film, during which the brigade, along with Ralf's boss and another co-worker, are shown attending the studio screening. The women, as well as Ralf and his co-workers,

are emotionally affected by the film and are shown smiling, some with tears in their eyes.

17. Both Ilse Nagelschmidt and Hildegard Maria Nickel pay special attention to the disproportionate number of women working low-wage jobs requiring few qualifications. They argue that this was a result of the SED's "Muttipolitik" and the naturalization of women as *reproducers* (i.e., primary caregivers, who would miss more work for reasons such as the *Babyjahr* and child sickness), as well as women's choices not to pursue advanced training while working full-time and performing a second shift in the home. See Nagelschmidt "Frauenliteratur der siebziger Jahre . . ." 65 and Nickel "Geschlechtertrennung" 11–12.

18. See Laura Mulvey's "Visual Pleasure and Narrative Cinema" and "Afterthoughts," Kaja Silverman's "Lost Objects and Mistaken Subjects," and Mary Ann Doane's "Film and the Masquerade."

19. Gaines, "Women and Representation" 81–83; Kaplan, "Aspects of British Feminist Film Theory" 54.

20. While participating in the DEFA Summer Film Institute in July 2003 at the University of Massachussetts-Amherst, I took part in a discussion that dealt specifically with artistic assumptions about the viewing audience. Several DEFA scholars and one former DEFA director in attendance suggested that the studios assumed a nonsegmented audience, that is, that DEFA was not creating texts with an elite or sub-audience in mind, but rather on both a utopian and a mainstreaming level, assumed a homogeneous audience with what could be considered mainstream textual expectations in terms of narrative and identificatory structures.

21. Bisky and Wiedemann present research that suggests that "female viewers find more affinities and motivations from the films they watch than male viewers do." While they argue against interpreting this

as indicative that women are *a priori* more influenced by films than men, they do suggest that more attention should be paid to "different interests and needs of male and female viewers. One should ask, therefore, if these differing interests and needs are being and could be better met by the variety of films offered to the viewing population" (*Der Spielfilm* 107).

22. Gaines, "Women and Representation" 83. Gaines begins her essay with a discussion of feminist critiques of pornography and focuses on arguments made by psychoanalytic and counter-cinema theorists (Mulvey, Johnston) who directly oppose classical conventions in order to withhold the indulgent pleasures of voyeuristic "looking" and narrative closure. Gaines argues that these approaches, following the examples of Godard and Brecht in attempting to revolutionize the cinema, demand the creation of a new language of desire made contingent on the destruction of "male" pleasure. But, she argues, in attempting to destroy spectator identification and create a critically distant viewer, these approaches neglect the possible political and utopian impulses of fantasy and pleasure (81–82).

23. Gaines, "Women and Representation" 84.

24. What I am teasing out in this chapter are the ways in which this film utilizes cinematic practices that have been defined as particularly "feminist," and how these practices are specifically related to questions of viewer pleasure. This is especially important considering that the film has often been referred to as "feminist," although the women working on the film have, sometimes vehemently, resisted such a label.

25. Rich, "Compulsory Heterosexuality and Lesbian Existence" 192.

26. Ibid.

27. Rich is concerned in her essay with three things: "the bias of compulsory het-

erosexuality" wherein lesbian experience is discursively constructed as "deviant" and "abhorrent," or "is simply rendered invisible"; the reasons and means by which "women's choice of women as passionate comrades, life partners, co-workers, lovers" has been invalidated or made invisible by being "forced into hiding"; and "the virtual neglect of lesbian existence in a wide range of writings, including feminist scholarship" ("Compulsory Heterosexuality and Lesbian Existence" 178).

28. Hillhouse, "Out of the Closet Behind the Wall" 587–588.

29. Ibid., 587.

30. McLellan, "Glad to be Gay Behind the Wall" 108; Hillhouse, "Out of the Closet Behind the Wall" 589.

31. Kuzniar, *The Queer German Cinema* 6.

32. Brückner "Women's Films Are Searches for Traces" 87.

33. See especially *Sun Seekers; Beschreibung eines Sommers* [*Description of a Summer*] (dir. Ralf Kirsten, 1963); *Divided Heaven; Berlin um die Ecke* [*Berlin Around the Corner*] (dir. Gerhard Klein, 1965); *Trace of Stones;* and *Lachtauben weinen nicht* [*Laughing Doves Don't Cry*] (dir. Ralf Kirsten, 1979).

34. Unlike most Hollywood films of the period, the space of the factory, specifically work on the assembly line, is prominently featured in *All My Girls*. A handful of Hollywood films actually do represent women in this kind of environment, including the contemporaries of *All My Girls, An Officer and a Gentleman* (dir. Taylor Hackford, 1982) and *Norma Rae* (dir. Martin Ritt, 1981). One popular sitcom, *Laverne and Shirley*, also portrayed its female protagonists as manual laborers. However, as I will argue shortly, the space of the factory is either downplayed in relation to the women's romantic interests or competes strongly with the "labor" aspects of the films.

35. I have already mentioned two of the most popular and important DEFA films in which the dominant space of film is the factory: *Trace of Stones* and *Berlin Around the Corner*. In both cases the protagonists are exclusively male. Two other DEFA films of the same period that illustrate women's manual labor are *On Probation* and *The Bicycle* (see chapter two). While *The Bicycle* emphasizes the role of unskilled labor in Susanne's alienation, it is a secondary concern in *On Probation*'s questioning of Nina's emancipation and self-fulfillment, and is therefore less pertinent to the development of the protagonist and viewer identification.

36. See especially Ina Merkel's . . . *und Du, Frau and der Werkbank!* When women are shown as part of the production process, Merkel argues, they are typically young women, who are constructed as gender-free. That is, they are neither "women" nor "men," but rather "workers," who "are desexualized . . . as comrades" (70).

37. The working title of the film was *Bewährungsprobe* [*On Probation*] before it was changed to *All My Girls*.

38. Anita's overt hostility (and covert interest) in Kerstin reveals the contradiction more clearly: while the "worker's and peasants' state" glorifies labor as the means "to widen, to enrich, [and] to promote the existence of the labourer," it simultaneously uses labor as a form of "political power . . . the organized power of one class [here, the Party] for oppressing another [here, its resistant subjects]" (Marx, *Manifesto of the Communist Party* 485, 490).

39. The use of labor as punishment is an occasional focus of critique in DEFA films, beginning with the rabbit-films of the 1960s. In *Karla* it is a former journalist who, after Stalin's death, wanted to write about the crimes of Stalin but was hindered. For him, labor is both a kind of self-induced punishment and refuge from the contradictions of a society that is based on

dialectical critique. In *Lot's Wife*, Katrin is sentenced to work for two years in a factory as a punishment for stealing. The critique of this practice in *Lot's Wife* comes from the only other teacher in the school who is willing to ponder why Katrin is driven to steal in the first place, rather than provide her with empty, hypocritical advice. In these films, the characters are ultimately shipped off to factories, and the viewer is left to wonder about their experiences.

40. In this respect, *All My Girls* particularly resembles the feminist films of West Germany. In *ReDuPers*, the female photography collective plays a discursive role similar to that of the collective in *All My Girls*: cooperatively comparing and combining their art—as a social, political, aesthetic act—they experience the emancipatory possibilities of camaraderie. In contrast, as Edda photographs and develops alone, her acts are broken down into repetitive movements—art becomes alienated labor—and are accompanied by a voice-over that describes the material specificity of that labor, the production and reproduction of everyday life. In one printing scene, Edda's work is accompanied by the (extra-)diegetic sound of an East German broadcast in celebration of International Women's Day, making the connections between East and West, the "holes in the Wall" as Edda calls them, particularly obvious.

41. Gusner, Interview.

42. cf. note 16.

43. It may be a stretch to call this an "orgy"; perhaps "group sex" is more applicable. Regardless, given taboos against representing any explicit sex on screen, the sex itself is absent—only hinted at. The scene, while chaste, emphasizes the erotic attraction and intimate attachments between the women (and more marginally, Ralf), and Anita's "dance of the veils" functions as an overt metaphor for the sex we are not allowed to witness. Anita's dance is

also the most obvious allusion in the film to Chytilová's *Daisies*.

44. Rich, "Compulsory Heterosexuality and Lesbian Existence" 193, my emphasis.

45. Irigaray, *The Sex Which is Not One* 63. Irigaray's interrogation of female sexuality occurs in the context of her critique of psychoanalytic theory, wherein she emphasizes the feminist need to "encourage a *precritical* attitude toward analytic theory" (63). Unlike Rich, Irigaray is more focused on female erogenous zones, but she mirrors Rich in her assertion of the multiplicity inherent in female sexuality (64).

46. For an interesting discussion of women's simultaneous identification and voyeuristic enjoyment of pornographic images, see Gaines, "Women and Representation" 84–85.

47. In *Her Third* a similarly charged scene takes place between the main character, Margit, and her best friend, Lucie. As Margit tries on wigs and talks of desiring Hrdlitschka, Lucie moves closer to her. Margit stands up, and they caress and kiss before Lucie goes home. In *Until Death Do Us Part*, Sonja leaves Jens and spends the night with Tilly, her best friend, one evening. After some wine, they jump into bed and pretend it's their wedding night, though there is no kissing or fondling as in the other two films.

48. Although *Her Third* also limits women's homoerotic desire to a brief, albeit provocative, kiss, the film's ending can thus be read in two ways. As argued in the preface, it undermines the "happy ending" as such, by refusing narrative closure. In addition, by literally framing the two women, Margit and Lucie, as the final couple, a queer reading would suggest that Hrdlitschka is the only thing standing (or lying) between them.

49. The pleasure the two women experience during their homoerotic performance is in direct contrast to Sonja's real marriage to Jens, who continues to physi-

cally and emotionally abuse her regardless of his success at work and in reaction to her desire to return to work.

50. We know that Marie's brigade is exceptionally productive, as evidenced by her pointing out to Ralf the awards they have received, which are hanging on her office wall.

51. As already discussed, Engler argues that East German manual laborers actually had no use for the Party (see *Die Ost-deutschen*, chapter one, note 44). He also discusses the precariousness of Party membership, which he sees as a main reason for workers' reluctance to join the SED in the first place (191–92).

52. In the following chapter I deal more explicitly with feminist debates in documentary theory regarding the negotiation of power hierarchies in the documentary process and collaboration with one's documentary object.

53. The lyrics to the song describe how, if one bird acts, the others follow suit: "Alle meine Entchen / schwimmen auf dem See, schwimmen auf dem See, / Köpfchen in das Wasser, Schwänzchen in die Höh'. // Alle meine Gänschen / watscheln durch den Grund, watscheln durch den Grund, / Suchen in dem Tümpel, werden kugelrund. // Alle meine Hühner / scharren in dem Stroh, scharren in dem Stroh, / Finden sie ein Körnchen, sind sie alle froh. // Alle meine Täubchen / gurren auf dem Dach, gurren auf dem Dach, / Fliegt eins in die Lüfte, fliegen alle nach." http://www.kleinkind-online.de/seiten/kinderlieder/index.htm.

54. Regarding the hierarchy of voices in documentary, see Sonja Michel, Bill Nichols, and Penny Summerfield, as well as Diane Waldman and Janet Walker's volume of collected essays.

55. Ralf's position at the beginning of the film is one of "no taboos" and is based on his belief that documentary filmmakers must show viewers the truth of the world,

regardless of people's feelings or of social or political taboos. He supports his position by referring to a Chilean documentarist who filmed his own murder as a "revolutionary." However, after the orgy sequence, Ralf decides to take Kerstin's critique to heart, deciding in the end to leave the footage of the argument in Marie's office out of the final cut.

56. De Lauretis, *Alice Doesn't* 118.

57. Ibid.

58. Ibid., 119.

59. While *All My Girls* is not a mythical tale, it does complicate the mythical status of labor in the GDR and the common association of the laborer with the male subject.

60. De Lauretis, *Alice Doesn't* 127–128, 129.

61. Ibid.

62. Engler has discussed the contradictory position of the "middle" and "upper" classes in the GDR, arguing that while it was likely that the intelligentsia would have somewhat higher salaries, slightly better apartments, and more access to consumer goods, their status as "workers" was constantly in question, a situation that led to a significant amount of political anxiety on their part. He argues that the official mistrust of the intelligentsia in a "worker's and peasants' state" required a level of political conformity and discipline that was not required of the workers and farmers themselves. While artists did achieve certain privileges as a result of national and international recognition, making them in some respects "untouchable," they also stood outside the "everyday" of the worker/farmer and were subject to the mistrust of the state, regardless of Party affiliation (*Die Ostdeutschen* 190–196).

63. Elke Schieber emphasizes the consistent lack of women directors at DEFA, while pointing out that women tended to work primarily as artistic directors, editors, make-up and costume artists. See "Anfang

vom Ende oder Kontinuität des Argwohns (1980–89)." During my personal interview with Tamara Trampe, she admitted to having originally chosen a male documentary director for the film *All My Girls*, Heinz Brinkmann, who had filmed an early documentary film about female workers in Berlin. Unfortunately, DEFA refused her choice, since this would have been Brinkmann's first feature film, and instead assigned Iris Gusner as director of the film, a choice that both Trampe and Kotte were unhappy with. All of the information regarding Tamara Trampe's and Gabrielle Kotte's participation in the making of *All My Girls* is based on my personal interview with Trampe.

64. Trampe, Interview.

65. Marx, *The German Ideology* 159.

66. This seems to be a genuinely Marxist attempt, on the part of the filmmaking collective, to eradicate the division of physical/mental labor in the GDR through their filmmaking practice: "The transformation, through the division of labour, of personal powers (relationships) into material powers, cannot be dispelled by dismissing the general idea of it from one's mind, but can only be abolished by the individuals again subjecting these material powers to themselves and abolishing the division of labour. This is not possible without community. Only in community [with others has each] individual the means of cultivating his gifts in all directions; only in the community, therefore, is personal freedom possible" (Marx, *The German Ideology* 197).

67. Gusner, Interview.

68. Heino Brandes, qtd. in Jordan "Die frühen Jahre" 33. *Destinies of Women* certainly idealizes labor, though primarily through melodramatic generic conventions. For one female character, Renate, labor becomes part of her period of incarceration, teaching her the benefits of labor by incorporating her as an individual who has strayed into the utopian produc-

tive force of the collective. In one scene in particular, the mise-en-scène of her hard at work is combined with an extra-diegetic soundtrack of women's voices singing the blessings of work and socialism.

69. In the essay "Classical Hollywood Cinema: Narrational Principles and Procedures," David Bordwell suggests that "commonplaces like 'transparency' and 'invisibility' are on the whole unhelpful in specifying the narrational properties of the classical film. Very generally, we can say that classical narration tends to be omniscient, highly communicative, and only moderately self-conscious" (22). He argues that most classical films contain only codified moments of self-consciousness—in the credit sequence and the first few opening shots, in establishing shots, camera movements out from or in to significant objects, symbolic dissolves, or in musicals when characters sing directly to the viewer. "Most important is the tendency of the classical film to render narrational omniscience through spatial *omnipresence*" (24). However, as I have shown, *All My Girls*'s consistent problematization of the filmmaker's role as narrator/editor self-consciously questions the assumed omnipotence of the film's narrative.

70. Regarding closure, Bordwell argues that the principles of linearity and causality structure the narratives in classical Hollywood cinema, which necessarily leads either to a logical wrap-up, or to a generally arbitrary readjustment of the world knocked awry during the course of the plot ("Classical Hollywood Cinema" 20–21). He argues, however, that this closure, when perceived as forced, especially when certain strains of the plot remain unresolved, might be considered more of a "pseudo-closure" (22). If *All My Girls* offers the viewer any kind of closure, then it is a kind of pseudo-closure, in that it shows both the loss of Kerstin and her replacement by the new girl. This replacement does not, however,

imply a happy ending or a disavowal of that loss. In fact, it is the arrival of the new girl that instigates Anita's emotional outburst of remorse and guilt, making Kerstin's absence terribly present for the women on screen and for the viewer.

71. In her discussion of feminist documentary filmmaking practices, Sonya Michel quotes Loraine Gray as having attempted to create such an atmosphere in her film *With Babies and Banners* (1978). As Michel argued, the "talking heads" technique can be an important and critical way of creating oral history. This makes *All My Girls* even more interesting, given that the female collective talks, argues, and discusses only in the space of the factory: on the line, in the break room, and in Marie's office.

72. Focusing on melodramas of the early 1950s, Jackie Byars argues that the Working Woman and the Woman Alone were often conflated, which had not occurred in the films of the 1930s and 40s (*All That Hollywood Allows* 89). The real danger of the Working Woman/Woman Alone, Byars suggests, is best illustrated by Alice Tippet in *A Place in the Sun* (1951) and Blanche Dubois in *A Streetcar Named Desire* (1951), who conflate the Working Woman/Woman Alone with the promiscuous woman and the whore (100–104). While women in the 1970s are not portrayed as necessarily promiscuous, they are Women Alone who challenge "the notion that the family is both 'natural' and sacred, a notion still dominant, even in the face of newly changed circumstances" (101). In *Alice Doesn't Live Here Anymore, An Officer and a Gentleman, An Unmarried Woman,* and *Working Girl,* the films' resolutions reincorporate an independent working woman into the structure of the traditional nuclear family, thereby resolving the dangers associated with the Woman Alone.

73. Wood, "Images and Women" 337.

74. Ibid., 339. One exception would be *Norma Rae* (dir. Martin Ritt, 1981),

in which Sally Field plays a cotton mill worker who, with the help of a communist Jew from New York City, tries to start up a union. Unfortunately, the film spends much of its time emphasizing her romantic relationships, her role as a mother, and her individual struggle, rather than focusing on the collective. The film partially succeeds in representing the unionization struggle through the figure of Norma Rae in a way similar to Ken Loach's *Bread and Roses* (2001). Another possible example would be *Silkwood* (dir. Mike Nichols, 1983), based on the life of a technical worker at a nuclear power plant, who becomes involved with the union after she and another co-worker are exposed to radiation. Similar to *Norma Rae*, *Silkwood* does not focus on the collective struggle for justice, but rather on Karen Silkwood's personal struggle at work (with sexual advances from her male co-workers and with radiation exposure) and at home (with a live-in boyfriend who resents her activism, a live-in girlfriend who is in love with her, and three children who live in another state with her ex-husband.) Ultimately, the film is about an individual woman who is fighting against unbeatable odds.

75. While many of the West German films mentioned earlier in this chapter do emphasize women's agency (or lack thereof) in the factory space, those films are not feature films and would be categorized as feminist labor documentaries. The East European films already discussed— Forman's *Loves of a Blonde*, Mészáros' *Riddance* and the films of confinement—do not engage female collective agency within the space of labor at all, focusing instead on issues of isolation and institutional containment.

76. As noted above, many feminist historians point out that women's lack of agency was predominantly due to pay discrimination and women's (in)ability to enter into leadership and management po-

sitions. See Behrend, Dölling, Hornig and Steiner, Ehrhardt, Nagelschmidt, Nickel, and Röth.

77. Gusner, Interview.

4. REAL WOMEN: *GOODBYE TO WINTER* AND THE DOCUMENTARY WOMEN'S FILM

1. See Bill Nichols's *Introduction to Documentary*.

2. Winston, "Documentary: I Think We Are in Trouble" 21.

3. See Thomas Heimann, "Von Stahl und Menschen" 119, and Hans-Jörg Rother, "Auftrag: Propaganda."

4. Jordan, "Die frühen Jahre" 33.

5. Heino Brandes, qtd. in Jordan "Die frühen Jahre" 33.

6. For a discussion of the aesthetic constraints placed on DEFA, see Heimann, as well as Günter Jordan's "Die frühen Jahre 1946–52" and "Von Perlen und Kieselsteinen."

7. See Berghahn, "East German Cinema after Unification," and Feinstein, *The Triumph of the Ordinary*.

8. Gal's analysis of the semiotic fluidity of the public/private distinction is especially pertinent here.

9. Schieber, "Im Dämmerlicht der Perestroika" 186. The work of Gitta Nickel would be representative of the opposite trend. See also Schreiber, "Zeit der verpassten Möglichkeiten 1970 bis 1980."

10. Schreiber, "Zeit der verpassten Möglichkeiten 1970 bis 1980" 169, 171.

11. Lesage, "The Political Aesthetics of the Feminist Documentary Film" 223–224.

12. Ibid., 233.

13. Michel, "Feminism, Film, and Public History" 238, Lesage, "The Political Aesthetics of the Feminist Documentary Film" 230. The talking-heads technique is present in most of the documentary women's films already mentioned and can also be found in literary form in the very popular protocols compiled in the 1970s

and 80s. See especially Wander, Lambrecht, Müller, and Schmidt.

14. For an extensive analysis of these often contradictory official images of women, see Merkel.

15. See especially the work of the Personal Narratives Group.

16. Scott, "Experience" 63.

17. Smith and Watson, "Situating Subjectivity in Women's Autobiographical Practices" 12.

18. Summerfield, "Dis/composing the Subject" 91–92.

19. Ibid., 99.

20. Davies, "Collaboration and the Ordering Imperative in Life Story Production" 3.

21. Ibid., 8.

22. For a discussion on the hierarchy of voices in documentary constructed around the interview, see Nichols, *Introduction to Documentary* 54–56.

23. Mulvey, "Afterthoughts on 'Visual Pleasure and Narrative Cinema' . . ." 64.

24. Davies, "Collaboration and the Ordering Imperative in Life Story Production" 4.

25. Christina Schenk, "Zum Politik und Feminismusverständnis ostdeutscher Frauen" 61–63.

26. *Aktuelle Kamera* was the state-owned and -run television news station in the GDR.

27. Christine's *me'* is a rural pronunciation of *mir*, which is often inserted for *we* [*wir*] or one [*man*]. In English, the typical usage would correspond to a general *you*, since *one* is rarely used conversationally: "*You* wanted to enjoy *your* life, *you* wanted to enjoy *your* freedom."

28. For analyses of the treatment and socialization of the mentally ill in the

GDR see Klaus-Peter Becker and Robert Greenberg, Greg Eghiagian, Sabine Gries, and Gisela Helwig.

29. Wander, *Guten Morgen, du Schöne* 1.

30. See especially *Berlin—Schönhauser Corner* and *Born in '45*.

31. The most infamous *Jugendwerkhof* was in Torgau, Sachsen, where youth were regularly beaten and subjected to isolation treatment, sometimes for a week or longer. For a brief introduction to Torgau's work camp, see the homepage of the *Initiativgruppe Geschlossener Jugendwerkhof Torgau*. For a more extensive study of the *Jugendwerkhof* in the former GDR, see Gerhard Jörns.

CONCLUSION: AFTER THE FALL

1. Rentschler, "Predecessors" 213–215.

2. Ibid., 213.

3. Cook, Koepnick, and Prager, "Introduction: The Berlin School—Under Observation" 1, 3.

4. Ibid., 7–8, 14.

5. Ibid., 12.

6. Augé, *Non-Places: Introduction to an Anthropology of Supermodernity* 37, 103–105.

7. My own work on two post-*Wende* films, *Good Bye, Lenin!* (dir. Wolfgang Becker, 2003) and *The Lives of Others* (dir. Florian Henckel von Donnersmarck, 2006) reveals that post-unification representations of East German femininity continue to serve either as a radical critique of, or a reactionary support for, liberal democratic memories of socialism (Creech, "A Few Good Men"). See also Bammer, Betts, Bisky, Hein, Lindenberger, Maron, Staud, and Wierling.

DEFA Filmography

The DEFA Film Library at University of Massachusetts-Amherst houses an extensive collection of 35mm and 16mm prints, DVDs, books, periodicals, and articles. The following DEFA films are available for rental or purchase through the DEFA Film Library.

DEFA Film Library
502 Herter Hall
University of Massachusetts
161 Presidents Drive
Amherst, MA 01003-9312
Tel: 413-545-6681
Fax: 413-577-3808
defa@german.umass.edu
umass.edu/defa

Alle meine Mädchen. Dir. Iris Gusner. DEFA, 1979.

Berlin - Ecke Schönhauser. Dir. Gerhard Klein. DEFA, 1957.

Berlin um die Ecke. Dir. Gerhard Klein. DEFA, 1965.

Beschreibung eines Sommers. Dir. Ralf Kirsten. DEFA, 1963.

Beunruhigung, Die. Dir. Lothar Warneke. DEFA, 1982.

Bis daß der Tod euch scheidet. Dir. Heiner Carow. DEFA, 1979.

Bürgschaft für ein Jahr. Dir. Hermann Zschoche. DEFA, 1981.

Coming Out. Dir. Heiner Carow, 1989.

Dritte, Der. Dir. Egon Günther. DEFA, 1972.

Ernst Thälmann: Sohn seiner Klasse. Dir. Kurt Maetzig, 1954.

Ernst Thälmann: Führer seiner Klasse. Dir. Kurt Maetzig, 1955.

Fahrrad, Das. Dir. Evelyn Schmidt. DEFA, 1982.

Frauenschicksale. Dir. Slatan Dudow. DEFA, 1952.

Geteilte Himmel, Der. Dir. Konrad Wolf. DEFA, 1964.

Jahrgang '45. Dir. Jürgen Böttcher. DEFA, 1965.

Kaninchen bin ich, Das. Dir. Kurt Maetzig. DEFA, 1965.

Karla. Dir. Hermann Zschoche. DEFA, 1965/66.

Lachtauben weinen nicht. Dir. Ralf Kirsten. DEFA 1979.

Leben und Weben. Dir. Volker Koepp. DEFA, 1981.

Legende von Paul und Paula, Die. Dir. Heiner Carow. DEFA, 1973.

Lots Weib. Dir. Egon Günther. DEFA, 1965.

Mädchen in Wittstock. Dir. Volker Koepp. DEFA, 1975.

Sie. Dir. Gitta Nickel. DEFA, 1970.

Sonnensucher. Dir. Konrad Wolf. DEFA, 1958.

Spur der Steine. Dir. Frank Beyer. DEFA, 1965.

Stapellauf. Dir. Alfons Machalz. DEFA, 1956.

Stars. Dir. Jürgen Böttcher. DEFA, 1963.

Versteck, Das. Dir. Frank Beyer. DEFA, 1979.

Wäscherinnen. Dir. Jürgen Böttcher. DEFA, 1972.

Wieder in Wittstock. Dir. Volker Koepp. DEFA, 1976.

Winter adé. Dir. Helke Misselwitz. DEFA, 1988.

Wir von ESDA. Dir. Gitta Nickel. DEFA, 1976.

Wittstock III. Dir. Volker Koepp. DEFA, 1977.

Wittstock, Wittstock. Dir. Volker Koepp. BRD, 1997.

Works Cited

ARCHIVAL SOURCES

Bundesarchiv, Berlin (BA Berlin)
HV Film   DR1 14856a, DR1 14922,
    DR1 14992a, DR1 12856

**Bundesarchiv-Filmarchiv,
Berlin (BA Film)**
Newspaper clippings and *Abnahme*
[approval] files for DEFA films

**DEFA Betriebsarchiv (BA
Berlin DR117)**
Files A/0100a, 0204, 1155, 3081, 3109,
    6685, 7882, 8575, 14922

**Stiftung Archiv der Parteien und
Massenorganisationen der DDR im
Bundesarchiv, Berlin (SAPMO)**
Büro Kurt Hager   DY30
    IVB2/906/80, DY30 IVB2/906/84,
    DY30 IVB2/906/94–95, DY30
    IVB2/2024/94–95

ZK Kultur
"Einschätzung des Spielfilms *Bürgschaft
    für ein Jahr* zur staatlichen Zulassung."
    Abteilung Künstlerische Produktion.
    June 10, 1981. BA Film, Abnahme file,
    Protokoll Nr. 185/81.
"Einschätzung des Spielfilms *Lots Weib*.
    Abteilung Künstlerische Produktion.

May 26, 1965. BA Film, Abnahme file,
    Protokoll Nr. A/0100a.
"Kurzprotokoll über das Auswer-
    tungsgespräch zum DEFA-Film
    Bürgschaft für ein Jahr." Abteilung
    Wissenschaft und Information. Jan. 19,
    1983. BA Film, Abnahme file, Protokoll
    Nr. 185/81.
Mäde, Hans Dieter. "Stellungnahme zur
    Stattlichen Abnahme des Films *Alle
    meine Mädchen*." Aug. 13, 1979. Proto-
    koll Nr. 186/79.
———. "Stellungnahme zur Staatlichen
    Abnahme des Films *Bürgschaft für ein
    Jahr*." May 25, 1981. BA Film, Abnahme
    file, Protokoll Nr. 185/81.
———. "Stellungnahme zum Film
    Das Fahrrad." Sept. 11, 1981. BA
    Film, Abnahme file, Protokoll Nr.
    348/81.
Mäde, Hans Dieter, et al. Protokoll: Stu-
    dioabnahme *Bürgschaft für ein Jahr*. 13
    May 1981.
Müller, R. "Einschätzung des
    DEFA-Spielfilms *Das Fahrrad* zum
    staatlichen Zulassungsverfahren am
    25. September 1981." Sept. 23, 1981.
    BA Film, Abnahme file, Protokoll Nr.
    348/81.

PUBLISHED SOURCES AND FILMS

9 Leben. Dir. Maria Speth. Germany, 2001.

Abschied von Gestern. Dir. Alexander Kluge. West Germany, 1966.

Agde, Günther, ed. *Kahlschlag. Das 11. Plenum des ZK der SED 1965. Studien und Dokumente.* Berlin: Aufbau, 2000.

Alice Doesn't Live Here Anymore. Dir. Martin Scorsese. USA, 1974.

Allan, Seán, and John Sandford, eds. *DEFA: East German Cinema, 1946–1992.* New York: Berghahn, 1999.

Allan, Seán, and Sebastian Heiduschke, eds. *Re-Imagining DEFA: East German Cinema in its National and Transnational Contexts.* Oxford: Berghahn, 2016.

Alle meine Mädchen. Dir. Iris Gusner. DEFA, 1979.

Allseitig reduzierte Persönlichkeit, Die [ReDuPers]. Dir. Helke Sander. BRD, 1978.

Amants, Les. Dir. Louis Malle. France, 1958.

Anderson, Edith, ed. *Blitz aus heiterem Himmel.* Rostock: Hinstorff, 1975.

Artisten unter der Zirkuskuppel: ratlos. Dir. Alexander Kluge. West Germany, 1968.

Augé, Marc. *Non-Places: Introduction to an Anthropology of Supermodernity.* New York: Verso, 1995.

Bahr, Gisela. "Film and Consciousness: The Depiction of Women in East German Movies." *Gender and German Cinema: Feminist Interventions.* Vol I. *Gender and Representation in New German Cinema.* Ed. Sandra Frieden et al. Providence: Berg, 1993. 125–140.

Bammer, Angelika. "The American Feminist Reception of GDR Literature (With a Glance at West Germany)." *GDR Bulletin* 16.2 (1990): 18–24.

Barbara. Dir. Christian Petzold. Germany, 2012.

Barnouw, Erik. *Documentary: A History of the Non-Fiction Film.* New York: Oxford University Press, 1974.

Barrett, Michéle. Introduction. *The Origin of the Family, Private Property and the State.* Friedrich Engels. 1884. New York: Penguin, 1972.

Bathrick, David. *The Powers of Speech: The Politics of Culture in the GDR.* Lincoln: University of Nebraska Press, 1995.

Becker, Dorothea. *Zwischen Ideologie und Autonomie: Die DDR-Forschung über die deutsche Filmgeschichte.* Münster: LIT, 1990.

Becker, Klaus-Peter, and Robert A. Greenberg. *Educational Rehabilitation of the Handicapped in the German Democratic Republic and in the United States of America: An Overview.* New York: Pergamon, 1985.

Becker, Wieland, and Volker Petzold, eds. *Tarkowski trifft King Kong. Geschichte der Filmklubbewegung der DDR.* Berlin: Vistas, 2001.

Behrend, Hanna. "Frauenemanzipation made in GDR." Bütow and Stecker 32–49.

Bergfelder, Tim, Erica Carter, and Deniz Göktürk, eds. *The German cinema book.* London: British Film Institute, 2002.

Berghahn, Daniela. "East German Cinema after Unification." *German Cinema since Unification.* Ed. David Clarke. London: Continuum, 2006. 79–103.

———. *Hollywood Behind the Wall: The Cinema of East Germany.* New York: Manchester UP, 2005.

Berghahn, Daniela, and Alan Bance, eds. *Millennial Essays on Film and Other German Studies.* Oxford: Peter Lang, 2002.

Berlin - Ecke Schönhauser. Dir. Gerhard Klein. DEFA, 1957.

Berlin um die Ecke. Dir. Gerhard Klein. DEFA, 1965.

Beschreibung eines Sommers. Dir. Ralf Kirsten. DEFA, 1963.

Betts, Paul. "Remembrance of Things Past: Nostalgia in West and East Germany, 1980–2000." *Pain and Prosperity:*

Reconsidering Twentieth-Century German History. Ed. Paul Betts and Greg Eghigian. Stanford: Stanford UP, 2003. 178–273.

Beyer, Frank. Wenn der Wind sich dreht. Meine Filme, mein Leben. München: List, 2001.

Bis daß der Tod euch scheidet. Dir. Heiner Carow. DEFA, 1979.

Bisky, Jens. "Zonensucht: Kritik der neuen Ostalgie." Merkur 658 (Feb. 2004).

Bisky, Lothar and Dieter Wiedemann. Der Spielfilm. Rezeption und Wirkung. Berlin: Henschel, 1985.

Blunk, Harry. Die DDR in ihren Spielfilmen: Reproduktion und Konzeption der DDR-Gesellschaft im neueren DEFA-Gegenwartsspielfilm. München: Profil, 1984.

Bollinger, Stefan, and Fritz Vilmar. "Beiträge zur Zukunftsfähigkeit Deutschlands. Kritische Würdigung wichtiger sozial-kultureller Einrichtungen der DDR. Zur Einleitung." Die DDR war anders. Eine kritische Würdigung ihrer sozialkulturellen Einrichtungen. Berlin: Edition Ost, 2002.

Bordwell, David. "Classical Hollywood Cinema: Narrational Principles and Procedures." Narrative, Apparatus, Ideology: A Film Theory Reader. Ed. Philip Rosen. New York: Columbia UP, 1986. 17–34.

Brecht, Bertolt. "Theater for Pleasure or Theater for Instruction?" (1957) Brecht on Theater: The Development of an Aesthetic. Ed. John Willett. New York: Hill and Wang, 1964. 69–77.

Bread and Roses. Dir. Ken Loach. USA, 2001.

Bredel, Willi. Fünfzig Tage. Berlin: Verlag Neues Leben, 1950.

Brückner, Jutta. Interview with Marc Silberman (1982). Rpt. in Frieden et al., vol. 2, 253–58.

———. "Women's Films Are Searches for Traces" (1981). Rpt. in Rentschler 85–89.

Buck-Morss. Dreamworld and Catastrophe: The Passing of Mass Utopia in East and West. Cambridge: MIT, 2000.

Bürgschaft für ein Jahr. Dir. Hermann Zschoche. DEFA, 1981.

Bütow, Birgit, and Heide Stecker, eds. EigenArtige Ostfrauen: Frauenemanzipation in der DDR und den neuen Bundesländern. Theorie und Praxis der Frauenforschung, vol. 22. Bielefeld: Kleine, 1994.

Bullivant, Keith, Geoffrey Giles and Walter Pape, eds. Germany and Eastern Europe: Cultural Identities and Cultural Differences. Amsterdam: Rodopi, 1999.

Bundeszentrale für politische Bildung. Frauenbilder in den DDR-Medien. Medien-Beratung 2. Bonn: Bundeszentrale für politische Bildung, 1997.

———. Frauengestalten in Film und Fernsehen der DDR. Medien-Beratung 2. Bonn: Bundeszentrale für politische Bildung, 1997.

Butler, Judith. Gender Trouble: Feminism and the Subversion of Identity. New York: Routledge, 1990.

Byars, Jackie. All That Hollywood Allows: Re-Reading Gender in 1950s Melodrama. Chapel Hill: U of North Carolina P, 1991.

Byg, Barton. "GDR-Up: The Ideology of Universality in Long Term Documentary." New German Critique 82 (2001): 126–144.

———. "Introduction: Reassessing DEFA Today." Berghahn and Bance 1–23.

Carrière de Suzanne, La. Dir. Éric Rohmer, 1963.

Cheaper by the Dozen. Dir. Walter Lang. USA, 1950.

Claudius, Eduard. Menschen an unserer Seite. 1951. Berlin: Verlag Volk und Welt, 1953.

———."Vom schweren Anfang." Erzählungen. Berlin: Aufbau, 1951. 499–590.

Cléo de 5 à 7. Dir. Agnes Varda. France, 1962.

Cook, Roger F., Lutz Koepnick, and Brad Prager. "Introduction: The Berlin School—Under Observation." *Berlin School Glossary: An ABC of the New Wave in German Cinema*. Ed. Roger F. Cook et al. Chicago: Intellect, 2013. 1–25.

Cooke, Paul. *Representing East Germany Since Unification: From Colonization to Nostalgia*. New York: Berg, 2005.

Creech, Jennifer. "A Few Good Men: Gender, Ideology and Narrative Politics in *The Lives of Others* and *Good Bye, Lenin!*" *Women in German Yearbook* 25 (2009): 100–126.

Dalichow, Bärbel. "Die jüngste Regiegeneration der DEFA—Aufbruch oder Abgesang?" *Der DEFA-Film Erbe oder Episode?* Augenblick 14. Marburg: Schüren, 1993. 70–89.

Davidson, John E., and Sabine Hake, eds. *Take Two: Fifties Cinema in Divided Germany*. New York: Berghahn Books, 2007.

Davies, Carole Boyce. "Collaboration and the Ordering Imperative in Life Story Production." *De/Colonizing the Subject: the Politics of Gender in Women's Autobiography*. Ed. Sidonie Smith and Julia Watson. Minneapolis: U of Minnesota P, 1992. 3–19.

de Lauretis, Teresa. *Alice Doesn't: Feminism, Semiotics, Cinema*. Bloomington: Indiana UP, 1984.

Deutschland, bleiche Mutter. Dir. Helma Sanders-Brahms. West Germany, 1980.

Doane, Mary Ann. "Film and the Masquerade." Erens 41–57.

Dölling, Irene. "Die Bedeutung von Erwerbsarbeit für weibliche Identität in der ehemaligen DDR." *Differente Sexualitäten* 18.36 (1995): 40–52.

———. "We All Love Paula but Paul Is More Important to Us: Constructing a 'Socialist Person' Using the 'Femininity' of a Working Woman." *East German Film*. Spec. issue of *New German Critique* 82 (Winter 2001): 77–90.

Dritte, Der. Dir. Egon Günther. DEFA, 1972.

Eghigian, Greg. "The Psychologization of the Socialist Self: East German Forensic Psychology and its Deviants 1945–75." *German History* 22 (2004): 181–205.

Ehrhardt, Gisela. "Frauen und Karriere. Ein Rückblick auf die vermeintliche Chancengleichheit im Staatssozialismus." Schwarz and Zenner 120–131.

Eine Prämie für Irene. Dir. Helke Sander. BRD, 1971.

Emmerich, Wolfgang. *Kleine Literaturgeschichte der DDR*. Leipzig: Kiepenhauer, 1996.

Engels, Friedrich. *The Origin of the Family, Private Property and the State*. 1884. Tucker 734–759.

Engler, Wolfgang. *Die Ostdeutschen: Kunde von einem verlorenen Land*. Berlin: Aufbau, 2000.

———. "Strafgericht über die Moderne: Das 11. Plenum im historischen Rückblick." Agde 16–36.

Erens, Patricia, ed. *Issues in Feminist Film Criticism*. Bloomington: Indiana UP, 1990.

Es kommt darauf, sie zu verändern. Dir. Claudia von Alemann. BRD, 1973.

Et Dieu . . . créa la femme. Dir. Roger Vadim. France, 1959.

Fahrrad, Das. Dir. Evelyn Schmidt. DEFA, 1982.

Familiengesetzbuch der Deutschen Demokratischen Republik. 20 December 1965. Rpt. at http://www.verfassungen.de/de/ddr/familiengesetzbuch65.htm.

Fassbinder, Rainer Werner. *The Anarchy of the Imagination: Interviews, Essays, Notes*. Baltimore: Johns Hopkins UP, 1992.

Feinstein, Joshua. *The Triumph of the Ordinary: Depictions of Daily Life in the East German Cinema 1949–1989*. Chapel Hill: U of North Carolina P, 2002.

Femme mariée, Une. Dir. Jean-Luc Godard. France, 1964.

Femme est une femme, Une. Dir. Jean-Luc
Godard. France, 1961.

Forbes, Jill. "The French Novelle
Vague." *The Oxford Guide to Film
Studies.* Ed. John Hill and Pamela
Church Gibson. New York: Oxford
UP, 1998. 461–465.

Frauenschicksale. Dir. Slatan Dudow.
DEFA, 1952.

Frieden, Sandra et al, eds. *Gender and
German Cinema: Feminist Interventions.*
Vols. I and II. Providence: Berg, 1993.

Fröhlich, Margrit. "Behind the Curtain of
a State-Owned Film Industry: Women-
Filmmakers at the DEFA." Majer
O'Sickey and von Zadow 43–64.

"Fünf Mädchen, die auch zu uns gehören
könnten: Werktätige im Gespräch über
den Film *Alle meine Mädchen.*" *Freie
Presse* [Karl-Marx-Stadt] 18 Apr. 1980.

Gaines, Jane. "Women and Represen-
tation: Can We Enjoy Alternative
Pleasure?" *Jump Cut* 29 (1984). Rpt. in
Erens 75–92.

Gal, Susan. "A Semiotics of the Public/
Private Distinction." *Differences: A
Journal of Feminist Cultural Studies* 13.1
(2002): 77–95.

Gal, Susan and Gail Kligman. *The Politics
of Gender after Socialism: A Compara-
tive-Historical Essay.* Princeton: Princeton UP, 2000.

*Gesetz über den Mutter- und Kinderschutz
und die Rechte der Frau.* 1950. Rpt. at
http://www.verfassungen.de/de/ddr
/mutterkindgesetz50.htm.

Geteilte Himmel, Der. Dir. Konrad Wolf.
DEFA, 1964.

Goldberg, Henryk. "Iris Gusner: Des
Eigene und des Fremde." *DEFA:
Spielfilm-Regisseure und ihre* Kritiker.
Vol. 2. Ed. Rolf Richter. Berlin: Hen-
schel, 1983. 77–89.

Good, Jennifer. *Women Who Showed the
Way: Arbeiterinnen in DEFA Feature*

Film, 1946–1966. Diss. U of Massachusetts, 2005.

Gotsche, Otto. *Tiefe Furchen.* 1949. Halle:
Mitteldeutscher Verlag, 1960.

Gräf, Christel. Letter to Strafvollzugsanstalt Görlitz. 25 Mar. 1965. Stiftung
Archiv der Parteien und Massenorganisationen der DDR im Bundesarchiv, Berlin (SAPMO): DR 117 BA
A/0100a.

———. "Waren Ostfrauen wirklich an-
ders? Zur Darstellung von Frauen im
DEFA-Gegenwartsfilm." Pflügl and
Fritz, vol. 2., 107–17.

Green McGee, Laura. "'Ich wollte ewig
einen richtigen Film machen! Und
als es soweit war, konnte ich's nicht!'
The End Phase of the GDR in Films by
DEFA Nachwuchsregisseure." *German
Studies Review,* XXVI: 2 (May 2003).

Gries, Sabine. *Misslungene Kindheiten:
zum unsozialistischen Aufwachsen von
Kindern in der DDR.* Münster: Lit, 1994.

Günther, Egon. Personal Interview. 27
July 2003.

———. "Die verzauberte Welt. Nachden-
ken über Film und Politik." *Apropos:
Film 2000. Das Jahrbuch der DEFA-
Stiftung.* Ed. Ralf Schenk and Erika
Richter. Berlin: Verlag Das Neue Ber-
lin, 2000. 50–76.

Gusner, Iris. Interview. "*Alle meine Mäd-
chen:* Eröffnungsbeitrag des Nationalen
Spielfilmfestivals der DDR." *Sonntag*
[Berlin] 27 Apr. 1980.

Hake, Sabine. *German National Cinema.*
New York: Routledge, 2002.

Halle, Randall, and Reinhild Steingröver, eds. *After the Avant-Garde:
Contemporary German and Austrian
Experimental Film.* Rochester: Camden, 2008.

Hames, Peter. *The Czechoslovak New
Wave.* 2nd ed. New York: Wallflower,
2005.

Hanáková, Petra. "Voices From Another
World: Feminine Space and Masculine

Intrusion in *Sedmikrásky* and *Vrazda*
ing. Certa." Imre 63–77.

Harsch, Donna. *Revenge of the Domestic:
Women, the Family, and Communism in
the German Democratic Republic*. Princeton: Princeton UP, 2007.

Haskell, Molly. "The Woman's Film,"
*From Reverence to Rape: the Treatment
of Women in the Movies*. 2nd ed. Chicago: U of Chicago P, 1987. 153–88. Rpt.
in Thornham 20–30.

Heiduschke, Sebastian. *DEFA and Film
History*. New York: Palgrave, 2013.

Heimann, Thomas. "Von Stahl und Menschen." Jordan and Schenk 49–85.

Hein, Christoph. "Dritte Welt überall:
Ostdeutschland als Avantgarde der
Globalisierung . . . " *Die Zeit* 30 Septem-
ber 2004.

Hell, Julia. *Post-Fascist Fantasies: Psychoanalysis, History and the Literature
of East Germany*. Post-Contemporary
Interventions. Eds. Stanley Fish and
Fredric Jameson. Durham: Duke UP,
1997.

Helwig, Gisela. *Am Rande der Gesellschaft:
Alte und Behinderte in beiden deutschen
Staaten*. Köln: Verlag Wissenschaft und
Politik, 1980.

Hermand, Jost, and Marc Silberman, eds.
*Contentious memories: looking back at
the GDR*. New York: Peter Lang, 1998.

Hildebrandt, Karin. "Historischer Exkurs
zur Frauenpolitik der SED." Bütow and
Stecker 12–31.

Hillhouse, Raelynn J. "Out of the Closet
Behind the Wall: Sexual Politics and
Social Change in the GDR." *Slavic Re-
view* 49.4 (Winter 1990): 585–596.

Holzweißig, Gunter. *Zensur ohne Zensor:
Die SED-Informationsdiktatur*. Bonn:
Bouvier, 1997.

Hornig, Daphne and Christine Steiner.
"Der alltägliche Frauenk(r)ampf
zwischen Küche, Kirche und Kombi-
naten oder: ich weiß, es wird einmal ein
Wunder geschehen." *Mitteilungen aus*

der Kulturwissenschaftlichen Forschung
18:36 (1995): 55–79.

Hungerjahre in einem reichen Land. Dir.
Jutta Brückner. West Germany, 1979.

Imre, Anikó, ed. *East European Cinemas*.
New York: Routledge, 2005.

———. "Introduction: East European
Cinemas in New Perspectives." Imre
xi–xxvi.

In den Tag hinein. Dir. Maria Speth. Germany, 2001.

*Initiativgruppe Geschlossener Jugendwerk-
hof Torgau*. http://www.jugendwerk-
hof-torgau.de/index2.html.

Iordanova, Dina. *Cinema of the Other
Europe. The Industry and Artistry of East
Central European Film*. London: Wall-
flower, 2003.

Irigaray, Luce. *The Sex Which is Not One*.
1977. Trans. Catherine Porter. Ithaca:
Cornell UP, 1985.

Jahrgang '45. Dir. Jürgen Böttcher. DEFA,
1965.

Jörns, Gerhard. *Der Jugendwerkhof im
Jugendhilfesystem der DDR*. Göttingen:
Cuvillier, 1995.

Jordan, Günter. "Die frühen Jahre. 1946–
52." Jordan and Schenk 1–47.

———. "Von Perlen und Kieselsteinen.
Der DEFA-Dokumentarfilm von 1946
bis Mitte der 50er Jahre." Zimmermann
27–47.

Jordan, Günter, and Ralf Schenk. *Schwar-
zweiß und Farbe: DEFA-Dokumen-
tarfilme 1946–92*. Berlin: Jovis, 2000.

Jules & Jim. Dir. François Truffaut.
France, 1962.

Julia. Dir. Fred Zinnemann. USA,
1976/1977.

Jungnickel, Dirk. "Produktionsbedin-
gungen bei der Herstellung von
Kinospielfilmen und Fernsehfil-
men." *Filmland DDR: Ein Reader zu
Geschichte, Funktion und Wirkung der
DEFA*. Ed. Harry Blunk and Dirk Jung-
nickel. Köln: Verlag Wissenschaft und
Politik, 1990. 47–57.

Jürschik, Rudolf. "Erkundungen: Film-
bilder - Heldentypus - Alltag (1)." *Film
und Fernsehen* 4 (1981): 9–14.

Kaes, Anton. *From Hitler to Heimat: The
Return of History as Film*. Cambridge:
Harvard UP, 1989.

Kaninchen bin ich, Das. Dir. Kurt Maetzig.
DEFA, 1965.

Kaplan, E. Ann. "Aspects of British
Feminist Film Theory: A Critical
Evaluation of Texts by Claire Johnston
and Pam Cook." *Jump Cut* 2 (1974):
52–55.

———. *Motherhood and Representation:
The Mother in Popular Culture and
Melodrama*. New York: Routledge,
1992.

Kapczynski, Jennifer and Michael David
Richardson. *A New History of German
Cinema*. Rochester: Camden House,
2012.

Karla. Dir. Hermann Zschoche. DEFA,
1965/1966.

Kasman, Daniel. "Spatial Suspense: A
Conversation with Christian Petzold."
Notebook 16 October 2012 <http://
mubi.com/notebook/posts/spatial-
suspense-a-conversation-with-chris-
tian-petzold>.

Kerstin, Heinz. "Ein nichtfeministischer
Frauenfilm." *Frankfurter Rundschau* 9
June 1980.

Kleines politisches Wörterbuch. Berlin:
Dietz, 1978.

Kluge, Alexander. "On Film and the Public Sphere." 1979. *New German Critique*
24/25 (1981/82): 206–220.

———. "What Do the 'Oberhauseners'
Want?" 1962. Rentschler 10–13.

Kluge, Alexander and Oskar Negt.
*Öffentlichkeit und Erfahrung: Zur Or-
ganisationsanalyse von bürgerlicher und
proletarischer Öffentlichkeit*. Frankfurt
a.M.: Suhrkamp, 1972.

Knietzsch, Horst. "Helden gesucht!
DEFA-Spielfilme der Jahre 1983/84."
Prisma 16 (1985): 9–26.

———. "Versuche über das Glück: Zu
DEFA-Spielfilmen der Jahre 1986/87."
Prisma 19 (1990): 9–28.

Knight, Julia. *Women and the New German Cinema*. New York: Verso, 1992.

Kolano, Uta. *Kollektiv d'amour: Liebe, Sex,
und Partnerschaft in der DDR*. Berlin:
Jaron, 2012.

Königsdorf, Helga. *Der Lauf der Dinge*.
Berlin: Aufbau, 1982.

———. *Lichtverhältnisse*. 2nd ed. Berlin:
Aufbau, 1989.

———. *Respektloser Umgang*. Berlin:
Aufbau, 1986.

Kolinsky, Eva. "Gender and the Limits of
Equality in East Germany." *Reinventing
Gender: Women in Eastern Germany
since Unification*. Eds. Eva Kolinsky
and Hildegard Maria Nickel. London:
Frank Cass, 2003. 100–127.

Kramer, Karen Ruoff. "Representations of
Work in the Forbidden DEFA Films of
1965." Allan and Sandford 131–145.

Kristeva, Julia. "Women's Time." Rpt. in
*Feminisms: An Anthology of Literary
Theory and Criticism*. Ed. Robyn R.
Warhol and Diane Price Herndl. New
Brunswick: Rutgers UP, 1997. 443–462.

Kuhn, Annette. "Women's Genres: Melodrama, Soap Opera and Theory." Rpt.
in Thornham 146–156.

———. *Women's Pictures*. New York:
Verso, 1982.

Kuzniar, Alice A. *The Queer German Cinema*. Stanford: Stanford UP, 2000.

Lachtauben weinen nicht. Dir. Ralf
Kirsten, 1979.

Lambrecht, Christine. *Männerbekanntschaften: freimütige Protokolle*.
4th ed. Halle-Leipzig: Mitteldeutscher
V, 1986.

Landes, Joan B. "Further Thoughts on the
Public/Private Distinction." *Journal of
Women's History* 15.2 (Summer 2003):
28–39.

La Pointe Courte. Dir. Anges Varda.
France, 1954.

Laverne and Shirley. Dir. Gary Marshall. USA, 1976–1983.

Leben und Weben. Dir. Volker Koepp. DEFA, 1981.

Legende von Paul und Paula, Die. Dir. Heiner Carow. DEFA, 1973.

Lesage, Julia. "The Political Aesthetics of the Feminist Documentary Film." *Quarterly Review of Film Studies* 3.4 (1978). Rpt. in Erens 222–237.

Lewis, Alison. *Subverting Patriarchy: Feminism and Fantasy in the Works of Irmtraud Morgner.* Oxford: Berg, 1995.

Lim, Dennis. "Summoning Halcyon Days of Failed Ideals." *The New York Times* 7 December 2012 http://www.nytimes .com/2012/12/09/movies/christian-petzold-directs-barbara-starring -nina-hoss.html?ref=movies&_r=0.

Lindenberger, Thomas. "Die Diktatur der Grenzen." *Herrschaft und Eigen-Sinn in der Diktatur. Studien zur Gesellschaftsge-schichte der DDR.* Ed. Thomas Linden-berger. Köln: Böhlau, 1999. 51–101.

———. "Gewalt und Wahrheit: Verkehrte Welt in *Good Bye Lenin!*" *WerkstattGe-schichte* 2004, Nr. 37: 101–114.

Linville, Susan E. *Feminism, Film, Fas-cism: Women's Auto/biographical Film in Postwar Germany.* Austin: U of Texas P, 1998.

Lischke McNab, Ute. "Interview— Women, Film, and Writing in the GDR: Helga Schubert and the DEFA." Majer-O'Sickey and von Zadow 199–206.

Lohre, Mattias. "Zur Begrüßung den Schlüsselbund im Gesicht." 2005. http://www.das-parlament .de/2005/16/JugendimDialog/001 .html.

Loth, Rothraut. Letter to Arbeitsgruppe: "Roter Kreis." 1 Sept. 1965. Stiftung Archiv der Parteien und Massenorgan-isationen der DDR im Bundesarchiv, Berlin (SAPMO): DR 117 BA A/0100a.

Lots Weib. Dir. Egon Günther. DEFA, 1965.

Les Amants. Dir. Louis Malle. France, 1958.

Macht der Männer ist die Geduld der Frauen, Die. Dir. Cristina Perincioli, BRD, 1978.

Mädchen in Wittstock. Dir. Volker Koepp. DEFA, 1975.

Madonnen. Dir. Maria Speth. Germany, 2007.

Magnificent Seven, The. Dir. John Sturges. USA, 1960.

Majer-O'Sickey, Ingeborg, and Ingeborg von Zadow, eds. *Triangulated Visions. Women in Recent German Cin-ema.* Albany: State U of New York P, 1998.

Marciniak, Katarzyna. "Second World-ness and Transnational Feminist Prac-tices." Imre 3–20.

Maron, Monika. "Lebensentwürfe, Zeit-enbrüche: Vom Nutzen und Nachteil dunkler Brillen . . . ." *Süddeutsche Zei-tung* 13. September 2002.

Marx, Karl. *Economic and Philosophic Manuscripts of 1844.* Tucker 66–125.

———. *The German Ideology.* Tucker 146–200.

———. *Grundrisse.* Tucker 221–293.

———. *Manifesto of the Communist Party.* Tucker 469–500.

McCormick, Richard W. "Confronting German History: Melodrama, Dis-tantiation, and Women's Discourse in *Germany, Pale Mother.*" Frieden et al. vol. 2, 185–206.

McLellan, Josie. "Glad to be Gay Behind the Wall: Gay and Lesbian Activ-ism in 1970s East Germany." *History Workshop Journal* 74 (Autumn 2012): 105–130.

Merkel, Ina. . . . *und Du, Frau an der Werk-bank! Die DDR in den 50er Jahren.* Ber-lin: Elefanten, 1990.

Meurer, Hans Joachim. *Cinema and Na-tional Identity in a Divided Germany 1979–1989: The Split Screen.* Lewiston: Edwin Mellen, 2000.

Michel, Sonya. "Feminism, Film, and Public History." *Radical History Review* 25 (1981): 47–61. Rpt. in Erens 238–249.

Mihan, Hans-Rainer. "Die ganze Wahrheit - das ganze Vertrauen: Gedanken zum Gegenwartsspielfilm der DEFA (2)." *Film und Fernsehen* 9 (1982): 9–12.

———. "Sabine, Sunny, Nina und der Zuschauer: Gedanken zum Gegenwartsspielfilm der DEFA (1)." *Film und Fernsehen* 8 (1982): 9–12.

"Mit Vergnügen gesehen: *Tribüne*-Leser diskutieren *Alle meine Mädchen*." *Tribüne* [Berlin] 2 June 1980.

Monaco, James. *The New Wave: Truffaut, Godard, Chabrol, Rohmer, Rivette*. New York: Oxford UP, 1976.

Monticelli, Simona. "Italian post-war cinema and Neo-Realism." *The Oxford Guide to Film Studies*. Ed. John Hill and Pamela Church Gibson. New York: Oxford UP, 1998. 455–460.

Morgner, Irmtraud. *Leben und Abenteuer der Trobadora Beatriz nach Zeugnissen ihrer Spielfrau Laura*. 1976. München: DTV, 1994.

———. *Rumba auf einen Herbst*. Hamburg: Luchterhand, 1992.

Moving Images of East Germany: Past and Future of DEFA Film. Eds. Barton Byg and Betheny Moore. Harry and Helen Gray Humanities Program Ser. 12. Washington DC: American Institute for Contemporary German Studies and Johns Hopkins UP, 2002.

Müller, Christine. *James Dean lernt kochen*. 3rd ed. Frankfurt a.M.: Luchterhand, 1989.

Müller, Heinz. "Zeichen der Selbstbefreiung? Frauenschickale auf der Leinwand in Cannes '78." *Film und Fernsehen* 9 (1978): 40–43.

Mulvey, Laura. "Afterthoughts on "Visual Pleasure and Narrative Cinema" inspired by King Vidor's *Duel in the Sun* (1946)." *Visual and Other Pleasures*. London: Macmillan, 1989. 29–38.

———. "Visual Pleasure and Narrative Cinema." *Screen* 16.3 (1975): 6–18. Rpt. *The Sexual Subject: A Screen Reader in Sexuality*. New York: Routledge, 1992. 22–34.

Mushaben, Joyce Marie. "GDR Cinema De-/Reconstructed: An Introduction to the Forbidden Films." *GDR Bulletin* 19.1 (Spring 1993): 5–11.

Nagelschmidt, Ilse. "Frauenliteratur der siebziger Jahre als 'Brennspiegel' der Widersprüche und Ambivalenzen weiblicher Emanzipation in der DDR." Bütow and Stecker 63–74.

Naughton, Leonie. *That Was the Wild East*. Ann Arbor: U of Michigan P, 2002.

Neupert, Richard. *A History of the French New Wave Cinema*. Madison: U of Wisconsin P, 2007.

Nichols, Bill. *Introduction to Documentary*. Bloomington: Indiana UP, 2001.

Nickel, Hildegard Maria. "Geschlechtertrennung durch Arbeitsteilung: Berufs- und Familienarbeit in der DDR." *Feministische Studien* 8.1 (1990): 10–19.

———. "Women and Women's Policies in East and West Germany 1945–1999," *Social Transformation and the Family in Post-Communist Germany*. Ed. Eva Kolinsky. New York: St. Martin's, 1998. 23–56.

Norma Rae. Dir. Martin Ritt. USA, 1979.

"Oberhausen Manifesto." 1962.

O'Brien, Mary. *Reproducing the World: Essays in Feminist Theory*. Boulder: Westview, 1989.

Officer and a Gentleman, An. Dir. Taylor Hackford. USA, 1982.

Opgenoorth, Ernst. "Dokumentarfilm als Instrument der Propaganda in den 40er und 50er Jahren." Zimmermann 67–75.

Peppermint-Frieden. Dir. Marianne Rosenbaum. West Germany, 1983.

Personal Narratives Group. *Interpreting Women's Lives: Feminist Theory and Per-*

sonal Narratives. Bloomington: Indiana UP, 1989.

Pinkert, Anke. Film and Memory in East Germany. Bloomington: Indiana UP, 2008.

Pflügl, Helmut and Fritz, eds. Geteilte Himmel, Der: Höhepunkte des DEFA-Kinos, 1946–1992. Vols. 1 and 2. Vienna: Filmarchiv Austria, 2001.

Place in the Sun, A. Dir. George Stevens. USA, 1951.

Polizistin, Die. Dir. Andreas Dresen. Germany, 2000.

Rauhut, Michael. Beat in der Grauzone: DDR-Rock 1964 bis 1972 - Politik und Alltag. Berlin: Basisdruck, 1993.

———. "DDR-Beatmusik zwischen Engagement und Repression." Agde 52–63.

Reimann, Brigitte. Alles schmeckt nach Abschied: Tagebücher 1964–70. Berlin: Aufbau, 1998.

———. Ankunft im Alltag. Berlin: Aufbau, 1961.

Rentschler, Eric. Ministry of Illusion: Nazi Cinema and Its Afterlife. Cambridge: Harvard UP, 1996.

———. "Predecessors: The German Pre-history of the Berlin School." Berlin School Glossary: An ABC of the New Wave in German Cinema. Ed. Roger F. Cook et al. Chicago: Intellect, 2013. 213–221.

Rentschler, Eric, ed. West German Film-makers on Film: Voices and Visions. New York & London: Holmes & Meier, 1988.

Rich, Adrienne. "Compulsory Heterosexuality and Lesbian Existence." Powers of Desire: The Politics of Sexuality. Ed. Ann Snitow et al. New York: Monthly Review, 1983. 177–205.

Rich, B. Ruby. "She Says, He Says: The Power of the Narrator in Modernist Film Politics." Discourse 6 (1983): 31–46.

Richter, Rolf, ed. DEFA: Spielfilm-Regisseure und ihre Kritiker. Vol. 2. Berlin: Henschel, 1983.

Rinke, Andrea. "From Models to Misfits: Women in DEFA Films of the 1970's and 1980's." DEFA: East German Cinema, 1946–1992. Eds. Seán Allan and John Sandford. New York: Berghahn, 1999. 183–203.

———. "Eastside Stories: Singing and Dancing for Socialism." Film History 18.1 (2006): 73–87.

———. Images of Women in East German Cinema 1972–82. Socialist Models, Private Dreamers and Rebels. Lewiston: Edwin Mellen, 2006.

Rosenberg, Karen. "Goodbye to Winter: Women in the GDR. An Interview with Helke Misselwitz." International Documentary: the Newsletter of the International Documentary Association (Winter 1990): 4–9.

Röth, Ute. "Die Klassenlose Gretchenfrage. Über die Vereinbarkeit von Beruf und Familie." Schwarz and Zenner 132–144.

Rother, Hans-Jörg. "Auftrag: Propaganda. 1960 bis 1970." Jordan and Schenk 86–128.

Salecl, Renata. The Spoils of Freedom: Psychoanalysis and Feminism After the Fall of Socialism. New York: Routledge, 1994.

Sander, Helke. "Feminism and Film." 1977. Rentschler 75–81.

———. Interview. Marc Silberman. In Frieden et al. vol. 1, 163–165.

Sander, Helke, and R. Schlesier. "Die Legende von Paul und Paula: Eine frauenverachtende Schnulze aus der DDR." Frauen und Film 2 (Sept. 1974): 8–47.

Schenk, Christina. "Zum Politik und Feminismusverständnis ostdeutscher Frauen." Frauenleben—Frauenliteratur—Frauenkultur in der DDR der 70er und 80er Jahre. Ed. Ilse Nagelschmidt. Leipzig: Leipziger Universitätsverlag, 1997. 56–64.

Schenk, Ralf. "Abbilder des Lebens. Von der Kunst, Drehbücher zu schreiben:

Jurek Becker und Helga Schütz." *Film Dienst* 60:20 (2007): 16–17.

———. "Mitten im Kalten Krieg (1950–60)." Schenk 51–157.

———, ed. *Das zweite Leben der Filmstadt Babelsberg. DEFA-Spielfilme 1946–1992.* Berlin: Henschel, 1994.

Schieber, Elke. "Anfang vom Ende oder Kontinuität des Argwohns 1980 bis 1989." Schenk 265–326.

———. "Im Dämmerlicht der Perestroika. 1980 bis 1989." Jordan and Schenk 170–210.

Schittly, Dagmar. *Zwischen Regie und Regime: Die DEFA Filmpolitik der SED im Spiegel der DEFA-Produktionen.* Berlin: Ch. Links, 2002.

Schlüpmann, Heide. "Femininity as Productive Force: Kluge and Critical Theory." *New German Critique* 49 (1990): 69–78.

Schmidt, Sabine. *Frauenporträts und -protokolle aus der DDR: Zur Subjektivität der Dokumentarliteratur.* Wiesbaden: Deutscher Universitätsverlag, 1999.

Schönemann, Sibylle. "Stoffentwicklung im DEFA-Studio für Spielfilme." *Filmland DDR: Ein Reader zu Geschichte, Funktion und Wirkung der DEFA.* Ed. Harry Blunk and Dirk Jungnickel. Köln: Verlag Wissenschaft und Politik, 1990. 71–81.

Schreiber, Eduard. "Zeit der verpassten Möglichkeiten 1970 bis 1980." Jordan and Schenk 129–69.

Schütz, Helga. *Jette in Dresden.* Berlin: Aufbau, 1977.

———. *Julia oder Erziehung zum Chorgesang.* Berlin: Aufbau, 1980.

Schwarz, Gislinde and Christine Zenner, eds. *Wir wollen mehr als ein "Vaterland." DDR-Frauen im Aufbruch.* Reinbeck bei Hamburg: Rowohlt, 1990.

Scott, Joan W. "Experience." Smith and Watson 57–71.

Sehnsucht. Dir. Valeska Grisebach. Germany, 2006.

Sellier, Geneviève. *Masculine Singular: French New Wave Cinema.* Durham: Duke UP, 2008.

The Seven Samurai. Dir. Akira Kurosawa. Japan, 1954.

Sie. Dir. Gitta Nickel. DEFA, 1970.

Silkwood. Dir. Mike Nichols. USA, 1983.

Silberman, Marc. "Beyond Spectacle: Alexander Kluge's *Artists Under the Big Top: Perplexed.*" *German Cinema: Texts in Context.* Detroit: Wayne State UP, 1995. 181–197.

———. "Discipline and Gender: Hermann Zschoche's *On Probation.*" *German Cinema: Texts in Context.* Detroit: Wayne State UP, 1995. 162–177.

Silberman, Marc and Henning Wrage, eds. *DEFA at the Crossroads of East German and International Film Culture: A Companion.* Boston: DeGruyter, 2014.

Silverman, Kaja. "Dis-Embodying the Female Voice." *Re-Vision: Essays in Feminist Film Criticism,* eds. Mary Ann Doane, Patricia Mellencamp, and Linda Williams. Frederick, MD: U Publications of America, 1984. Rpt. in Erens 309–327.

———. "Lost Objects and Mistaken Subjects." *The Acoustic Mirror: The Female Voice in Psychoanalysis and Cinema.* Bloomington: Indiana UP, 1988. 6–32. Rpt. in Thornham 97–105.

Smith, Sidonie, and Julia Watson. "Situating Subjectivity in Women's Autobiographical Practices." Smith and Watson 1–56.

Smith, Sidonie, and Julia Watson, eds. *Women, Autobiography, Theory.* Madison: U of Wisconsin P, 1998.

Soldovieri, Stefan. "Censorship and the Law: The Case of *Das Kaninchen bin ich* (*I am the Rabbit*)." 146–163.

Something's Gotta Give. Dir. Nancy Meyers. USA, 2003.

Sommer, Stefan. *Lexikon des DDR-Alltags.* Berlin: Schwarzkopf & Schwarzkopf, 1999.

Sommer vorm Balkon. Dir. Andreas Dresen. Germany, 2005.

Sonnensucher. Dir. Konrad Wolf. DEFA, 1958.

Spur der Steine. Dir. Frank Beyer. DEFA, 1965.

Stapellauf. Dir. Alfons Machalz. DEFA, 1956.

Stars. Dir. Jürgen Böttcher. DEFA, 1963.

Staud, Toralf. "Die ostdeutschen Immigranten." *Das neue Deutschland: Die Zukunft als Chance*. Ed. Tanja Busse and Tobias Dürr. Berlin: Aufbau, 2003. 266–281.

Stegmann, Vera. "*Frauenschicksale*: A DEFA Film Viewed in Light of Brecht's Critique 481 of the Opera and Eisler/Adorno's Theory of Film Music" *German Studies Review* 28.3 (Oct. 2005): 481–500.

Streetcar Named Desire, A. Dir. Elia Kazan. USA, 1951.

Summerfield, Penny. "Dis/composing the Subject: Intersubjectivities in Oral History." *Feminism and Autobiography: Texts, Theories, Methods*. Transformations: Thinking Through Feminism. Ed. Tess Cosslett, Celia Lury, and Penny Summerfield. New York: Routledge, 2000. 91–106.

Sylvester, Regine. "The Forbidden Films." *Viewsletter: News on Midwest Media Art/A Legacy Productions' Publication* 8.3 (Fall 1992).

"Sympathische Frauen und Mädchen aus unserer Mitte: Zuschauer diskutieren *Alle meine Mädchen*." *Tribüne* [Berlin] 12 June 1980.

Szaloky, Melinda. "Somewhere in Europe: Exile and Orphanage in Post-World War II Hungarian Cinema." Imre 81–102.

Tag für Tag. Dir. Volker Koepp. DEFA, 1979/1980.

Thornham, Sue, ed. *Feminist Film Theory: A Reader*. New York: New York UP, 1989.

Töchter. Dir. Maria Speth. Germany, 2014.

Trampe, Tamara. "Filmmaking after the *Wende*: A Personal Story." Berghahn and Bance 72–84.

———. Personal interview. 1 Aug. 2003.

Trumpener, Katie. "DEFA: Moving Germany into Eastern Europe." *Moving Images of East Germany: Past and Future of DEFA Film*. Ed. Barton Byg and Bethany Moore. Harry and Helen Gray Humanities Program, ser. 12. Washington DC: American Institute for Contemporary German Studies and Johns Hopkins UP, 2002. 85–104.

Tucker, Robert C., ed. *The Marx-Engels Reader*. 2nd ed. New York: Norton, 1978.

Turovskaya, Maya. "Auf der Suche nach einer 'freundlicheren Welt.'" *Film und Fernsehen* 1 (1981): 20–24.

———. "Der 'Frauenfilm', was ist das?" *Film und Fernsehen* 4 (1982): 15–23.

Ulbricht, Walter. Schlußwort auf der 11. Tagung des ZK der SED 1965. Stiftung Archiv der Parteien und Massenorganisationen der DDR im Bundesarchiv, Berlin (SAPMO): Dy 30/iv 2/1/191. Agde 266–81.

Unmarried Woman, An. Dir. Paul Mazursky. USA, 1978.

Urang, John Griffith. *Legal Tender: Love and Legitimacy in the East German Cultural Imagination*. Ithaca: Cornell UP, 2010.

———. "Realism and Romance in the East German Cinema, 1952–1962." *Film History* 18.1 (2006): 88–103.

Verdery, Katherine. *What Was Socialism and What Comes Next?* Princeton: Princeton UP, 1996.

Verfassung der Deutschen Demokratischen Republik, die. 1949. http://www.documentarchiv.de/ddr/verfddr1949.html#b1.

Versteck, Das. Dir. Frank Beyer. DEFA, 1979.

Vivre sa vie. Dir. Jean-Luc Godard. France, 1962.

Von der Emde, Silke. "Irmtraud Morgner's Postmodern Feminism: A Question of Politics." *Women in German Yearbook* 10 (1995): 117–142.

Voss, Margit. "Frauenprofile gefragt. Resümee des Filmangebots aus Frankreich, Italien, Schweden und den USA im Spielplan 1979/80." *Prisma* 12 (1981): 165–184.

———. "Vertrauen—Prüfstein für alle." *Film und Fernsehen* 7 (1980): 8–9.

Wagner, Brigitte. *DEFA After East Germany*. Rochester: Camden House, 2014.

Wäscherinnen. Dir. Jürgen Böttcher. DEFA, 1972.

Waldman, Diane, and Janet Walker. *Feminism and Documentary*. Minneapolis: U of Minnesota P, 1999.

Wander, Maxie. *Guten Morgen, du Schöne*. 1977. Berlin: DTV, 1995.

What Women Want. Dir. Nancy Meyers. USA, 2000.

White, Hayden. "The Value of Narrativity in the Representation of Reality." *Critical Inquiry* 7 (1980): 5–27.

Wieder in Wittstock. Dir. Volker Koepp. DEFA, 1976.

Wierling, Dorothee. "The East as the Past: Problems with Memory and Identity." *German Politics and Society* 15.2 (Summer 1997): 53–75.

Williams, Raymond. *Marxism and Literature*. Oxford: Oxford UP, 1977.

Winston, Brian. "Documentary: I Think We Are in Trouble." Ed. Alan Rosenthal. *New Challenges for Documentary*. Berkeley: U of California P, 1988. 21–33.

Winter adé. Dir. Helke Misselwitz. DEFA, 1988.

Wir von ESDA. Dir. Gitta Nickel. DEFA, 1976.

Wischnewski, Klaus. "Die zornigen jungen Männer von Babelsberg." Agde 355–371.

With Babies and Banners. Dir. Loraine Gray. USA, 1978.

Wittstock III. Dir. Volker Koepp. DEFA, 1977.

Wittstock, Wittstock. Dir. Volker Koepp. BRD, 1997.

Wolf, Christa. *Der geteilte Himmel*. Berlin: Aufbau, 1963.

———. Foreword. *Guten Morgen, du Schöne!* München: dtv, 1977. 11–22.

———. *Kassandra*. 1983. München: DTV, 1996.

———. *Kindheitsmuster*. 1976. München: DTV, 2000.

———. *Nachdenken über Christa T*. 1969. Hamburg: Luchterhand, 1993.

Wolf, Dieter. *Gruppe Babelsberg: unsere nichtgedrehten Filme*. Berlin: Das Neue Berlin, 2000.

Wolter, Christina. *Die Alleinseglerin*. Berlin: Aufbau, 1982.

Wood, Robin. "Images and Women." *Hollywood from Vietnam to Reagan*. New York: Columbia UP, 1986. 202–222. Rpt. in Erens 337–352.

Working Girl. Dir. Mike Nichols. USA, 1988.

Yella. Dir. Christian Petzold. Germany, 2007.

Zimmermann, Peter, ed. *Deutschlandbilder Ost. Dokumentarfilme der DEFA von der Nachkriegszeit bis zur Wiedervereinigung*. Vol. 2. *Close Up. Schriften aus dem Haus des Dokumentarfilms*. Konstanz: UVK-Medien/Ölschläger, 1995.

———. "Der Dokumentarfilm der DEFA zwischen Propaganda, Alltagsbeobachtung und subversiver Rezeption." Zimmermann 9–24.

Žižek, Slavoj. *Did Somebody Say Totalitarianism? Five Interventions in the (Mis)Use of a Notion*. New York: Verso, 2001.

———. *For They Know Not What They Do: Enjoyment as a Political Factor*. London: Verso, 1991.

Index

Page numbers in italics indicate illustrations.

JENNIFER L. CREECH is Associate Professor of German at the University of Rochester, where she is also Affiliate Faculty in Film and Media Studies and Associate Faculty at the Susan B. Anthony Institute for Gender, Sexuality, and Women's Studies. Her research and teaching interests include late twentieth-century German literature, film, and culture; cinema studies; and materialist and feminist theories. She has published on East German and post-unification cinema in *Seminar* and *Women in German Yearbook* and is the co-editor of *Spectacle: German Visual Culture*, vol. 2, and of *The Body: German Visual Culture*, vol. 5.

CPSIA information can be obtained
at www.ICGtesting.com
Printed in the USA
LVOW04s0128020916

502842LV00027B/396/P